Mastering

Inkscape

Transform Your Creative Vision with the Ultimate Guide to Professional Vector Design for Beginners & Pros Alike

Elliot Mercer

TABLE OF CONTENTS

INTRODUCTION

Welcome to the world of Inkscape, a powerful and versatile vector graphics software designed to elevate your digital artistry. Whether you are a seasoned designer or a beginner eager to explore your creative potential, Inkscape provides the tools you need to bring your artistic visions to life. This comprehensive guide will take you on a journey from the fundamental principles of vector design to the advanced techniques that will set your work apart.

We begin with the basics, guiding you through the creation of simple shapes and lines, gradually building up your skills to handle intricate and detailed illustrations. But Inkscape's capabilities extend far beyond simple drawings. You will learn how to design professional logos, craft eye-catching icons, and produce stunning posters, all with the precision and flexibility that vector graphics offer.

Inkscape is not only a tool for artistic expression; it's also a practical solution for various design needs. Whether you're creating graphics for a school project, designing marketing materials, or exploring digital art as a hobby, Inkscape provides a rich feature set that caters to every requirement. Best of all, this powerful software is completely free, making it accessible to everyone.

Prepare to immerse yourself in the limitless possibilities of Inkscape. This guide will equip you with the knowledge and skills to make the most of this remarkable tool. Get ready to unleash your creativity and transform your ideas into extraordinary digital artworks. Let's get started and make your creative dreams a reality with Inkscape!

CHAPTER 1
ABOUT INKSCAPE

What is Inkscape?

Inkscape is an application that allows for the production and modification of interactive vectors. This piece of software is often utilized to create and modify a wide variety of artworks, drawings, charts, graphs, and other forms of visual representations. There is compatibility between this program and the file format known as SVG, which is an abbreviation for Scalable Vector Graphics. This software allows us to import a variety of file formats, including JPEG (Joint Photographic Experts Group), PNG (Portable Network Graphics), BMP (Bitmap), and many more. Additionally, we can export a variety of file formats, including PNG (Portable Network Graphics) and many others. Additionally, it was compatible with the Linux operating system, macOS, and Windows operating system when it was first made available to the public in November 2003. Besides being offered in the English language, it is also accessible in a great number of other languages. To comprehend any program, it is necessary to be familiar with the features that are associated with that program.

Consequently, let's talk about some of the most essential aspects of the Inkscape program in a style that is both incredibly intriguing and easy to understand:

1. This piece of software is developed with a large number of Drawing and Shaping tools, as well as Calligraphy approaches, and it also includes a Pen and Pencil command in the form of tools.
2. A few other tools include the **Rectangle tool, the Square tool**, and others. These tools allow you to build a rectangle and a square, respectively.
3. The 3D boxes tool is yet another intriguing function that can be found in this application. Creating a three-dimensional box that can be modified in the XYZ plane is one of its uses. After ungrouping the sides of the box, to make more modifications, you may also independently change each side of the box.
4. The following characteristic is connected to the fact that it is possible to color. Within this function, we have a paint bucket tool that allows us to fill any particular location, and this tool also provides us with the ability to colorize our project in whatever way we see fit.
5. This program allows you to simplify the various sorts of paths so that they are more suitable for your particular needs.
6. With the help of this program, you can accurately trace any kind of Bitmap image, regardless of whether it is in path-oriented or colored image form. This allows you to make the image usable for your project work and ensure that your project is successful.

7. The fact that the Inkscape program, like other vector graphics software, is also capable of dealing with layer systems is a feature that proves to be quite useful when working with this software.
8. With the help of the Inkscape program, you can have both an anti-aliased Display facility and an object grouping facility.

Advantages of Inkscape Software

It is important to note that the Inkscape program is distinct from other vector graphics software due to its numerous fascinating advantages.

Allow me to go over some of its benefits, which will be of use to you when modifying vector graphics:

1. Node modifying is the most interesting benefit that this program offers. This means that vector graphics in this software include a frame region that contains a node, which allows for a broad range of flexibility while modifying the design. The Inkscape program makes it easier for you to edit nodes by providing you with some intriguing aspects of the node. These features include the ability to add nodes in any segment, delete nodes from any segment, move nodes from one location to another in any segment, and assist in the creation of curves and symmetry with nodes, among other things.
2. This piece of software allows users to access a broad variety of tools, including the *Pen tool, the Pencil tool, the Calligraphy tool, the text tool,* and a great deal more. These tools each have their set of capabilities, such as the Pencil tool, which is used for freehand drawing work, the Pen tool, which is used for precision work by creating art with the line segment, and the Calligraphy tool, which provides you with an artistic manner of drawing anything with your concept. Consequently, the use of these tools offers you the liberty to incorporate your practical ideas into your work without any limitations.
3. Because it is a gadget that is supported by the web, it may be utilized for the objectives of either small businesses or medium businesses.
4. This program provides us with the most intriguing benefit, which is the **Z-order**. Z-order is an abbreviation that refers to order sequences of drawn objects. The term "high Z-order" refers to objects that are drawn at the very end of the process, whereas "lower Z-order" refers to objects that are drawn at the very top. You can manually move a specific object at any sequence according to your requirements, or the layer system can handle the order of the objects. Both options are available to you.
5. **Create Tiled Clones** is a unique tool that is included in this program, which brings us to the next advantage of using this software. Using this tool, you will be provided with a framework that serves as a guide for you to perform tasks with more accuracy and excellence. Using the Create Tiled Clones tool, you may create any kind of guide according

3

to your idea, and you can use it to produce work that is virtually one hundred percent precise.

Now that you have this information, you will have no trouble becoming familiar with the Inkscape program, and you will be able to utilize it for your business purposes without any reservations. You will be able to move your company to the next level of vector graphics tasks with the assistance of this program. If you are interested in acquiring this program, you can go to its official website, where you can also get a subscription that is tailored to your needs and utilize its capabilities in your vector graphics projects.

Installation and Setup

Stable version and Development one

Before beginning the process of installing Inkscape, the first thing you should investigate is whether you would like a *stable version or a development one*. Version numbers have been assigned to **stable versions,** which have been formally discharged from the development process. The term **"stable"** does not imply that a version is flawless and does not experience any crashes; rather, it indicates that this version has been subjected to a sufficient amount of testing, has more comprehensive documentation, and is the version that the majority of users employ. The most significant benefit of using a stable version is that it is the version that other users run, which means that other Inkscape artists are more likely to be able to assist you. Apart from the fact that it is stable, this is the most significant advantage. Generally speaking, I would suggest that you begin with a stable version of Inkscape, but you should think about upgrading to a development build if you discover that you enjoy using Inkscape and would like to contribute to its development, or if you require the new capabilities that have been introduced since the release.

Making use of a **development build** comes with its own set of benefits. To begin, these builds have all of the most recent and finest features, which may be considerable in comparison to the stable version (particularly if the stable release has been out for more than a few months). In many cases, these newly added features include patches for the significant flaws that were present in the stable version. Additionally, by using the development version, you are assisting the development community in locating and fixing any new flaws that may have been introduced. Since it is only natural that active developers would be more interested in the development version, you will have a greater chance of receiving rapid assistance straight from the active developers. However, what about its consistency? Development builds are indeed, on average, more prone to include bugs and crash more frequently. Nevertheless, if you come across a new problem that is driving you crazy and if the bug is not addressed promptly, you always have the option to revert to the most recent stable version that does not have this bug. Please don't forget to save frequently, regardless of the version you're using!

4

Downloading and installing Inkscape on different operating systems

After selecting Download Now from the menu on the Inkscape website **(https://inkscape.org/),** you will be able to select either the most recent development version or the previously stable version. After that, select a version that corresponds to your operating system.

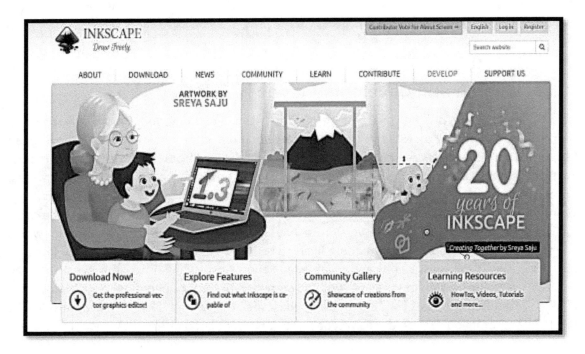

Windows (Windows)

You can choose to install the software using either the.exe or.msi file type. Run the.exe file, and for the.msi file, right-click and select the Install option from the context menu. After that, select the language, folder, and any other options that are available by following the instructions. When you are finished, you will have an icon of Inkscape that can be clicked on both on your desktop and in the Start menu. Additionally, the Windows App Store is where you may get Inkscape for use on Windows. **NOTE**: Archive files with the extension.7z are used for development or alpha/beta versions which are designed for Windows. There is a free unarchiver available for download at http://www.7-zip.org. With such a build, all that is required of you is to unarchive the file into a folder, and it will function perfectly from that point on.

Linux

Several options are available. If all you want is a stable version, the majority of Linux distributions already have one; all you have to do is select it in the software installation program that you are using (for instance, on Ubuntu, start Ubuntu Software Center or just execute apt-get install Inkscape from the command line). On the other hand, this version can be rather outdated. Inkscape.org has some downloaded packages that may be utilized with Linux package managers. These packages can be used to obtain a more recent stable version or the development version that is considered to be on the cutting edge.

macOS

To use the Mac, you will need to download a disk image file (.dmg). There is also the option to install Inkscape using MacPorts. On a reasonably consistent basis, typically daily, new development versions are typically made accessible. If, on the other hand, you want Inkscape that is completely up to date, you may obtain the most recent version of the Inkscape code from GitLab and then build it. In general, it is simpler to set up development on Linux than it is on Windows or Mac. We are not going to go into detail about this because it demands a higher level of computer expertise than the typical person.

CHAPTER 2
UNDERSTANDING VECTOR GRAPHICS

Vector vs. Raster Graphics

Before we begin with what vector graphics and raster graphics are, we must understand a few basic terms:

- **Pixel:** A pixel, also known as a dot or a picture element, is a physical point that is present in an image. Pixels are used in computer graphics. The smallest addressable piece of an image that is displayed on a screen is referred to as a pixel on the screen. It is raster images that make up the vast bulk of the photos that we view on our computer screens. Another example of a raster image is the selfie that you take with your mobile phone using the camera setting. A bitmap is a collection of pixels that is used to create an image through the process of image creation.

- **Bitmap**: A bitmap is a mapping from some domain (for example, a range of numbers) to bits, which are values that are either zero or one. Bitmaps are used in computer graphics. Additionally, it is referred to as a bit array or a bitmap index. A pixmap is a broader phrase that refers to a map of pixels, including the fact that each pixel can hold more than two colors, resulting in the use of more than one bit for each pixel. Frequently, bitmap is also utilized for this purpose. Bitmap is used to refer to images that have one bit per pixel in some settings, whereas pixmap is used to refer to images that have several bits per pixel.

You may sometimes hear the term **"scalable vector graphics" (SVG)** used to refer to vector graphics. These graphics are comparable to the connect-the-dot activities that you may have participated in when you were younger. They are made up of anchoring dots that are connected by lines and curves. The graphics in question are referred to as resolution-independent because they are not based on pixels. This property enables them to be indefinitely scaled. Regardless of their size, their lines are well-defined, and there is no reduction in the quality or level of detail. Therefore, the quality of these graphics is not reliant on the number of dots that are accessible on a printer or the number of pixels that are displayed on a screen. Additionally, these graphics are device-independent. The size of the file is pretty minimal because it is composed of lines and anchor points. The production of raster images is accomplished through the employment of pixels, which are very small dots that employ color and tone. Whenever the image is magnified or zoomed in, the pixels display themselves as if they were little squares on graph paper. These pictures are produced by digital cameras, by scanning images into a computer, or by using software that is based on raster images of the image. A predetermined number of pixels is the only thing that can be contained within an image; the quality of the image is determined by the number of pixels. Resolving this issue is what we call it. A greater number of pixels results in a higher-quality image at the same or bigger dimensions as the original. However, this also results in an increase in the size of the file as well as the amount of space that is required to store the file. There is a direct correlation between the number of pixels and the resolution. The maximum size that an image may be scaled up without revealing its pixels is determined by the resolution of the image. A high-resolution image that is printed at a tiny size, on the other hand, will cause the pixels to "cram" together, which will result in the image seeming as unprofessional as if there were not enough pixels in a huge image.

When to choose vector versus raster?

Because of its short file size and flexibility to scale, a vector image is particularly well-suited for usage in digital printing, which may be used for everything from billboards to business cards. In addition, they are utilized in the bottom thirds of films, as well as in the rendering of web-based objects and 3D or 2D computer animation. It is necessary to have their native files to create coins, laser engraving, t-shirts, patches, and other items. It is recommended to use raster images for digital photographs and printed products. Vector is the greatest option if your project calls for scalable shapes and solid colors, whereas raster is the best option for projects that call for sophisticated color mixes.

What Vector Graphics Is and Why It Matters

Inkscape is a vector graphics editor. What does that mean?

In today's world, the majority of the images that are saved and processed on computers are represented as rasters, which are also referred to as bitmaps. A basic representation is referred to as a raster image, which is nothing more than a grid of tiny rectangular rectangles known as pixels. The color of each pixel and, in some cases, its transparency is the sole pieces of information that are recorded for that pixel. An illustration of this would be a bitmap image that has a black circle on a white background (as seen in the left image). However, the image does not include a black circle in its original form. Seeing the image is the only way to determine whether or not you have the concept of a black circle in your head. All that the computer is aware of regarding the image is the fact that some of its pixels are black, while others are white, and a few of them are gray that falls somewhere in between.

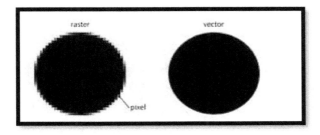

As a result, the computer is limited in its ability to manipulate such an image without the assistance of a person. Even though it can convert all of the white pixels to blue, it is unable to move the circle easily since it does not consider it to be a separate object. You will have to use some tools that are fickle and unreliable to "*select*" the circle, and this is especially difficult to do if, for example, the edge of the circle is anti-aliased (that is, some pixels on the edge have intermediate values between black and white), as shown in the image above. This is a task that may be difficult even for humans, as anyone who has used GIMP or Photoshop can attest. Everything is different when it comes to vector graphics (the image on the right). When using a vector format, the actual circle is saved as an object, together with all of its properties. This indicates that it is distinct from any other object, which signifies that you are free to do whatever you want with it. Your computer is capable of doing a wide range of intelligent tasks automatically when it is provided with such an image. For instance, it may remove all circles, paint all red objects with green, or scale all black circles to twice their size automatically. Getting rid of those annoying pixel selections is as simple as selecting any object at any moment and editing it as required. Inkscape operates in this manner, and this is the primary distinction that sets it apart from other raster editors on the market, such as Photoshop.

Let's look at the most prominent advantages of the vector approach:

- **Scalability**: The scalability of vector graphics is one of the most significant advantages that have been associated with them. Vector graphics, in contrast to raster graphics, are based on mathematical equations rather than pixels and can appear pixelated when scaled up. As a result, they are capable of being scaled to any size without compromising their quality. Your artwork will always seem clean and sharp, regardless of whether you are working on a little symbol or a massive billboard from start to finish.
- **Resolution Independence**: Vector graphics are not reliant on resolution, which means that they may be reproduced at any scale without sacrificing quality. This is because vector graphics are not dependent on resolution. These characteristics make them an excellent choice for print design, which requires output of a high quality. Your artwork will appear just as wonderful in print as it does on screen, regardless of whether you are printing a little business card or a massive billboard.
- **Small File Sizes**: When compared to raster graphics files, vector graphics files are often substantially smaller in size. This is because vector graphics files are more compact. The reason for this is that vector graphics simply save the mathematical instructions that are required to construct the image, as opposed to saving each pixel specific to the image. When it comes to web design, where loading speeds are of utmost importance, vector graphics are great because of their smaller file sizes.
- **Editability**: The editability of vector graphics is yet another advantage of using these types of digital graphics. It is simple to edit and change vector graphics using software such as Inkscape since they are made up of separate objects and shapes, each with its own set of

properties. You may alter the colors, make adjustments to the shapes, and rearrange the pieces without sacrificing the quality of the image or having to repaint the entire thing.

- **Versatility**: Vector graphics are extremely adaptable and may be utilized for a broad variety of applications, ranging from logos and drawings to diagrams and animations. This versatility allows them to be used for almost anything. Because it provides users with a comprehensive collection of drawing tools and functionalities, Inkscape gives users the ability to produce nearly any kind of vector artwork that can be imagined.
- **Compatibility**: Vector graphics are extensively supported across a variety of systems and software programs, ensuring compatibility. SVG (Scalable Vector Graphics), PDF, EPS, and some other file formats are among those that may be exported by Inkscape, which is an open-source tool in and of itself. Your artwork will be able to be readily shared and utilized in a variety of scenarios thanks to its compatibility with text.
- **Non-Destructive Editing**: The process of editing a vector graphic in Inkscape is known as non-destructive editing. This means that you are not definitively altering the original artwork. Rather than that, you are composing a set of instructions that will direct the computer on how to show the image. Utilizing this non-destructive editing approach gives you the freedom to explore and make adjustments without worrying about destroying your artwork.

Applications of Vector Graphics

The Trace Bitmap tool is one of the best things about Inkscape. Many designers and artists love the Trace Bitmap tool, which is one of the best parts of Inkscape. It lets people change raster images, like JPEG or PNG files, into a vector version that can be edited. This translation is very important because it lets people change the size of their art without losing any quality. Vector graphics are also great for printing and making graphics for a variety of media because they don't depend on resolution. In addition to being able to scale, the Trace Bitmap tool gives you a lot of artistic options. Some parts of an image can be taken out by designers and changed to fit their needs. They can also put together different vectorized images to make new designs. The **Trace Bitmap tool** in Inkscape can be very helpful if you want to make drawings, logos, or icons. Now that we know why the Trace Bitmap tool is important, let's look at how to use it in Inkscape step by step.

Choosing the Picture

Select the image that you want to turn into a vector file to begin. You can pick a JPEG or PNG picture. To make the tracing process easier, make sure the image has a neutral background, like white.

Adjusting the Brightness Cut-off

Go to the **Path** menu and select "**Trace Bitmap**" after you've chosen the image. This will bring up a dialogue box with different options to help you adjust the tracing process. Set the "**Brightness cut-off**" setting and start with the "**Single scan**" option. The vectorization is set by this setting. Due to the images light levels. Move the tool around until you get the result you want.

Using Edge Detection

The Trace Bitmap tool also has an option called **"Edge detection**." For images with clear edges, like cars or still-life objects, this tool works well. The method will concentrate on finding and tracing the edges of the image to produce a vector representation when edge detection is enabled.

Using Auto Trace

The "**Auto Trace**" tool is useful if you want to quickly and automatically trace your image. This option speeds up the tracing process and doesn't need many changes. To get the amount of accuracy you want, play around with the error bar and filter rounds.

Multiple Scans for Color Tracing

The "**Multiple scans**" option is best for images with a lot of different colors. It lets you split colors into their layers, which makes a vector image that is bright and full of details. Change the number of scans based on how complicated your image is, making sure that the amount of detail is balanced with the time it takes to process.

Tips and Tricks for Effective Tracing

Keep these tips in mind to get the most out of the Trace Bitmap tool:

- Try out different places to work: The Trace Bitmap tool has a lot of different options and sliders that you can use to get the result you want.
- Put together several tracings: If you need to, use various settings for various parts of the image and then put them all together to get the result you want.
- Use the Preview function: Always use the preview function to see a sneak peek of the traced image before making the settings official.
- Always save your work: As you try out different settings and do more than one scan, make sure you save your work often so you don't lose any progress.

CHAPTER 3
INKSCAPE'S "HELLO, WORLD!"

"Hello, World!" is a common way to start learning a new computer language. The only thing this simple, real, and working program does is print "**Hello, World**!" somewhere and then stop. Now I'll show you a simple but real Inkscape editing session that includes opening the program, making some objects, changing them, and then saving the changes. You can start Inkscape the same way you start any other app. You can click the icon, select it from a menu, or put Inkscape into the command line, depending on your operating system and personal tastes. If you choose a different document or press Esc to close the welcome dialog, Inkscape will start its main working window. Inkscape's basic interface is depicted in the image below.

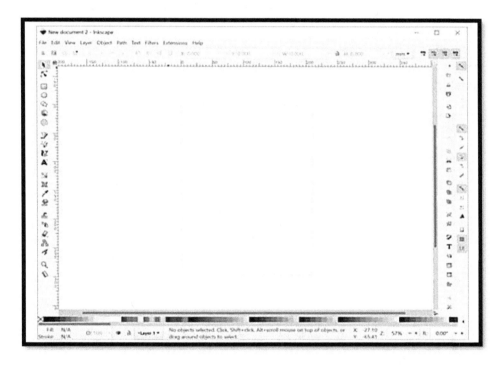

The white area in the middle of Inkscape's window is called the canvas. Along the sides are some tools and settings. You don't need to select **File>New** because Inkscape has already made a new, empty document for you in the canvas. You can get to work on it right away. Click the icon with the blue square in the list of icons on the left. You can make and edit squares using this tool, the Rectangle tool. Now, drag (or tap and drag on a computer) using the mouse button anywhere on the image. There will be a blue rectangle. When you let go of the mouse, the rectangle will become a new object in your document.

12

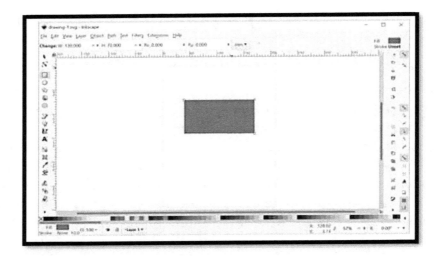

The Text tool will now be selected when you click the A button on the left. Inside the box, click but don't drag. The place where you clicked will have a text pointer blink. Type "**Hello, World**!" The second object in your document is a text object that you just made.

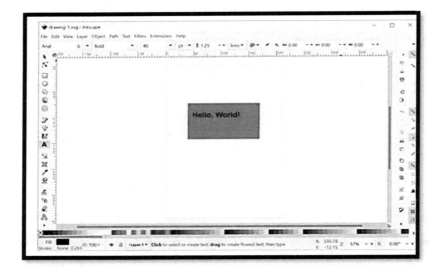

You may now have a better idea of what your objects are made of, where they are, or what color they are. Simple fix! Click the button at the very top of the left menu that looks like an arrow. This is the tool called Selector. You can now drag the objects around on the surface to move them anywhere you want. There is a color palette at the bottom of the window. To change the color of an object, just drag and drop the color you want on it. Enough of the tweaks. This document looks great. It's only flawed by not having been saved to a file yet. Select **File > Save**, then type in a title

13

and select the desired folder. That's it. With graphics and text, you just made a new SVG document. Excellent work!

A Look at the Inkscape Interface

You can use Inkscape by dividing the screen into groups that are set up like shelves for the things you want to use. There will be a lot of pictures, so you won't have to remember everything right now. This is more of a tour than a list of things to remember. Use it as a help when you can't remember what something was called. That thing, you know? That thing with the buttons... Yes, that one. There's a hot new dark mode in Inkscape that you can use right away. The **Dark mode switch** can be found in the **Startup dialog** box, which is also called the **Welcome Screen**. To exit Dark mode, flip the switch.

Also, I chose to use the old Inkscape icons since they are easier to see. You can do so too by using the **Appearance** dropdown beside the **Dark** mode switch.

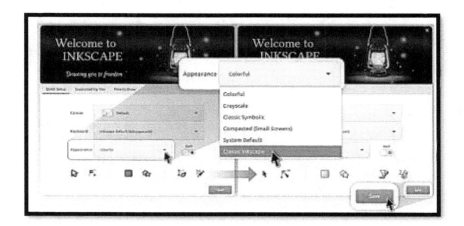

14

That certainly looks more like it! However, there's one more; depending on how wide your screen is, Inkscape may look slightly different than in some of the images here. What kind of screen do I have? Inkscape can tell and give me a bigger view instead. Because your view might be a little different, you might want to change it to **Wide** instead. This can be done by selecting **wide** from the **View** menu at the top of the screen.

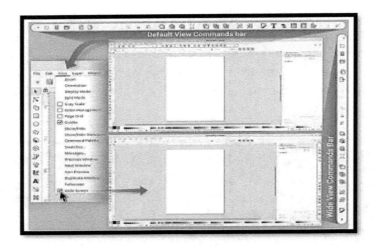

Changing views is completely optional and won't change anything except where the Commands bar is located. We will go over this bar, but we won't use it much because most of the things on this menu are easier to access with hotkeys. It also gets in the way of the much more useful Tool control bar, which we will use a lot. To keep your vertical screen room for drawing and clear things up, I suggest moving it to the side. For a description of the components, see the image **below. I've broken up the Wide Screen interface into pieces here so that you can see the different parts we'll be talking about better:**

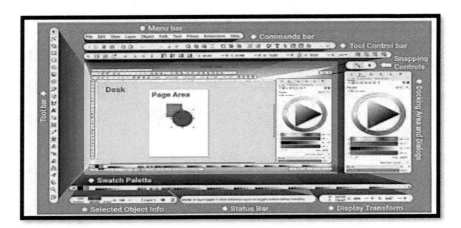

There are some rules that Inkscape follows that will help you find your way around before we get into the specifics of the different parts of the interface:

- **Hover to discover**: Place your mouse over an icon or box and hold it there for a moment to see what it does (see image below for an example of how to do this):

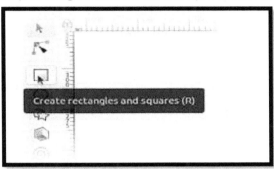

- **Hotkeys**: A hotkey is a key on your computer (or a group of keys) that lets you do something right away without having to go through menus or the icon bar. Whether it's in the Menu bar or the "**hover**" information (as mentioned in the last bullet point), Inkscape will usually show you the button that goes with the item.

You will be able to work faster and spend less time clicking since you will remember these hotkeys better. In the end, hotkeys will let you think about doing something and then do it at the same time. Spending a little time on this during your projects will save you a huge amount of time in the future.

- **Instant Search**: As of Inkscape 1.1, there is a new Command Palette that can be opened with the **Shift +?** key. This lets you do an instant search. You can type what you're looking for into this bar, and Inkscape will show you the results right away. You should remember the button because it helps you find things quickly. Have a question? Press the **"Shift +?"** key.

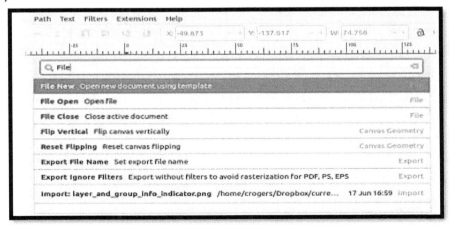

- **Buttons**: To do something with these, you only need to click them once. These include the Save and Load buttons in the Command Palette and the + and − keys inside the Spin Boxes, which let you change the number in the box more than once.
- **Toggles**: There are also toggles, which look like buttons but do more than just one thing. They can turn something on or off. These options are often found in the Tool control bar, which makes it easy to see at a glance which tools or locking options are picked. They are either on or off.

When the switch is turned on, the background of the icon will get a little darker to show that the button is hit. Now, if you press it again, it will turn off again, and the dark background will go away.

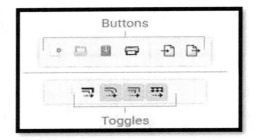

- **Spin Boxes**: These are boxes that hold numbers that can be increased or decreased by pressing the + and − buttons inside them. The + button adds one, and the − button takes away one. To edit the number directly, you can also click inside the box.

Here are some cool things you can do with Spin Boxes:
- Double-click on the **Spin Box** to select either the whole number or the decimal part of it. After that, you can type a new value, which will replace the part of the number that is underlined.
- Click three times in the Spin Box to make the whole number stand out. You can type in a new number, just like before. The **Ctrl + C** and **Ctrl + V** hotkeys can also be used to copy and paste the amount.
- Use the math tools in the Spin Box to do calculations. That's correct! You can multiply, divide, add, and take away right in the Spin Box. When you press the **Enter key**, Inkscape will turn your math into a number. You don't need a computer!

Math Operation	Entry in Spin Box	Result after pressing Enter
Add (+)	24.5+10	34.5
Subtract (-)	24.5-10	14.5
Multiply (*)	24.5*10	245
Divide (/)	24.5/10	2.45

- To convert from one measurement to another, simply add the units to the number you are working with. For instance, if you are working in centimeters (cm) and you are producing something that has to be 24 inches, you may convert it into centimeters by simply putting 24 inches into the Spin Box and then hitting the Enter key after you are finished:

- Right-clicking the Spin Box and selecting a value from the menu that appears will allow you to select a preset.

Would you say that we are prepared for the big tour now that we have all of these tiny tips and techniques for getting around? Amazing! It's time to get started.

Panning and Zooming

The tools that allow you to navigate about an endless vector canvas and zoom in and out for a more comfortable perspective are highly significant. These tools also allow you to move around the canvas. It is possible to pan (scroll) and zoom in Inkscape in a variety of methods, which is sufficient to meet every taste. The canvas scroll bars, of course, are perfectly capable of scrolling the canvas; nevertheless, they are not particularly useful, which is why I often conceal them by hitting the Ctrl-B key combination. Rather, the middle drag is the one that I utilize the most frequently. While dragging the canvas in any direction, press the middle mouse button and move it to any location on the canvas. It is possible to use middle drag in any tool or mode.

NOTE: It is quite probable that your mouse does not have a center button in the traditional sense; instead, you should attempt to push (rather than roll) the wheel that the majority of mice have (located between the left and right buttons). In most cases, you can click this wheel in the same way that you would click a button. Naturally, turning the wheel also works to scroll the canvas in a vertical direction; turning it while simultaneously pressing Shift scrolls the canvas in a horizontal direction. However, the majority of the time, my right hand is focused on the keyboard rather than the mouse. In that situation, the most convenient method for scrolling the canvas is to press the ***Ctrl-arrow keys*** simultaneously. For instance, if you press and hold the **Ctrl-↑** key, the canvas will begin to scroll downward (that is, your perspective will begin to ascend), first at a modest pace but gradually picking up speed. After you have gotten the hang of it, it will seem quite natural to you. The ability to zoom in and out is very simple. If you want to zoom in or out, all you have to do is hit the **plus (+) or minus (-)** keys on your keyboard. This is in contrast to the majority of other applications, which need you to use the Ctrl or Shift keys. Instead, you may use the basic plus and minus keys, which can be found on the main keyboard or the keypad. You can zoom in by using the middle click on your mouse, and you can zoom out by using the Shift-middle click. Alternatively, you may switch to the Zoom tool, which allows you to zoom in by using the usual left-click shortcut, zoom out by using the Shift-left click shortcut, or zoom into a rectangle region by dragging with the left mouse button.

The Menu bar

Since this bar is a standard component of the majority of desktop apps, you are undoubtedly already familiar with it. In most cases, the information that you are looking for is often arranged in menus that are located at the very top of the screen.

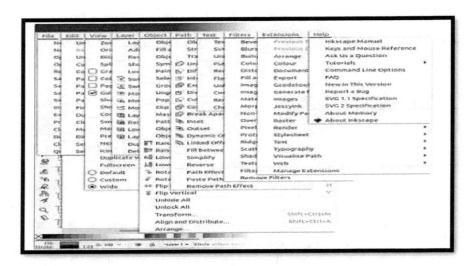

Even though this may appear to be a substantial amount of information, you will notice that everything is organized logically, and as you grow accustomed to the locations of the various objects, it will become second nature to you.

Just for the time being, the following are some samples of the sorts of items that may be found on each menu:

- **File**: This section includes elements that pertain to loading and saving files, printing, cleaning up, and modifying the properties of your document.
- **Edit**: This menu includes action options like copy, paste, and select, in addition to the Inkscape Preferences dialog box.
- **View**: This menu allows you to reveal and conceal various components of the Inkscape user interface. It also includes zoom controls, display modes, and a wide range of customization options.

- **Layer**: The Layer menu is where you'll find shortcuts and controls for the layers. Within this menu, the Layers dialog box is also displayed. Although it is more probable that you will use the Layers dialog than the items in this menu, the items in this menu are still helpful references for the hotkeys that are used to raise and lower layers, as well as other modifiers.
- **Objects**: This menu has a wide variety of helpful tools for interacting with objects, such as elevating and lowering them in the object stack (more detailed information on this topic will be provided later). Additionally, the Objects dialog, the Align and Distribute dialog, and the Arrange dialog are all brought up when you choose this option as well.
- **Path**: This is a veritable toolkit of functions that allows you to edit the nodes and curves (lines/strokes) of your shapes. Additionally, it allows you to convert from an object into a path to make shapes editable. Adding, removing, and cutting shapes with other shapes may also be accomplished with the use of handy path operations. The fact that this menu provides quick ways to obtain the shapes that we want to construct without the need to edit them node by node means that we will spend a significant amount of time searching through it.
- **Text**: This option allows you to bring up the Text and Font dialog, connect text to paths, flow text through objects so that your paragraphs take on the shape of non-rectangle objects, and, of course, bring up the **Check Spelling dialog**, which is an extremely essential dialog.
- **Filters:** In addition to allowing users to design shapes, Inkscape provides them the opportunity to apply effects to those shapes. The effects that are available in this menu should be utilized with caution for some different reasons. On the other hand, this has some interesting effects, and you have the potential to create your own, so we will have some fun with that later.
- **Help**: This menu has an excellent assortment of fast links that may be utilized for learning the fundamentals of Inkscape, obtaining assistance, and even engaging in real-time conversation with members of the Inkscape community on the Inkscape chat server.

Tools and Panels

The Toolbar and Tool control bar

Together, these two are inseparable. On the left side of the screen are the tools and the controls for the tools are located at the very top. When you select a tool from the bar on the left, the Tool control bar will show you all of the available options for that particular tool. For instance, if you select the **Star and Polygon** tool, the region of the Tool control bar will display the number of points, regardless of whether the shape in question is a star or a polygon, and it will even round the points! Changing to the **Text tool** reveals all of the different fonts, letters, line, and character spacing, and other types of formatting options.

If the Star and Polygon tool is selected, the Tool control bar displays many options for the tool, such as the number of corners that the star possesses, as seen in the image that follows:

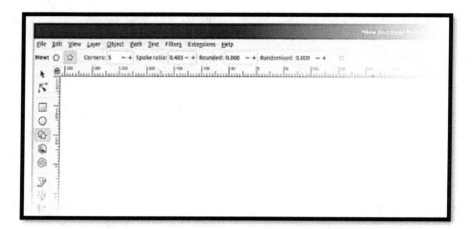

When you double-click on a tool in the Toolbar, you will be presented with options for that tool. One of these options is the **Last used style**, which you will most likely want to activate. This will allow Inkscape to remember the fill color and stroke thickness of the most recent shape you created, as well as the font you used for the most recent text file, and so on. To access the **Preferences** dialog for a particular tool, simply double-click on the tool in question.

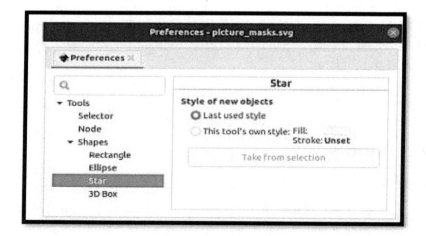

The Desk and Page areas

You will be drawing using the numerous tools that are located on the Toolbar in this area, which is depicted in the image below. A4-sized pages are the default setting for the Page area; however, you can modify this setting by selecting File > Document Properties or by hitting **Ctrl + Shift + D:**

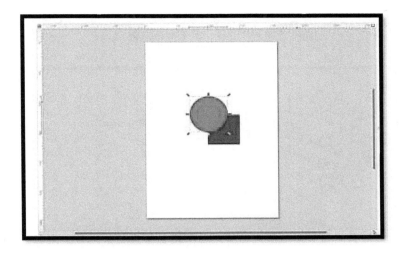

Even though you are free to create wherever you choose within the **Desk** area, the **Page** area is excellent for storing your primary graphics. It is what will be displayed in the thumbnail preview of your web browser and file browser, as well as what someone see when they open the PDF that you will have saved. Additionally, it is the region that is exported when the Page option is selected in the PNG Export dialog box.

When it comes to exploring the Desk and Page sections, here are some helpful hints:

- **Zoom in and out**: While holding down the Ctrl key, roll the mouse wheel to zoom in and out of the image. If your computer is equipped with a touch screen, you can also zoom in and out by pinching the screen, or you may use the plus and minus buttons. Even though there is a Zoom tool on the Toolbar that resembles a magnifying glass, I advocate using the other techniques because there are so many other excellent ways to zoom without having to switch tools.

- **Panning the view**: Paging is the process of moving the vision from one side to the other or from one level to another. You can indeed move the little scrollbars that are located at the bottom and left side of the canvas. However, you also have the option of just holding down the spacebar, which will grasp the canvas and move it depending on how you move the mouse.

It is also possible to pan by holding down the middle mouse button if you have one, but once you become accustomed to the spacebar approach, it will become your preferred method of positioning the mouse. After a time, you will find yourself wishing if your other programs performed the same thing.

- **The context menu**: Can you imagine a scenario in which you could access certain things on the menu bar without having to take your mouse off the canvas? An even more desirable scenario would be if you could just right-click on the canvas or an object on the canvas, and then immediately be presented with a subset of actions that are specific to that sort of object. To put it simply, that is precisely the purpose of the context menu!

22

Simply right-click on the **Desk, Page**, or any other object that you have selected, and you will be offered a selection of helpful things to choose from.

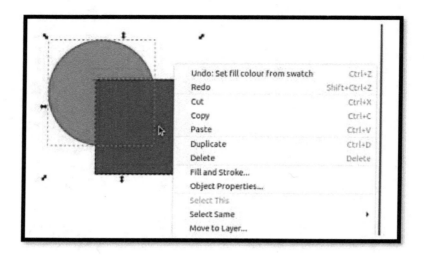

Now that you are familiar with how to navigate the **Desk** area, let's have a look at some of the different ways that you can color your shapes using the Swatch Palette.

The Swatch Palette

If you want to color quickly, the Swatch Palette is a fantastic choice, as seen below. One of these will fill any shape that has been picked with that color if you click on it:

When you click a swatch while holding Shift, a stroke of that color will be assigned to the swatch. Alternatively, you may right-click a swatch and select **Set stroke** from the popover menu. When you click the hamburger menu (the one with three lines) on the far right, you will be given the option to view more color palettes and to swap between them. In addition, the up and down arrow buttons located to the left of the hamburger menu will scroll the available swatches in the palette that is now chosen. Additionally, the mouse wheel and hovering the mouse cursor over the swatches will also scroll the available swatches inside the palette. You may see that the first swatches on the left are significantly larger than the others. Because these are pinned colors, you can add and delete them from this section to keep your preferred colors. Let's say, for instance, that you have a strong preference for the brightest red, and you would want it to be pinned. To select the **Pin color**, simply right-click on the red swatch and select it from the menu that appears, as seen in the following image.

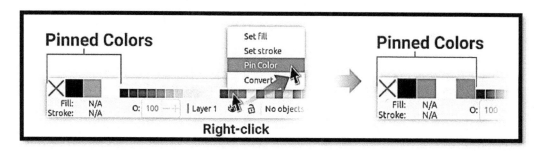

The color indicators

The **fill and stroke (outline)** colors for the selected shapes are shown by the color indicators corresponding to those colors. Until a shape is picked, these indicators will be blank and display the abbreviation **N/A**, which stands for **not applicable**. If you click on the color bar, you will be sent to the **Fill and Stroke** dialog, which contains more options. Additionally, there are some other custom option pickers that you may use to select your colors. When the color bars are right-clicked, a menu of attractive presets will appear. Additionally, you will have the option to copy, paste, and switch colors between strokes and fills that are displayed.

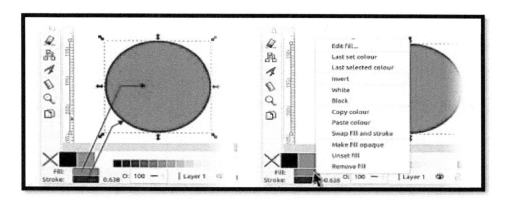

Within the vicinity of the **Stroke** color bar is a numerical value that denotes the width of the stroke, which in this instance is 0.638. If you click on that number, the **Fill and Stroke** dialog will bring up the **Stroke Style** tab, where you will be able to make adjustments to the value of that number. The opacity value, which affects the transparency or opacity of the chosen object, is the value that is located to the right of the width of the stroke in the box marked with the letter O. According to this number, the opacity slider that is located at the bottom of the **Fill and Stroke** panel should be adjusted. If you want to adjust the opacity value, you may utilize either one of

24

these. You will note that there are more options directly to the right of the color indicators, but those are the fundamentals of the color indicators. May I suggest that we have a look at the Layer Info Indicator and see what it is all about?

The Layer Info Indicator

These are just a handful of the tools that may be used quickly to deal with the layer or group that is now chosen. These controls are also accessible through the **Layers dialog** as well as the **Objects** dialog interface.

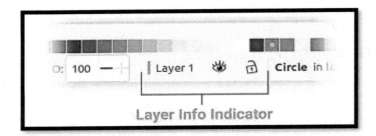

Clicking the **Eyeball Toggle** icon will either conceal or display the layer or group that is now active, and clicking the **Lock Toggle** icon will either lock or unlock the layer or group. When you lock a layer, it prevents you from selecting it, which is useful when you are working on top of backdrop shapes that you do not want to select by accident. You also have the option of clicking the layer name, which will cause the **Layers and Objects** window to display the layer and object that is now chosen. This is the **Status bar**, which is located farther to the right and has a space that is filled with a message.

The Status bar

This readout, which displays helpful information about the current status of Inkscape, is a section of the interactive interface that is sometimes neglected.

This section displays a variety of items, depending on what is selected among the following:

- **When there are no shapes selected**, the Status bar displays helpful information on the tool that is now active.
- **The selection of an object** causes the Status bar to display information about the object as well as the type of object that has been selected.
- The Status bar displays the number of nodes that are currently included inside **the path that is currently chosen.**
- **When a group is chosen**, the Status bar displays the number of objects and paths that are included inside the group, as well as whether or not the group contains any additional groups.
- **When an image is selected,** the Status bar displays the measurement of the image in pixels, as well as the information on whether or not the image is linked to the document or embedded inside it.
- You have attempted to subtract one shape from another using path operations, but one of the objects you are working with is not a path. This is an example of a situation in which something goes wrong. Here, Inkscape will display an error notice to inform you that one of your shapes is an object, and until you convert it, it will not be able to be used for this operation (more on this later).

Before we go on, let's have a look at the dialogs and the Docking area.

The Docking area and dialogs

This area will display all of the dialogs you open and offer a custom space where you can keep one or more of them close at hand while you work:

You might not see any text boxes the first time you open Inkscape. You can open these dialogs in some ways, such as by clicking on the Fill and Stroke color bars (as we've already said) or by using the Menu bar to access similar options (for example, **Object > Fill and Stroke**). To move the tabs at the top of each dialog box around in the Docking area, click and drag them. As for Inkscape 1.1, you can even dock them to the other side of the screen next to your Toolbar if you want to. Look at the three dots on the left side of the text boxes. You can change the size of the dialogs with this handle. Handles are also present between dialogs to do the same thing. **Tip:** It takes a lot of work to make the space needed for some of the bigger dialogs smaller right now. On the other hand, you can drag a chat box out into a floating window and then stop it. When you call up the dialog box again, Inkscape will remember your choice and float it so that it doesn't take up space in your dock all the time. You can turn the Docking area on and off with the F12 key, so if it's getting in the way of your drawing, you can briefly hide it and then bring it back when you need it. Moving further to the right, there is another bar of icon buttons, though you probably won't need these as often. The Command bar looks interesting.

The Commands bar

This bar has some of the most-used features from the Menu bar's different options, like save/load, undo/redo, and even some dialogs that you can open. Even though I don't use them, these are a nice touch for people who aren't used to using the Menu bar or hotkeys to select things, which is how I like to do it. **You should use hotkeys to do the things that are on the Command bar instead of clicking buttons:**

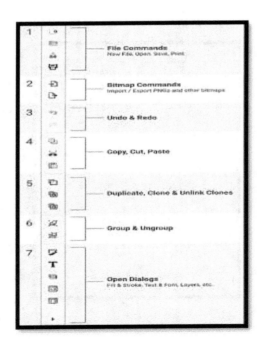

You can click the button at the bottom to see more text boxes that don't fit on the screen. This line might or might not show up on your screen, depending on its size. The last set of buttons is here, and this is about as far to the right as we can go without going off the screen. As we already said, these are toggles that make up the Snap control bar.

The Snap control bar

The mouse may instantly snap to different parts of the drawing area or other shapes you have already drawn as you move your objects around the page or draw new ones. You can use this to help with alignment. The image below shows how snapping usually works. When you drag an object to a new spot, Inkscape finds the shape's closest point (or line) to your cursor and offers places to align or snap it to a nearby shape. **After that, just let go of the mouse button and the shape will be perfectly lined up:**

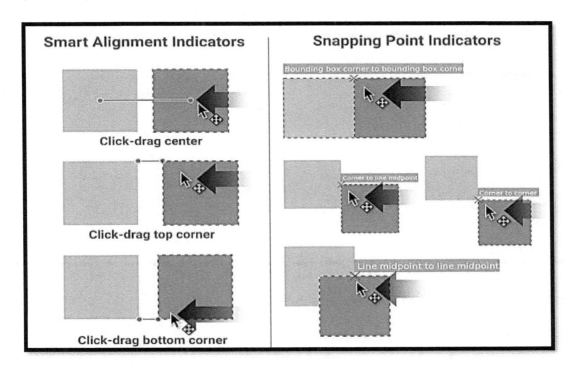

When an object snaps to another, a line will show up to let you know what Inkscape is switching to before you let go of the mouse button. The **Snapping Controls** button lets you choose what Inkscape uses to snap. You can turn on or off snapping by clicking the **Snapping Controls** button. By default, the arrow next to it opens the **Simple Snapping** options. When you click on the "**Advanced Options**" link at the bottom, you can see a full list of all of Inkscape's locking options.

28

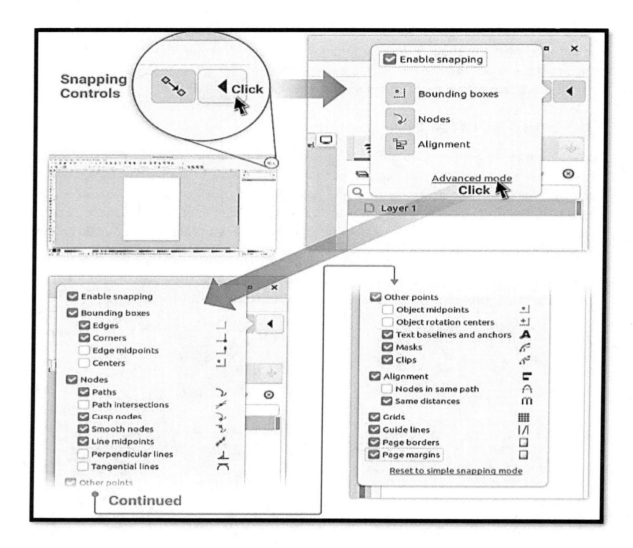

The following summarizes what these checkboxes do:

- **Enable Snapping**: This button will turn on and off all snapping, making it simple to turn it on or off. You can also turn this on and off with the % key.
- **Bounding Boxes**: A dashed rectangle shows up around an object when you select it. This is called the "bounding box," and this choice lets you choose whether to snap to this unseen line. This area has indented options. These let you choose which parts of the bounding box Inkscape snaps to.
- **Nodes**: The points in the shape that are between the lines are called nodes. If you turned your object into a path, you can use one of the nodes in this part to snap one object to another. Inkscape lets you tell what kinds of nodes you want to snap to, just like the Bounding Box part.

- **Other Points**: This is a catch-all group for snapping options that don't fit neatly into one of the other groups. For example, you could snap to the baseline of a line of text and anchors or the rotational center or middle of an object. When we discuss rotating and changing shapes, we will learn more about them.
- **Snap to Grid**: The grid doesn't show up by default in Inkscape. If you turn this option on, moving objects will be snapped to the invisible grid. Tap the # key, which resembles a grid, to activate the grid, or select **View > Page Grid** to turn it on and off.
- **Guide lines**: To make snapping lines, click on a ruler and drag it out onto the Desk or Page. To make a line going across the screen, click and drag from the top ruler. To make a line going up and down, click and drag from the top-left ruler. To make a 45-degree breaking line, you can also click and drag from the top left corner, where the lines meet.

After that, all you have to do is use this snapping toggle to connect your objects to the new lines you made. Select **View > Guides** or press **the > key** to turn these lines on and off. You can also get rid of a guide by dragging it back to the ruler or by pressing the Delete key while your cursor is over it.

- **Page Borders**: Yes, this setting lets you snap your shapes to the page's edge.
- **Page Margins**: You can snap objects to page borders that you set with the Pages Tool property.

The Display Transform Control

This part of the Inkscape window is in the bottom right corner and has a custom control for the **Desk view. It shows the X and Y positions of the mouse when it's over the Desk (from the page's upper left corner), has a zoom control, and can rotate the view:**

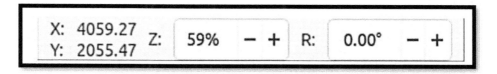

If you right-click on the zoom or rotation buttons, you can see some nice pre-set options. Some of these are also in the View menu:

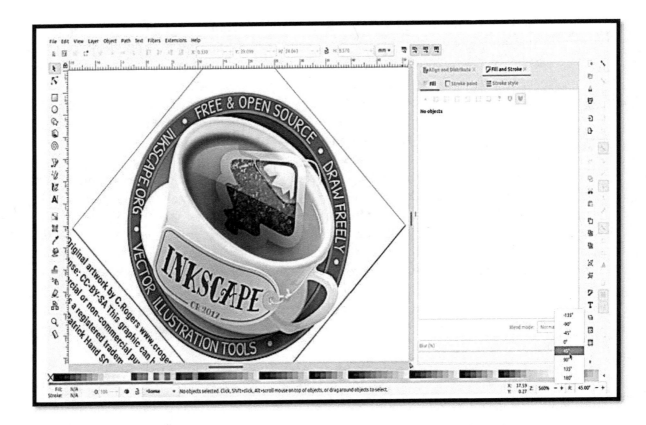

Inkscape: Changing the Document Properties and Preferences

Since the settings (SVG pixels) are not a measure that most people are familiar with, the first thing you will want to do when you start using Inkscape is set up the **Document Properties** and **Global Inkscape Preferences** to fit your design style. You can change some Global Preferences and have Inkscape apply them to all of your documents. You will have to set up other things (**Document Properties**) every time you make a new file. Most of the settings will work fine if you aren't looking for a certain size. There are units of measurement option boxes all over the place, so you can change your units of measurement at different points in the planning process.

Global Preferences

You can click **Edit > Preferences** or the last icon in the second row to get to the **Preferences** menu.

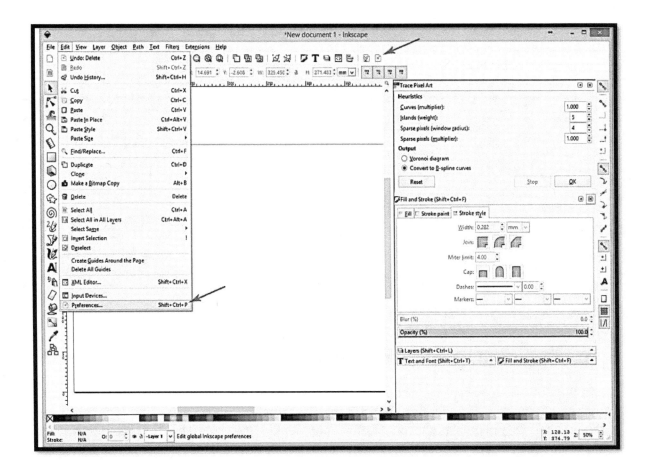

It's possible to give shapes (like squares and ellipses) their style in the **Shapes** options that you can find here. If you don't, the tool will remember the settings you last used the next time you use it.

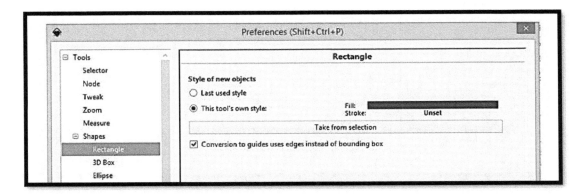

To set **Grid** values that will stay the same, scroll down to the part called "**Interface**." Some people like to create in inches and people who like to use millimeters. If you have a taste, you can set a universal grid style here.

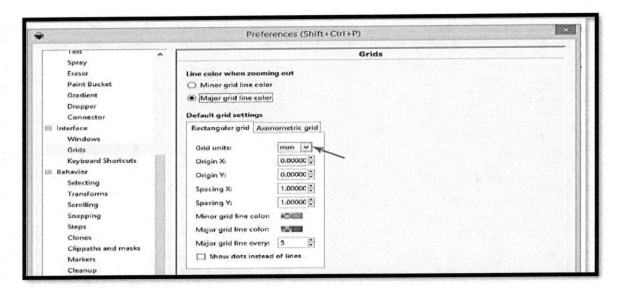

Last but not least, you can change how far the **Keyboard Arrow Keys** will move nodes and change the size of your shapes under **Behavior > Steps**. Two pixels is a very small value. You can change the numbers to mm or inches if you'd rather, and then use the arrow keys to move the handle by that amount.

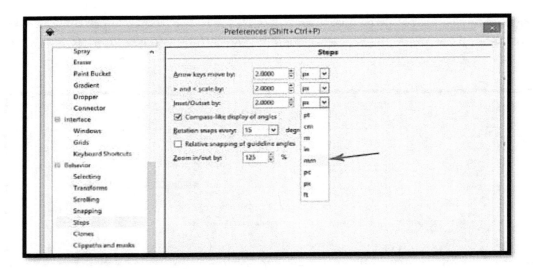

Document Properties

It is saved with each document that the **Document Properties** are used. By going to **File > Document Properties**, you can choose which units of measurement to use for the document (inches, mm, or cm). These units don't have to match the units used for the page size. (Inkscape changes everything to the units you choose.) The **Landscape** mode for your page is another option you will want to select.

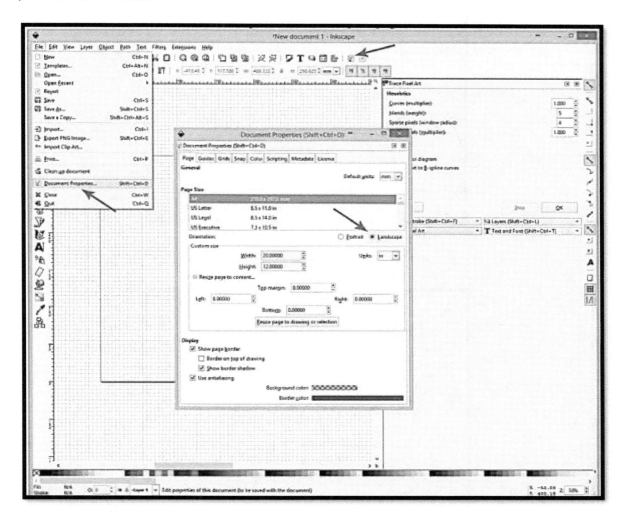

One more useful setting you can change in the Document Properties box is the **Snap** setting. These might need to be changed based on the numbers you picked for the Major Grid. You can also choose to always snap to the grid, objects, or directions.

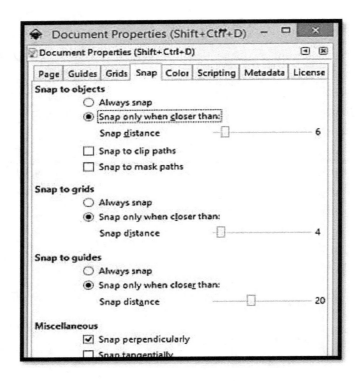

And last, Inkscape offers a nice little selection of Licenses that you can apply to your artwork.

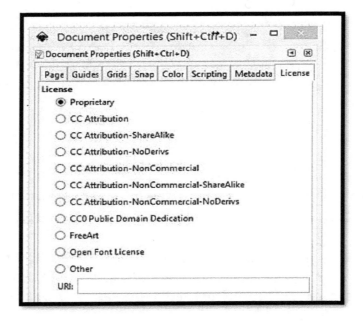

CHAPTER 4
BASIC DRAWING TECHNIQUES

All about Shapes

In Inkscape, shapes are the first step in making beautiful artwork. Shapes are the building blocks of all visual design. Inkscape has a lot of different shapes, from simple geometric shapes like triangles, circles, and squares to more complicated custom shapes made with Bezier curves. The drawing tools in Inkscape are easy to use, so you can quickly make shapes that fit your design needs. Shapes give your art the structure and framework it needs, whether you're making a simple design or a complicated drawing. Inkscape shapes can be used in a lot of different ways. You can easily change their size, rotation, and placement, giving you full control over how your design is put together. You can also change how shapes look by changing their custom properties, such as fill color, stroke color, and shape width. Inkscape also has strong tools for changing and mixing shapes. Boolean functions like Union, Difference, Intersection, and Exclusion let you add to, subtract from, or join shapes, which let you make complex designs and visual effects. Inkscape also lets you clone shapes to make drawings and patterns that repeat. It's simple to make copies of shapes that are tied to the original. This lets you try out different arrangements and setups. Finally, Inkscape has many shape effects that you can use to make your drawings look better. You can give your art more depth and volume with these effects, which include colors, shadows, blurs, and more.

Making your first shape

Of course, we will need to draw a shape before we can color and style it. You can make a brand-new rectangle by choosing the **Rectangle** tool, pressing somewhere on the canvas, and then dragging while holding down the left mouse button.

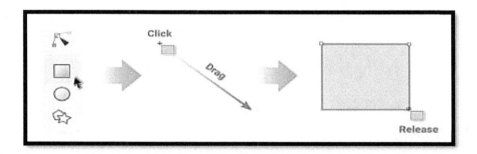

To make a smooth shape, like a square, you can also hold down the **Ctrl key** and drag. Your new square might look different from the one in the image above depending on how you have Inkscape configured. That's fine, though. Let's use **Fill and Stroke** to make it look the way we want it to.

Fill and Stroke

Inkscape's vector shapes all have a **Fill**, which is the color that the object is filled with, and a **Stroke**, which is the color and thickness of the shape's edge. For example, the **Fill and Stroke properties** in the image below match the numbers in the **Color Indicator** area:

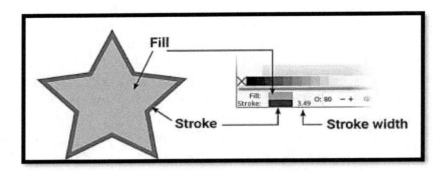

If you click on a color in the Swatch Palette at the bottom of the screen, you can give the chosen object a fill color. When you click the swatch while holding down the Shift key, the **Stroke Color** changes. To see more options, double-click on the fill or stroke bar in the **Color Indicator** area. This will open the **Fill and Stroke** dialog box. Also, clicking on the **Stroke width** number will show you the **Stroke style**, which lets you, change the thickness of the stroke and give you other **options. All of the Fill and Stroke options can be seen next to each other here:**

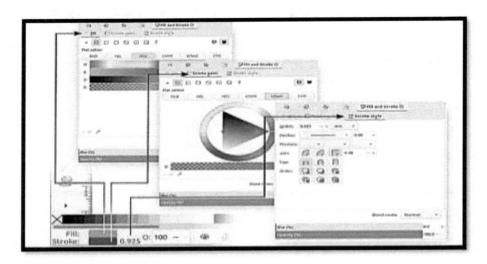

You may have noticed that the image above has different color mixes for Fill and Stroke paint. Wheel can be your color changer for both fill and stroke paint, which is something to keep in mind. Since HSV or HSL color mixers with slider bars are usually the default, I put this one here to show that it's an option. You might have trouble with the stroke width field being grayed out or going back to 0 if you try to change it if you are using an older version of Inkscape (before 1.1). In this case, all you need to do is set the color of your stroke by holding down Shift and clicking on a swatch or right-clicking on a swatch and selecting **Set stroke**. The old Inkscape will be like, "What stroke, man?" if there isn't a stroke set. After setting one, the stroke will now work as it should. Now we know some basic shapes and how to dress them. However, you'll want to move, spin, and transform your rectangle in different ways after you've drawn and styled it to perfection. Let's learn how to move our shapes around in Inkscape like pros!

Making use of the Select and Transform tool

You'll want to select, move, spin, and delete the shapes as you use the shape tools to make your amazing art. Since we've already drawn one rectangle, let's do it again and draw three rectangles next to each other, like in the image below.

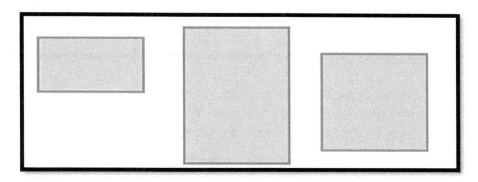

You will see that when you make a rectangular, it is already chosen and has a dashed line and handles around the object. This makes it simple to change the color, make the sides round, and do other things. But first, let's talk about how to use the Select and Transform tool to make simple selections. The **Arrow tool** is another name for the **Select and Transform** tool. It is the one at the very top of the menu that looks like an arrow tip on a mouse. When the **Select and Transform** tool is active, the Tool control bar changes. Click on it to turn it on. This gives us access to some useful features:

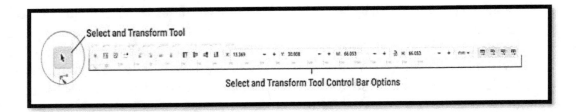

Select and Transform Tool

Select and Transform Tool Control Bar Options

A lot of basic shape selection and transformation tasks can be done with this tool. In the parts that follow, we'll look at some of the certain benefits.

Choose and reject different shapes

When using the Select and Transform tool, all we need to do to select a shape is click on it, as shown below:

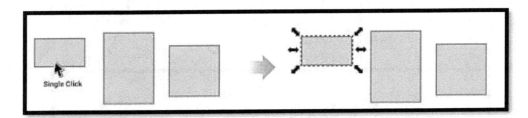

Single Click

If you've ever drawn a rectangle or any other shape, you may have noticed that it instantly gets chosen. We might not want it to be chosen, though. We can remove it from the selection by clicking on the canvas or another shape, or we can press the Esc key on the keyboard.

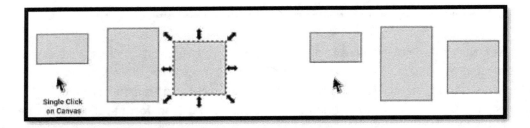

Single Click
on Canvas

To take an object out of the selection, hold down the Shift key again and click on a shape you want to take out of the selection. Keep in mind that you can also remove a shape by Shift-clicking it again if you accidentally chose it. The fact that you can skip this part of the selection means you don't have to start over.

Selecting multiple shapes all at once

It works fine to shift-click on each shape to add it to a selection when there are only a few shapes to add. But if there are a lot of shapes, this method gets old very quickly. **Rubber-band Select** can help you out in this situation! Holding down Shift lets you click and drag a selection box around objects to select them all at once. Anything inside the box will be added to the selection. When you move the mouse, the selection box turns into a wavy line. This line is known as a "**rubber band**" because it can be stretched around things. Keep in mind that you don't need to hold down **Shift** to do this if you click and drag on a blank drawing area. Since clicking and dragging is also how you move objects, if the surface you are working on doesn't have any space, you might accidentally grab an object. When you hold down Shift, Inkscape knows that you want to add to a selection instead of moving an object. To get into the habit, it's best to hold Shift every time you make a rubber-band selection. In this way, you will never move something by mistake.

Here's how this method works:

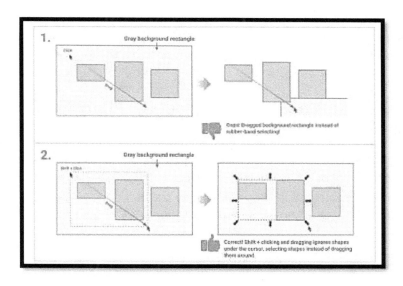

If you start to drag a selection box over an object, make sure you hold down Shift. First, you'll forget, but after a while, it will just happen without you having to think about it.

Selecting everything

You might just want to select everything occasionally. To select all shapes in the current text, Inkscape uses the common **Ctrl + A** hotkey. You can also use **Edit > Select All** or the button in the Toolbar that says "**Select All.**"

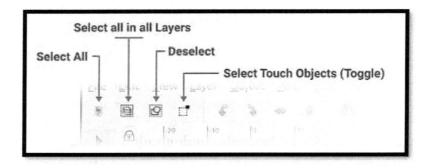

Pressing **Ctrl + A** will select everything in a group. If you're not in a group, pressing Ctrl + A will select everything on the image. **Layers** will also narrow the selection to the current layer just to be sure. To select all objects in all layers, however, go to **Edit > Select All in All Layers**. This will select every unlocked object in your document.

Fancy selecting with the Alt key

Currently, we have investigated a few different ways to select, but there are instances when the circumstance demands more sophisticated selection options. Let us have a look at a few other possibilities.

Selecting by using Touch-Path Select (holding Alt and dragging the mouse)

There are occasions when a rectangular rubber band is simply not the right shape for which you are looking to select. Your good fortune lies in the fact that you can drag a red selection line along the shapes you want to select if you keep the **Alt key** pressed down. Whenever you let go of the mouse pointer, the selection will be expanded to include every shape that it has touched, as seen in

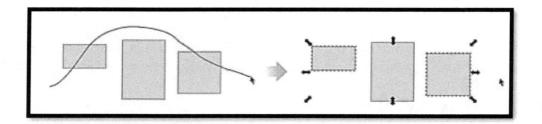

Remember that For this to function, there must be nothing previously chosen in the other options. As long as the Alt key is held down when dragging an object that is chosen, the object will be moved regardless of where the cursor is located on the page. It is sufficient to press the Esc key

many times to deselect whatever is now chosen; after that, the Touch-Path Select option will function properly.

Selecting an object behind another object using X-Ray Select (holding Alt and rotating the mouse wheel)

You may find yourself in a situation where you have many objects piled on top of each other, and you would like to select a shape that is concealed behind another object. For this, you will need to hold down the Alt key and click the top shape until the shape that is underneath it is chosen. In addition, you may accomplish this by holding down the Alt key and scrolling the mouse wheel. This will cause an **X-Ray Select** action to be carried out, which will momentarily make all of the objects that are under the cursor transparent, but the object that is selected will remain opaque. The selection of each object will occur in turn as you turn the mouse wheel. To select the opaque object that is displayed, you need just let go of the Alt key.

A demonstration of this effect is shown below;

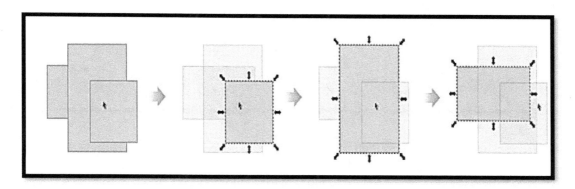

To deselect everything, you can either click on a space on the canvas or tap the *Esc* key.

Selecting objects with the same attributes

Consider the following scenario: you have a large collection of shapes, and you want to select only the rectangle objects from the collection. Or perhaps you would want to choose all of the shapes that are the same color to select? What about the objects that have a black stroke? Through the **Edit > Select Same** menu option, Inkscape has you covered.

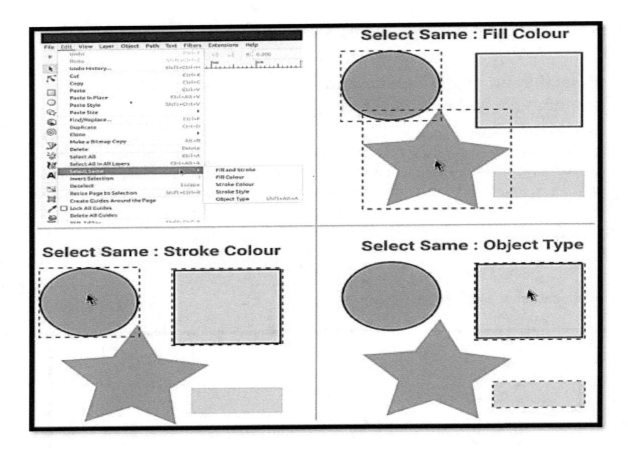

It is important to take note that the shape that was picked before the operation is indicated by the mouse cursor.

Invert selection

You might be interested in selecting everything other than the items that are currently selected. You have the option of selecting the items that you do not want to be chosen first and then selecting **Edit > Invert Selection**. Alternatively, you may hold down the Shift key and hit the! key simultaneously **(Shift +!).** Let's move on to the next topic, which is how to move shapes across the canvas, now that we've covered how to select shapes.

Moving shapes

When you have finished selecting your shapes, you may move them by simply clicking and dragging them with the mouse pointer around the screen. To force drag without having to click and hold the objects that are chosen, you can alternatively utilize the **Alt key** to do this action. This is especially helpful in situations when the object you wish to move is located behind another object, as it prevents you from altering the selection with the first click. When you are holding down the **Alt key**, you may click anywhere on the canvas to move the objects that are chosen. This is demonstrated in the image that follows. To ensure that we are just moving the items that are already chosen, we are holding down the Alt key in this example since the rectangle that we have selected is hidden behind other shapes.

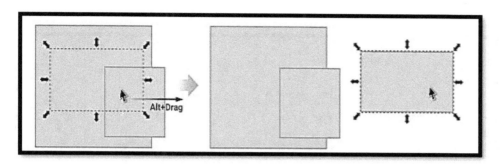

We have a fairly decent handle on it when it comes to moving shapes about in a variety of different ways, but what if we want more of the same shape... or maybe we're simply sick of our shape and want it gone completely? Let's take a look at how to remove shapes in Inkscape, which includes how to copy, cut, and paste them.

Cutting, copying, pasting, and deleting shapes

If you are familiar with the procedures that are performed in other applications, then this is not a very novel feature. **Cut, Copy, and Paste** are all supported by Inkscape using the conventional hotkeys **(Ctrl + X, Ctrl + C, and Ctrl + V).** Please take note that the Commands bar has buttons that correspond to these functions, as seen in the image that follows. If you want to utilize the hotkeys instead, I suggest you do so because they are much quicker to use:

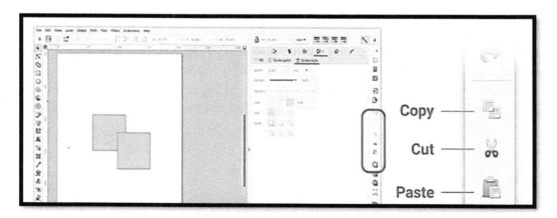

In addition, Inkscape provides Paste in Place (**Ctrl + Shift + V),** which will paste an object in the same position as the copied object (useful for copying/pasting between layers and groups). Duplicating **(Edit > Duplicate or Ctrl + D)** is another method of **Paste in Place** without the need to copy first. In addition, you may drop copies of an object that you have selected while you are dragging it by hitting the spacebar at various points along the route. I use this method to replicate objects regularly since it is by far my preferred method, and I do so out of habit:

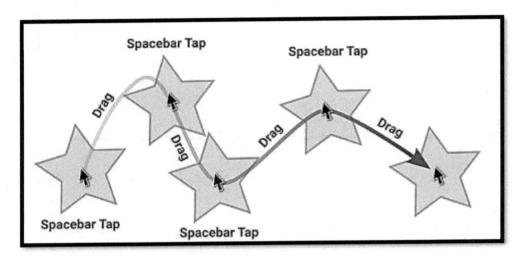

Pressing the **Delete key** is all that is required to delete the shapes that have been selected. There is a distinction between this and **Cut** in that the object that is destroyed is not transferred to the clipboard of the system.

Sizing up the shapes

The handles at the corners of a newly created rectangle (or another object) will transform into resizing arrows when you click on the **Select and Transform** tool. This will occur while you are working with a newly drawn rectangle. When you grab them, you will be able to change the size of the shape or shapes that you have picked. You should be aware that if you hold down the **Control key** while dragging a handle, the aspect ratio of the shape will be preserved in a manner that is very similar to how it is preserved when you are drawing shapes. For instance, if you enlarge a square, it will not transform into a rectangle but rather remain a square. This is because of the way that this works.

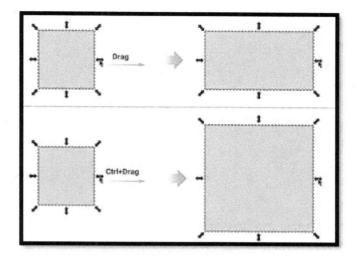

Resizing the height and width values with the Select and Transform tool

Whenever you have a shape chosen, you might have noticed that the Tool control bar displays the values for the shape's **height (H) and width (W).** You may use these numbers to manually adjust the height and width of the shape that has been selected, and you can even specify the **units (mm, inches, pixels, and so on) that you wish to resize using as well:**

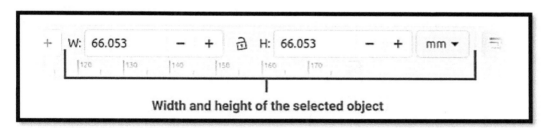

Width and height of the selected object

The capability to select one of the scaling handles as the point of reference for scaling (or moving) an object using the Tool control bar options is a function that was introduced very recently in Inkscape since it is a relatively new feature. Inkscape will automatically resize the shape starting from the top left corner of the screen. Let us assume, however, that we would want to scale our rectangle starting from the bottom-right corner. The bottom-right scaling handle can be selected by clicking on it, and then a very thin cross will emerge behind it. This cross will go up and down, left and right until it reaches the border of the page. Now, when you scale using the **W: and H:** values in the Tool control bar, Inkscape will scale them from that reference point rather than from the middle of the image.

46

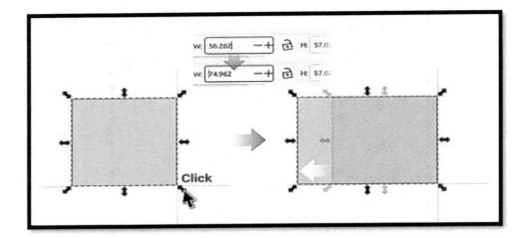

It is all well and good, but what if we want to size objects to the same height and width without having to go through the laborious process of copying and pasting the values for height and width? We can! First, let's investigate in greater depth.

Resizing shapes with Paste Size

Whereas, if you want one shape to be the same size as another shape, what should you do? Take, for instance, the possibility that you would like it to have the same height as another object that you have drawn in the past. Using the three rectangles that we started with, let's analyze how we can copy and paste the dimensions of one object onto the dimensions of other objects. To get things started, let's assume that we want all of our rectangles to have the same height as the one in the middle. To duplicate the middle rectangle, select it and then copy it. Followed by selecting the remaining two rectangles, select **Edit > Paste Height > Paste Height Separately** from the menu that appears. All of the rectangles will have the same height as a result of this.

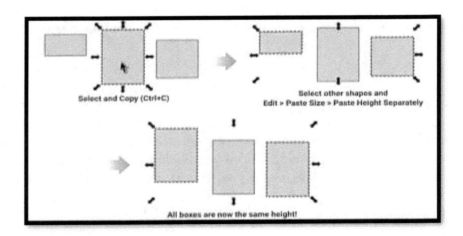

You will note that there are quite some different options for pasting size while you are operating within the Paste Size submenu. These options include:

- **Paste Size**: Using this function, you may take one or more selected shapes and reduce the size of the whole selection to match the size of the selected shape.
- **Paste Width**: This function takes one or more selected shapes and compresses the entire selection such that it is the same width as the object that was selected.
- **Paste Height**: This function takes one or more selected shapes and compresses the entire selection such that it is the same height as the selected shape.

I've never encountered a circumstance in which I needed to cram numerous selected shapes into the region of the duplicated shape, but these function well with a single selected shape. I've seen situations when I needed to do that.

It is far more beneficial to select one of the other three options in the submenu:

- **Paste Size Separately**: This feature takes all of the selected shapes and resizes them so that they contain the same dimensions as the copied shape.
- **Paste Width Separately**: This feature takes all of the selected shapes and resizes them separately to the same width as the shape that was copied.
- **Paste Height Separately**: This feature takes all of the selected shapes and resizes them independently making sure that they are the same height as the copied shape.

On the other hand, the majority of the time, you will probably want to rescale objects appropriately without compressing or stretching them before doing so. Exactly what should you do? The option to **paste the height separately proportionally** is nowhere to be seen. In the image that follows, I would like to take this opportunity to introduce you to my very dear buddy the **Lock Proportions** button.

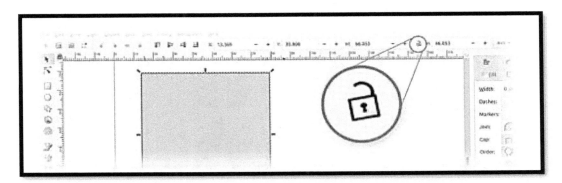

Suddenly, the **Paste Size** options become far more helpful thanks to this little button. By way of illustration, if you click it into the locked position before selecting **Paste Height Separately**, you will be able to make all of your rectangles the same height without extending them. You may have three gorgeous images of Jack-o'-lanterns, but you want to make sure that they are all the same height in the Halloween party file. The image that follows illustrates the results that occur **when proportions are left unlocked as opposed to being locked:**

As can be seen, stretching is not a very beneficial activity. This appears to be either a mistake or, at the very least, a lazy design. The lesson to be learned from this is that when using Paste Size, it is best to make sure that the Lock Proportions button is turned on.

Scaling styles

At this point, we are aware of how to scale shapes; however, what about the strokes that are used on those shapes? Is it possible to scale the object while maintaining the stroke in its current state? My dear readers, the answer is yes to that question! As a result of the fact that it is frequently essential to maintain a consistent stroke in illustration work, Inkscape provides you with the ability to lock the stroke width so that it remains the same regardless of how large or small you make your illustration when you are performing resizing. Take, for example, the cute youngster with the flower.

As you can see, she has a bit of difficulty with that big bloom. We could do her a favor by making the top of it smaller, but when we do, our stroke also goes smaller (seen on the left), which looks dreadful. By switching the Scale Stroke button off (it's in the Tool control bar), we may scale, and

Inkscape will retain our stroke the same width (seen on the right). When it comes to turning off the other style buttons, the process is the same. With the **Gradient Scaling/Moving** toggled off, the shape will be scaled, but the gradient will remain in its original position. By turning off **Pattern Scaling/Moving**, you will be able to maintain the pattern in place while you scale the shape. Additionally, although we have not yet covered corner rounding on rectangles, turning off **Corner Scaling** will ensure that the corners of the rectangle remain the same shape regardless of how large or small you make the rectangle.

Rotating shapes

Selecting one of our rectangles will be the first step. Take note of the handles that allow you to resize the window in the corner. Changing the handles to rotate will be accomplished by clicking on the rectangle you have picked once again. Another way to toggle this is to press **Shift and S** simultaneously. Additionally, a rotation pivot will appear in the middle of the rectangle. Changing the position of this pivot will enable you to spin the shape from a new vantage point. You may move it around. Below is a representation of rotation as well as rotation after the pivot point has been moved.

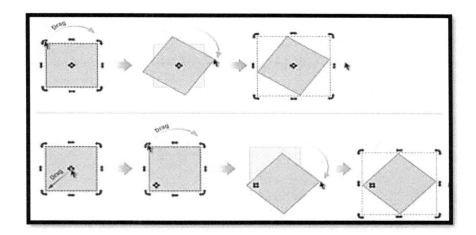

While you are rotating, you may lock the rotation to 15-degree increments by holding down the Ctrl key or the Alt key. This helps achieve some quick accuracy. You may also rotate while holding down the Shift key, which is another helpful tip. By doing so, the shape will be rotated from the other corner of the handle that you are now using. For instance, if you hold down the **Shift key** while grabbing the rotation handle at the top-right corner of the selection box, Inkscape will begin rotating about the bottom-left corner of the box. Allowing the shift to be released at any point throughout the rotation will cause the rotation to restart from the pivot point. It is also possible to bring up the Transform dialog by selecting **Object > Transform** and then selecting the **Rotate** tab. This is useful in situations when you need to rotate a shape to a certain amount that is not a multiple of **15**. This is the place where you may input whatever value you want, and you can also select whether you want to rotate all of the objects that you have selected collectively or rotate them individually by checking the checkbox that is seen in the image below.

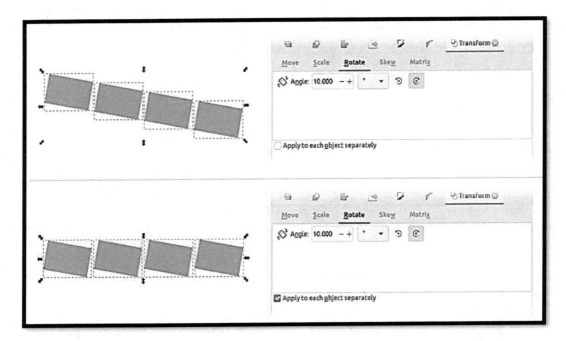

Upon closer inspection, you will observe that the Transform dialog contains additional options to Scale, Move, Skew, and so on. Because they can be helpful in specific situations, I strongly suggest that you explore with them. Nevertheless, rather than bombarding you with a lengthy discussion of each option, let's move on to the next topic, which is the rising and lowering of shapes.

Raising and lowering shapes

When you create a new shape in Inkscape, it will automatically draw it on top of the previous shape you created. What happens, however, if we want to draw a new rectangle and then move it such that it is positioned beneath one or more of the rectangles that we have previously drawn? All that is required to do this is to select the rectangle that we want to slide down behind the others and then click the **Raise or Lower** button that is located in the Tool control bar. To illustrate what happens to our rectangle when we use each of these buttons to raise and lower the shape that we have picked, the image that follows is presented:

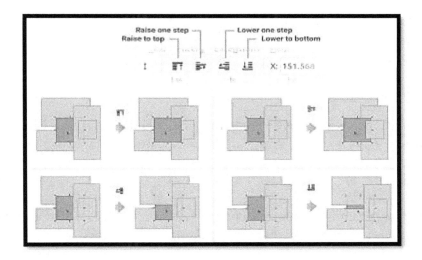

To raise and lower the selected object without having to click buttons, you can alternatively utilize the **Page Up and Page Down** hotkeys. This is the way that I like to use it because it eliminates the need to click individual buttons. Additionally, pressing the **Home and End** keys will place the selected object at the very top or bottom of all the other shapes, respectively, depending on which key you press. It is important to take note of the fact that the symbols representing the raise and lower operations appear to create a stack as if the shapes were seen diagonally. Stacks are formed by all shapes in Inkscape, which is something that we will discover. From a top-down viewpoint, you may think of your shapes as a stack of cutout paper shapes that are all overlapping each other. This applies to your shapes for the time being. The image that follows illustrates what this may look like if you were able to see our top-down overlapping rectangle stack from the side to see the stack of paper objects:

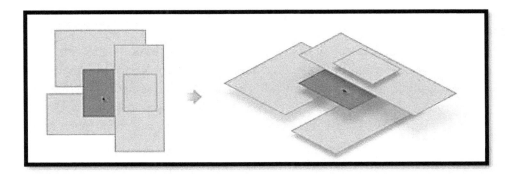

As your experience with Inkscape increases, this will appear more natural to you. Therefore, if you find this peculiar at this moment, you shouldn't be concerned about it. Simply said, it is a method of visualizing. It is essential to remember that you can raise and lower objects as well as make them overlap in a variety of various ways. The shapes can be raised and lowered, but what happens if we wish to group them? When you think about it, repeatedly picking the same shapes might be a monotonous process. How about we have a look at how to temporarily glue shapes together using groups?

Grouping shapes

You can occasionally find yourself wishing that objects would adhere to one another. Consider the case of a window that is constructed up of five rectangles. We would not have to select all of the shapes to move them together as a single unit. With the help of grouping, we can select all of them with a single click, just as if they were a single object.

Using the **Group** button in the Commands bar, we may select **Object > Group**, or we can simply click **Ctrl + G** to group chosen shapes into a single object.

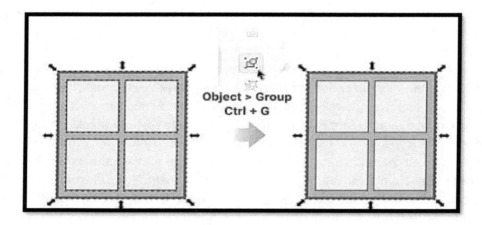

We can now move, scale, and rotate the entire thing by simply clicking once on any of the shapes in the group if we deselect our shapes. This allows us to do all of these things. However, what happens if we wish to change the color of one of the window panes or move it around? We could ungroup all of our window shapes by selecting **Object > Ungroup** (or by pressing **Ctrl + Shift + G** or by using the **Ungroup** button in the Commands bar), but the good news is that we do not have to destroy the group to make changes. We can easily enter our group by just double-clicking on it, which will allow us to do so. As a result, it is now feasible to select our pane and make the necessary adjustments.

53

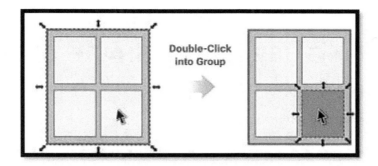

Once we have done so, we may either click anywhere outside of the group or press the Esc button twice to leave the group. When we perform a single click on one object within the group in the future, it will respond in the manner that we desire and select the entire group. Isn't it neat? Although it is a basic feature, it is incredibly strong. As a result of the fact that we can create sub-groups inside groups, grouping is an extremely effective tool for structuring an image. What if, however, we would prefer to have our shape mirrored? Let's figure out how to flip them.

Flipping shapes

Because it is symmetrical, flipping a rectangle is not a particularly fascinating activity. The concept of flipping can be better shown with the help of a line of elephants, should we, instead? In place of simply waiting in queue, we would like these elephants to engage in some social interaction with one another and chat with one another. To flip one of them around, we could use the **Flip Horizontal or Flip Vertical** buttons that are located in the Tool control panel. However, why would we go through the bother of doing so when we could just use the **H and V** keys on the keyboard to do the same task?

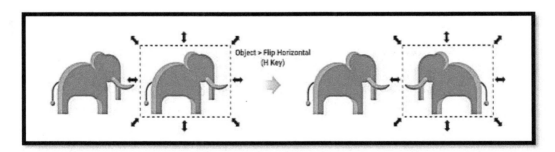

Yes, you read that correctly! If you select one of our elephants and press the H key, you will be able to engage in a full-fledged discussion with a pachyderm. Just be sure you don't choose to overlook the obvious problem! In a similar vein, pressing the V key will cause our elephant to flip over on its back; however, I am unable to see why you would want to do that to our elephant.

CHAPTER 5

MAKING USE OF THE SHAPE TOOLS

The Rectangle Tool

Select the **Rectangle** tool from the Tool control bar.

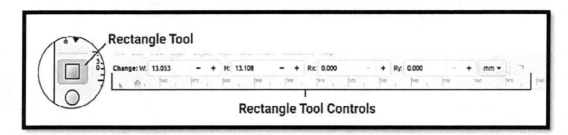

In this section, you have some manual control over the **width (W) and height (H)** of the rectangle, as well as two **Corner Radius values (Rx and Ry)** that correlate to the Corner Rounding Handles attribute that is located in the upper-right corner of the shape.

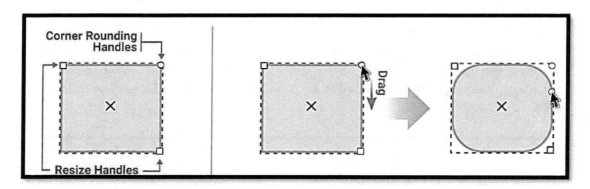

If you drag either of these handles, you will be able to round the edges of your rectangle in an even manner on all four corners. It is also possible to move the other handle thereafter to create an elliptic corner instead; but, I must confess that in all of my years as a designer, I have never wished to do this. Every time, it is completely and utterly unattractive. If you move both of the handles by accident and find yourself stuck with an elliptical corner, all you need to do is press the button labeled **"Make Corners Sharp"** located in the Tool control bar, and it will reset it for you accordingly.

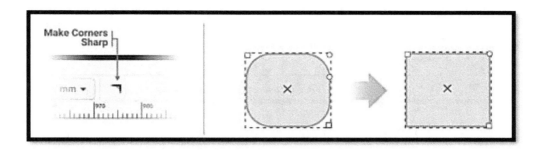

Another method for symmetrically rounding the corners is to hold down the Ctrl key and drag one of the handles. The handles located at the top left and bottom right of the rectangle will scale the height and width of the rectangle regardless of whether or not the rectangle is rotated. To clarify, the rectangular shape will be maintained throughout the process. Even while rounded rectangles are quite thrilling, you might like a circle or an ellipse instead...

The Circle, Ellipse, and Arc tools

Let us create some arcs, circles, and ellipses, which are essentially extended circles. To keep things simple, we will just call this tool the Circle tool, even though we are aware, based on the name of the tool, that it may also be used to create other shapes. To make circles, we will proceed in the same manner that we did when we made rectangles. Make sure that the size of your shape is to your liking by clicking and dragging one of the corners out. Simply holding down the **Shift key** will cause the circle you construct to be dragged out from the center rather than the corner. This is the case if you wish to drag a circle out from the center rather than the corner. If you also hold down the **Ctrl key (that is, Shift + Ctrl),** you will also obtain a perfect circle.

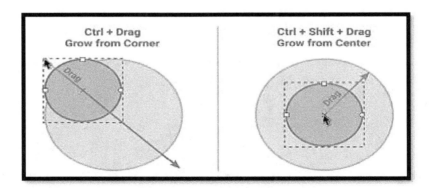

In a manner analogous to that of the rectangle, the Tool control bar has some unique properties and options that we may experiment with.

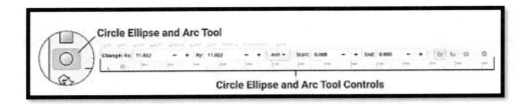

Circle Ellipse and Arc Tool

Circle Ellipse and Arc Tool Controls

It should be noted that **Rx and Ry** are there; however, this time, they correspond to the X and Y radius of the whole shape, which allows them to determine the size of the ellipse. Additionally, there are two values consisting of angles measured in degrees. These values are referred to as **Start and End**. You can recall from your geometry class in elementary school that angles may be expressed by degrees. For example, a quarter circle is equal to 90 degrees, a half circle is equal to 180 degrees, and a whole circle is equal to 360 degrees. If you look at the image below, you **can see that utilizing these degree values also enables you to easily create pie charts and other semicircular shapes by sliding the start and end handles:**

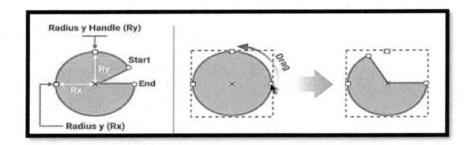

Through the use of the matching icons located in the Tool control bar, you can do a style change on the shape. You also have the option to reset the ellipse or circle to make it complete once more by selecting the button labeled "**Make Whole Ellipse**."

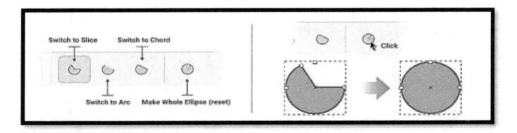

It seems simple enough, doesn't it? Let's construct a brand-new pie chart and utilize a real-world example as our inspiration. To obtain your pie piece, you may make use of the equation **P/100 * 360,** where **P** is the percentage of the pie chart that you wish to fill up. Consider the following scenario: we have a pie chart with parts that indicate fifty percent, forty percent, and ten **percent.**

When entered into the **End Spin Box** section, the following equations will produce the appropriate shapes for the pie pieces:

- **50/100*360**
- **40/100*360**
- **10/100*360**

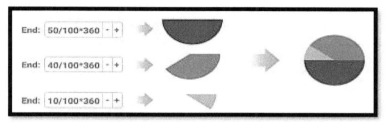

Are you ready for some shapes that are even more interesting? There is no need to look any further than the tool that creates polygons and stars.

The Polygon and Star tool

When it comes to an object that has options! To create a wide variety of clean shapes, the **Polygon and Star** tool is indispensable. A look of the tool control bar for this tool, which is **packed with options, is as follows:**

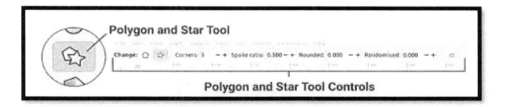

You can control whether the shape is a polygon or a star by using the first two toggles that are located by the word **Change**. This can be seen in the **image presented below (left). The Corners:** The Spin Box is responsible for determining the number of points that the star possesses or the number of corners that the polygon possesses, as seen in the **image on the right below**:

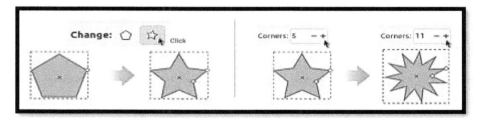

The portion of our star known as the **Spoke Ratio** is responsible for determining the degree of sharpness of the spokes, as shown in the **image on the left below**. Generally speaking, however, it is simpler to manipulate by sliding the spoke handles, which enables you to manually adjust it to be as sharp as you desire without having to fiddle with the **Spin Boxes**. The **Rounded:** field is a fun one, letting you make anything from a floral or splotch shape to one of those Spirograph thingies from the 1980s.. They are indeed nearly entirely ineffective as a design feature; yet, if you look me in the eye and tell me that it is not entertaining to play with, I will not believe you.

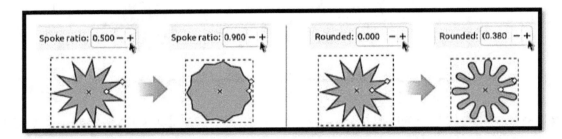

The **Randomised:** Spin Box controls the amount of randomization that's added to each point of the star to create a jitter effect. You should use this setting if you want your stars to appear to be drawn more randomly and to have a lesser degree of regularity. This randomization is **depicted in the image on the left, which can be found below; the greater the value, the more distorted the image becomes:**

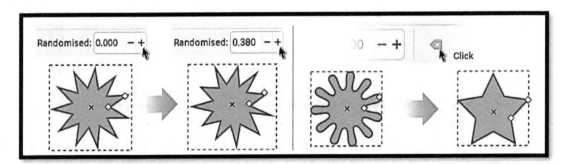

To reset the parameters of your polygon or star to their initial state, you may do so by using the Reset Shape Parameters button, as seen in the image on the right below. Additionally, you can **make freehand adjustments to your star qualities by using the following modifier keys:**

- **Snap to Angle**: When drawing your star or polygon, you may lock it to exact incremental angles by holding down the Ctrl key.
- **Lock Spoke Symmetry**: Hold the *Ctrl* key while dragging one of the spoke handles to make the spokes symmetrical

- With the **Change Rounding feature**, you can control the corner rounding by holding down the Shift key while dragging a spoke handle.
- **Change Randomization**: Hold the *Alt* key to increase or decrease the randomization value as you are dragging the spoke handles

During the process of drawing your stars, you could have seen that when there are a significant number of spokes, the sharpness of the tips has diminished. The reason for this is something that is referred to as the **mitre limit**. In Inkscape, the stroke may be created in three distinct join styles: round, bevel, and mitre. These join styles are suitable for situations in which the stroke connects at a sharp corner. If mitre is selected, Inkscape will produce a pointed point. If the point is too lengthy, however, Inkscape can automatically transform the corner into a bevel. Increasing the mitre limit value, which is the value that is located in the Spin Box next to the mitre join toggle, will cause Inkscape to attempt to join your corner with a sharp mitre edge at a greater distance. You can see that the **mitre limit** value has been reached in the image that is below. As a result, Inkscape has chopped off the corners and replaced them with bevel joints. If you want to obtain excellent sharp points again, you should increase the mitre limit setting, which is the maximum length of the mitre.

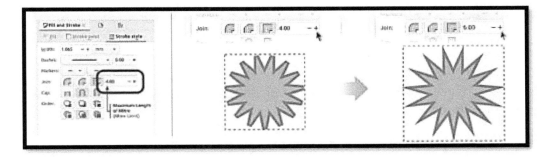

The **Star and Polygon** tool has one more secret gem. You can now make a polygon rhombus (or diamond, if you like my bad puns about lost wealth) in Inkscape 1.1. To get this new shape, just change the Corners number to 2. Before, this wasn't possible, and it's a very useful shape to have.

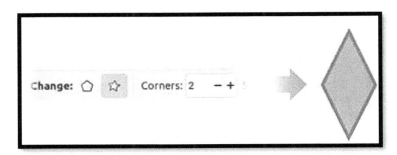

That's all there is to the Polygon and Star tool. You thought this tool was cool? Just wait until you see the 3D Box tool!

The 3D Box tool

When you use a two-point view with the 3D Box tool, you can draw... Well, 3D boxes. As you can see in the picture below, there are some annoying Angle buttons and settings that have lines next to them. If you don't know exactly what you're doing, changing these values will only make **things more confusing and frustrating than the last tools, so I strongly advise you to leave them alone and use the handles instead:**

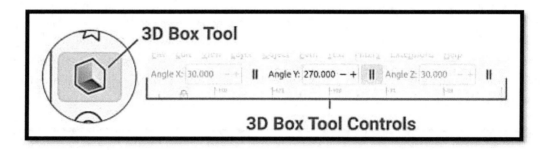

If you're going to use this tool, I suggest drawing your first box on the page and then changing the vanishing points by clicking and dragging them to extend beyond the page borders. Things can also get weird when you try to draw a box outside the page area. That way, you won't step into the fourth dimension by mistake and get messed up.

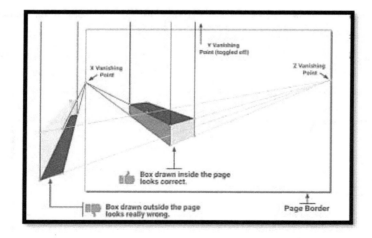

Since the vanishing points are on the page's sides by default, drawing a box off the screen makes it look really...interesting. You can change the vanishing points after you've drawn on the page. If you set the **Y Vanishing Point** setting to limited (off), you can see things from three points of view. By default, it is turned on (**infinite**). Keep in mind that the Vanishing Point (VP) buttons each have a picture of two straight lines. This is because the VP lines are parallel instead of merging when they are turned on. This means they never cross, which means the lines don't make a vanishing point. If you've worked with perspective pictures before, you probably already know that you can turn the other two VPs on and off to make one-point perspective and isometric boxes. To make isometric shapes more easily, you can use the axonometric grid. The 3D Box tool is mostly used to make boxes, as you can see here. Depending on how good you are at drawing, you can use those boxes as a base for designing packages, building mock-ups, and other fake 3D shapes. If you like that kind of thing, it can also help you plan out 3D scenes.

The Spiral tool

Each once in a while, you might want to curl up. Yeah, the Spiral tool is the best one for that. It has a lot of options on the Tool control bar.

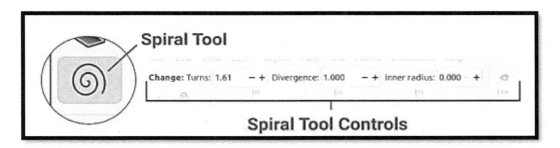

Turns Spin Box: This box controls how many times the spiral goes around the middle point (revolutions); *Divergence Spin Box*: This box controls how fast the spiral grows between revolutions. In other words, the spiral gap gets bigger as you move away from the center, like in a nautilus shell. **Here are some examples of turns and divergence:**

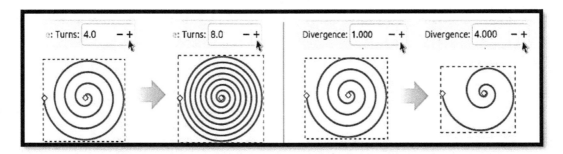

By dragging the handles, you can change where the spiral's beginning and ending points are.

You can also edit your spiral while pulling a handle by using these helpful modifier keys:

- **Snap to angle**: Holding down the Ctrl key moves the Start or End Node property to a small angle around the center.
- **Resize**: Holding down the Shift key changes the size of the circle when you drag the End handle property.
- **Rotate**: To rotate the whole spiral, hold down the Alt key and drag the End handle property.
- **Change Divergence**: You can change the Divergence number by hand by holding down the Alt key and moving the Start handle property.

You can also set a decimal percentage number between **0.0 and 1.0** in the Inner radius Spin Box. Let's say you wanted the circle to begin halfway between the center and the outside. That's 50% of the distance, **or 0.5.** Below is an image of the outcome. The **Reset Shape Parameters** button, which is depicted in the image below (right), allows you to return the spiral to its original settings.

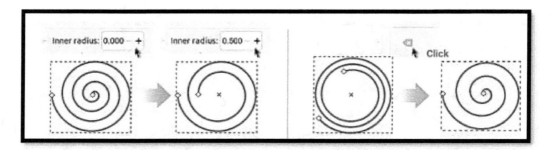

We're done with the object tools now! With what we've learned so far in this part, let's make something from start to finish before we learn how to change these base shapes in more ways.

Do it yourself.

That might not be the most interesting thing to make, but we're just talking about basic shapes, and a turntable (also called a record player) has many shapes that use most of the tools we've talked about so far. We'll make it more interesting by adding a modern view screen with an adjuster already built in.

How to do it

1. Use the **Rectangle tool** to begin and make the shapes in the image below. As shown in the image below (right), I drew them in this manner so that you could see the various shapes before we arranged them to make the main body of our turntable.

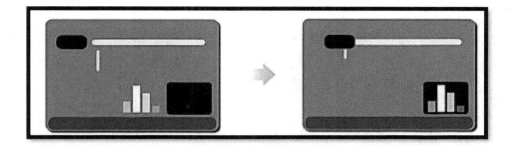

2. Give the arm some shadows and highlights by picking all of its parts and selecting **Group** from the **Object Menu** in the menu bar (**Object > Group** is the short form for this).

3. Once the parts are grouped, they can be moved around as a single object. We'll press Ctrl + C to copy this group and then press Ctrl + V to paste it. To turn all the shapes in this group black, just click the black color swatch in the **Swatch Palette**.

4. To make this shadow shape semi-transparent, enter a value of **50** in the **O:** Spin Box next to **Color Indicators**.

5. Now, use the **Page Down** key or the **Lower Selection one Step** option in the **Select and Transform** tool area to move the new shadow under the arm.

6. To make the reflection on the metal part of the arm and our equalizer window look the same, make rectangles with 50% opacity. This time, change the color to white instead of black and move the rectangles over the arm and the equalizer, respectively, instead of under them.

Before and After

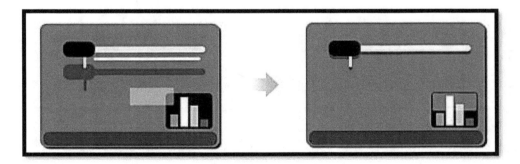

7. Now, add all of our round shapes with the **Circle and Ellipse** tools. As shown in the image below (left), begin by creating round metal pieces that resemble pie charts.

8. Once we have this, we can just group it and make a copy of it (you can copy and paste or press the spacebar to drop copies while moving). The metal base for the record player is obtained by scaling the pie chart shape up, while the metal for our four control dials is obtained by scaling it down, as shown in the image below (right). Keep in mind that the record's shiny edge is a circle in Arc mode with a white stroke; the fill value is set to **None**.

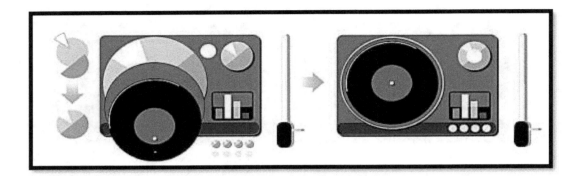

9. We'll add the track with the spiral to our record by setting the **Inner Radius** to 0.5, which is 50% of the spiral's width, and the Turns number to 31.

10. Hold down the Shift key and click on a gray color swatch to change the **Stroke** option to a light gray.

11. Click on the number next to the Stroke Color Indicator area to make the stroke's width very thin. The Fill and Stroke dialog box that appears with the stroke's Style tab and Width Spin Box can then be used to modify the value until it is ready to accept your new value.

12. Click on the red X swatch on the far-left side of the Swatch Palette to change the fill to None.

13. After that, we can move our spiral into place like this:

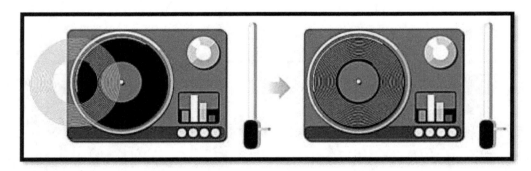

Now that it looks good, we need to connect the tonearm to the turntable. We could just turn it around a bit and then move it into place, but the pen might not be where we want it to be, so we'd have to turn and move it again. We need to move the joint that turns the tonearm to the back of it. Finally, we can move it once to line up the back of the tonearm with the base of the tonearm, and then turn it into place like a real turntable.

14. To do that, click again after selecting the tonearm (or simply press Shift + S) to get our turning handles and pivot point, and then drag the pivot to the back of the tonearm, as shown in the image below (left).

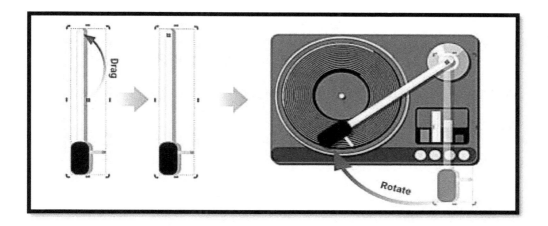

15. Place the tonearm on the base and turn it to the exact position you want, as shown in the image above (right).

16. To finish, we'll put a star on the record cover. Okay, so this drawing probably doesn't need much of an explanation at this point. But here's a nice picture to show you what it looks like:

Excellent work! You've used Inkscape to make your first full picture. Let's use File > Save to save it. Because that's what Inkscape works with, you should save it as an **.svg file**. Name the file something useful, like **turntable.svg,** so you can find it again.

CHAPTER 6
MASTERING COLORS AND FILLS
Using the Fill and Stroke Dialog

1. **Opening the Fill and Stroke Dialog**:
   - You can access the Fill and Stroke dialog by navigating to "Object" in the menu bar and selecting "Fill and Stroke..." or by pressing **Shift + Ctrl + F** on your keyboard. Alternatively, you can click on the Fill and Stroke icon in the toolbar, which looks like a paint bucket and a pencil.

2. **Controlling Fill Properties**:
   - In the Fill tab of the dialog, you can control the fill color, opacity, and gradient settings of your selected object.
   - To change the fill color, simply click on the color swatch next to "Fill" and choose a color from the color picker or select one of the predefined colors or swatches.
   - You can adjust the opacity of the fill by moving the Opacity slider or entering a specific value.
   - If you want to apply a gradient fill, you can choose from linear, radial, or conical gradients and customize the gradient stops and colors.

3. **Adjusting Stroke Properties**:
   - Switch to the Stroke paint tab to control the properties of the object's stroke (outline).
   - Similar to the fill, you can change the stroke color by clicking on the color swatch next to "Stroke" and selecting a color.
   - You can also adjust the opacity of the stroke and choose from various stroke styles, such as solid, dashed, or dotted lines.
   - Further customization options include adjusting the stroke width, joining, and capping styles for creating different line effects.

4. **Managing Stroke Style and Effects**:
   - In the Stroke style tab, you can fine-tune additional stroke properties, such as dash patterns, arrowheads, and markers.
   - You can create custom dash patterns by specifying the length of dashes and gaps.
   - Arrowheads and markers allow you to add directional indicators or decorative elements to the start or end of your strokes.

5. **Using the "Fill and Stroke" Dialog with Multiple Objects**:
   - When you have multiple objects selected, you can use the Fill and Stroke dialog to apply consistent fill and stroke settings to all selected objects simultaneously.
   - Any changes made in the dialog will be applied to all selected objects, making it efficient for managing the appearance of multiple elements in your design.

Applying Gradients

Gradients are how different colors blend. They are an important part of both graphic design and digital art in general. There are two tools in Inkscape that we will use to make gradients: the **Gradients Tool and the Mesh Tool**. To further edit the curves and add color, we'll also use the **Fill & Stroke menu**.

Different Kinds of Gradients

You can work with four different kinds of shades in Inkscape:

- **Linear gradients**: Transitions between colors that follow a straight (or "linear") path.
- **Radial gradients** make the colors move in a circle path.
- **Mesh shades** are when colors are added to a grid.
- **Conical gradients** are a type of gradient where the colors move in a partly circular path.

To help you understand how the four types of gradients work in Illustrator, here is a picture of them:

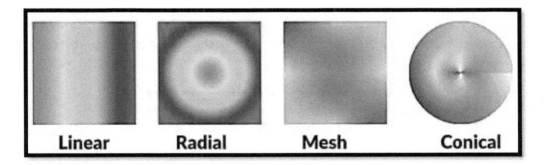

Linear Gradients

We will learn how to make linear curves in Inkscape in this first part of the lesson. Most of the time, you'll be working with these kinds of slopes. Select the object you want to apply the linear gradient to, then open the Fill & Stroke menu by pressing **Control + Shift + F** on your keyboard or by going to **Object > Fill & Stroke** to do so. The **Fill & Stroke** menu should show up on the right side of your screen as a dockable window. Look for the button that says "**Linear Gradient**" when you move your mouse over the **Fill** tab near the top of the menu.

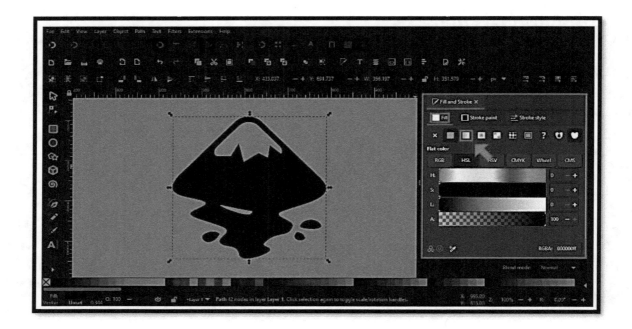

When you click that button, your object will become a gradient fill. The left side of the gradient is the original color, and the right side is clear. **Everything in the middle is a bridge between those two fills:**

To further edit this gradient, select the **Gradient Tool** from the toolbox on the left side of your screen or press **G** on your keyboard. To select the gradient path, use the **Gradient Tool** and click on either of the nodes on the left or right side of it. You can change the color of an object just **like you would any other object once it is chosen.**

The other node can then be selected, and its color can also be changed:

To add more colors to your gradient, double-click the path with the Gradient Tool to make a new node and change its color the same way you did before:

Lastly, you can move your gradient by clicking and dragging the end nodes around the image with the Gradient Tool:

You can also move the nodes back and forth between the end nodes to change where the colors are in the gradient.

Radial Gradients

Let's talk about radial gradients, which are the second most popular type you'll work with. Inkscape works the same way with radial gradients as it does with linear gradients. The only thing that differs is that the colors move in a circle rather than a straight path.

To make radial gradients in Inkscape, do the same things you do to make linear gradients:

1. Pick out an object and open the **Fill & Stroke** tab.
2. After going to the **Fill** tab, move your mouse over the button that says "**Radial Gradient**" and click on it.
3. Get the **Gradients Tool** and click on each gradient node to change its color on its own.

Just to the right of the linear gradient option is the radial gradient option:

The path of your radial gradient will be a circle. There is one node in the middle that shows the first color in the gradient, and two nodes on the ends that show the last color in the gradient:

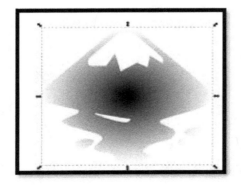

71

They may look like two different nodes, but they are related and do the same thing. **You will be able to do the following with the Gradient Tool, just like we did for our linear gradient:**

- Double-click the path to add more colors to the gradient.
- By clicking and dragging the center node, you can move the gradient around on the screen.
- To change the gradient's radius, click and drag one of the nodes on the sides.

Mesh Gradients

The colors in a mesh gradient are spread out on a grid instead of a path, which is different from linear and radial gradients. Inkscape's ability to make mesh patterns is a fairly new feature that doesn't work the same way we used to with other tools.

Select your object and pick up the Meshes Tool from the toolbox in Inkscape to create a mesh gradient:

You will see some options for the mesh gradient you're about to make in the tool settings menu **bar at the top of your screen. Before making the gradient, we need to use these options. Here are some of them:**

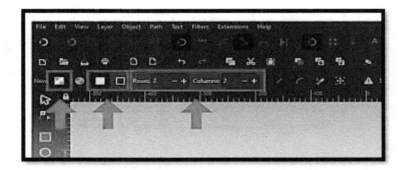

- The **Mesh box** lets you make a mesh gradient instead of a conical gradient.
- The **Fill box** lets you add the gradient to the object's fill instead of its stroke.
- How big the grid for your gradient will be is set by **Rows and Columns**.

We will use two rows and two columns for this example, which should give us four boxes in our grid. You will need more rows and columns if you want to use a bigger grid with more colors. After setting up your tool options, use the **Meshes Tool** to click and drag your gradient across your object.

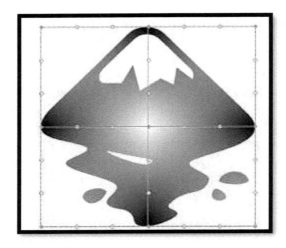

To change the gradient colors, you can now click on each node in the grid individually:

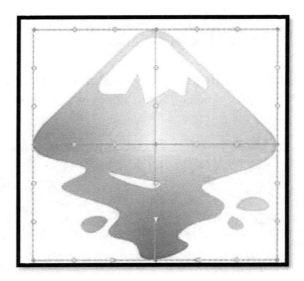

Additionally, you can click and drag any of the grid's nodes to move them in the gradient.

73

Conical Gradients

A circle path is followed by conical gradients, just like radial gradients. The main difference is that their paths aren't completely continuous, so different colors can follow the same circle. This isn't possible with radial gradients, where each path can only have one color.

The steps we took to make mesh gradients are also the steps we took to make conical gradients in Inkscape:

- Take the **Meshes Tool** and select the object you want to work on.
- In the tool settings menu near the top of the screen, choose the **Conical** option instead of the **Mesh** option.
- Figure out how many **rows and columns** you want in your cone-shaped or circle grid.

Making a circular gradient with **three rows and three columns** is what I will do for this example. **After you've set your options, click and drag across your object to make a cone-shaped gradient:**

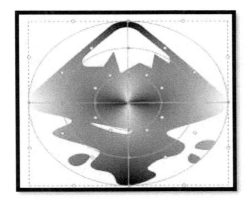

Like in the previous steps, all you have to do is click on any of the nodes in the cone-shaped grid to select it and change its color:

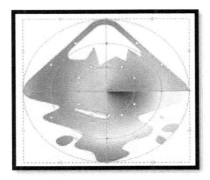

The nodes can also be moved by clicking on them and dragging them across the grid. That's all there is to this lesson.

Working with Color Palettes

Inkscape comes with a lot of color schemes already set up. A custom color palette can also be created and saved. For color reference, custom palettes can be made from images or drawings. We will show you how to use an image to make a color scheme and save it. Inkscape saves palettes as.gpl files, which are Gimp Palettes. You can't add themes that were made for Procreate or any other editing program, which is a shame. You can, however, make a palette from a resource file or a JPG or PNG file that comes with the product.

Start by opening Inkscape and choosing New Document.

Step 1 - Setup the color palette

At the very bottom of the screen is the color gallery. There is a button to the right of the palette that opens the **Palette Menu** when clicked. Although you can select from a variety of colors, **Inkscape Default** is typically chosen. Our palette will be made up of **Create squares and squares**. To make a square that is **1 inch by 1** inch, choose the tool and click and drag it. At the top, you can change the width and height. To help line up the squares, click on **Enable Snapping** on the right side. Select **Duplicate** from the drop-down menu that appears after right-clicking the square. The copy should be moved to the right of the square until it clicks into place. Make copies of the squares until there are eight rows across and eight rows down. You can change how many colors you want to add by adding more or less.

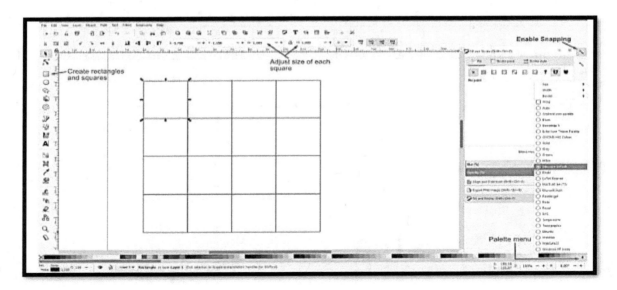

75

To add the reference image to the document, drag and drop it there. The **Import** menu will show up when you use this method. Don't change anything; just click "**OK**." Click on a square, then click on the left side button that says "**Pick colors from image**." Select a color by moving your mouse over it on the image. The color will fill up the square.

Repeat until you get the colors you want for the custom scheme. The example image should be deleted before moving on to the next step.

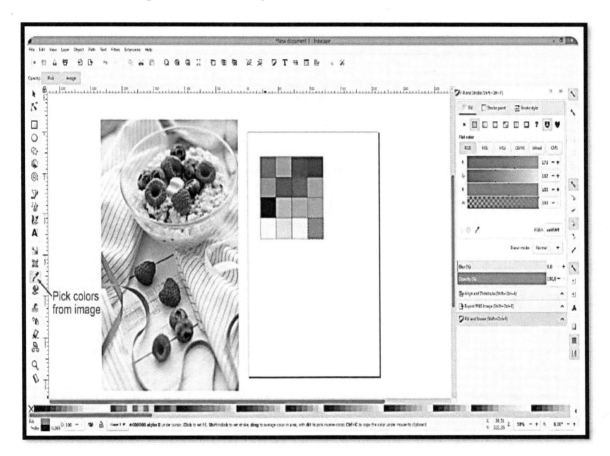

Step 2 - Save your custom color palette
It's time to add the palette to the **Palette Menu**. Here are a few more steps you need to take. Select **Document Properties** after clicking **File**. After that, go to the top and click on **Page**. Then, under **Custom Size**, click on the button next to the Resize **page to content**. Pick **Resize page to drawing or selection** from the menu.

The page will be about the right size for coloring. Click File > Save As to save this selection. Select **GIMP Palette (*.gpl)** as the **Save As Type** after giving the palette a name.

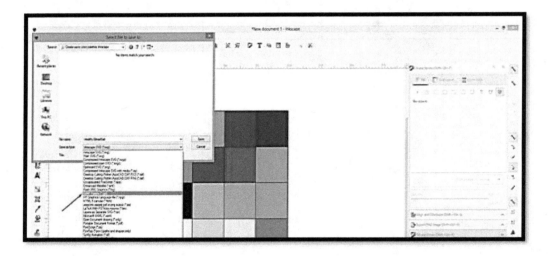

Step 3 - Add a new palette to the Palette Folder

Inkscape is different from other programs in that it needs you to move new colors to the Palette Folder. First, click **File**, **Close**, and then **Close without saving** to stop Inkscape. We already saved the color scheme, so we don't need to keep the **Square design**. Find the spot on your computer where the Inkscape folder is kept. Most of the time, you can find this in Program Files. First click on the **Share fold**er, then on the **Inkscape folder**. Select the **Palettes folder** by scrolling down and clicking on the Inkscape folder that is located in the Share folder. Every image we saw in the image menu is kept in this folder. This is where you should put your custom color. Get rid of the folder and start Inkscape up again.

Click on the farthest right button in the **Color Palette** at the very bottom. The Palette menu should be open. Click on the name of your custom palette. Our color scheme is called "**Healthy Breakfast**." After that, it will be added to the Color Palette.

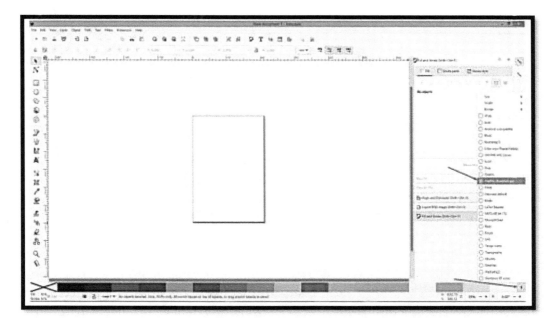

At any time, you can change the Color Palette selection back to Inkscape Default. The Palette Menu is easy to get to; just click the arrow and choose the palette you want. You will need to enter the Palette Folder and delete the palette there to get rid of it.

CHAPTER 7
MASTERING STROKE AND MARKERS

Stroke Width

The width of the stroke is the most important thing about it. There are several ways to measure width in Inkscape, just like there are several ways to measure any other length. You can see and change the stroke width of the chosen objects in two places in the UI right now: the marked style in the status bar (to the right of the stroke swatch in the bottom left corner of the window) and the Stroke style tab in the **Fill and Stroke** menu.

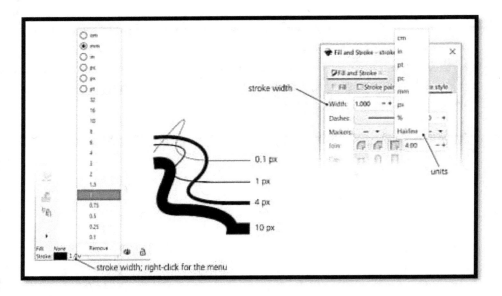

If you right-click on the number next to the stroke swatch in the chosen style indicator and pick a value from the menu that appears, you can change the stroke width. The unit for stroke width can be changed in the same menu. The unit that is used by default is ***px (SVG pixel).*** You can also drag the stroke width value into the canvas to change the stroke width of the selection directly, similar to how you edit fill or stroke colors with color movements. If you drag from where you started to the 45-degree no-change line-up and the left, the stroke in chosen objects gets wider (up to 50 times its original width). If you drag from below and to the right, it gets narrower (down to zero). In this case, if you start with a 1 px stroke, dragging up and to the left will make it 50 px, and dragging right and down will make it 0 px. You can quickly change the stroke width this way, without having to open any dialogs or options. You can type any number into the normal editable space in the Fill and Stroke dialog, and there is also a unit selection. Please note that if the whole Stroke style tab is grayed out, it means that the object you have chosen does not have any stroke paint. To turn it on, go to the Stroke Paint tab in the same dialog box and pick a single color or any other paint for the stroke. When the Hairline option is chosen from the units drop-down for the Width value, the Width value itself is turned off. No matter how much you zoom in or out, the strokes of the chosen objects will always look like they are a constant 1 px wide. It will still be possible to zoom in and out on the object, but the stroke will never look smaller or larger.

Hairline Width in SVG

As a result of the fact that the **vector-effect:non-scaling-stroke CSS property** is a relatively new addition to SVG, not all SVG viewers can handle it. Hairline width is accomplished using this property. When this article was being written, it was also not supported when exporting to PDF. When you use the outline mode, all of the objects in the document appear to have a hairline stroke that is always 1 pixel wide, regardless of how far you zoom in. Within the Visible Hairlines option, you can scale the stroke upwards, but not downwards; thus, it will always be at least one screen pixel wide, regardless of how far you zoom out. On the other hand, in contrast to the Hairline setting in the Fill and Stroke menu, these modes are only a more convenient editing option that is exclusive to Inkscape and does not have any impact on the SVG code of the document.

Stroke Width in Multiple Objects

The selected style indicator takes the average of the stroke widths of all of the objects in the selection that have any stroke. This occurs when the selection comprises numerous objects that have various strokes. Suppose, for instance, that one of the two objects that have been selected, has a stroke of three pixels and the other has a stroke of one pixel, the indicator will display two, and the tooltip will indicate that this is an averaged value. At this point, if you set any width by dragging or using the right-click menu, the same width will be allocated to all of the chosen objects that had any stroke in the first place. For instance, if one of the objects has a stroke that is three pixels in width and the other does not have a stroke, the stroke paint swatch will display three as the stroke width and say that it is different. However, any new width that you choose will only be allocated to the object that had a stroke that was three pixels in width. Different behaviors are displayed by the Fill and Stroke dialog. While the selection is being made, the stroke width unit will change to the percent unit (%) and the displayed value will be 100%. This occurs when different stroke widths are identified in the selection. For instance, if you alter it to 200% and then click **Enter**, the stroke width of each stroke in the selection will increase by a factor of two, making it twice as broad as originally. All of the diverse stroke widths will continue to be distinct, and the value that is presented will once again be one hundred percent. Within the same dialog, you can swap the unit selection from percent to any absolute unit, and you can also apply the same stroke width to any number of objects that have been chosen. However, even if you only have one object chosen, you may still switch to the percent unit and provide a new width as a % of the previous one. This is possible even if you have only one object selected.

Join

The path that a stroke takes is always a path, and a path might feature acute twists that are referred to as cusps. A sharp cusp may be generated even in the center of a Bézier curve, even though a cusp is often a node that happens to be the point at which two path segments meet at an angle. However, a node is not required to create a cusp. The two style properties that are modifiable on the Stroke style tab of the Fill and Stroke dialog are join type and miter limit. These properties influence how the stroke behaves at the cusps of the stroke. The round join, the bevel join, and the miter join (the default) are the three types of joins that are conceivable, and they are represented by the three toggle buttons.

Round join

Using this method, the effect is similar to that of tracing the join with an exactly round pen. At the moment that the cusp comes into view, the outer shape is a smooth circular arc with its center located on the path centerline. When it comes to paths that are primarily curvilinear and where occasional cusps could appear out of character if they are not rounded, this option is the most obvious choice.

Bevel Join

It is essentially the same as a Miter join (for more information, see below), with the exception that the miter limit is set to 0. The corner is cut off by a bevel, which is a straight line that is perpendicular to the bisector of the cusp angle. This implies that the corner can be cut into any angle.

Miter join

In this sort of join, the appearance of the join is determined by the degree of sharpness of the cusp angle. Until these straight lines intersect, the outer contour of the stroke at the cusp point is continued by two straight line fragments that are tangential to the stroke on both sides of the joint. This is done for angles that are not excessively acute. As a result of this, the joint is ornamented with a pointed peak that is known as a miter. This miter grows longer and more pointed as the angle at the joint lowers, and it may even extend beyond the location of the cusp node. On the other hand, this results in difficulty. What is the maximum length that the miter can reach? It should come as no surprise that the miter will be indefinitely long until the angle at the junction reaches zero, which is entirely lawful. Miter limit control is responsible for ensuring that this does not occur by establishing the maximum length of a miter in terms of stroke width.

For instance, if the default miter limit is set to four, any miter that is less than four-stroke widths will continue to have a sharp tip. However, if you lower the angle to make the miter longer than that, it will be cut, or beveled, at a distance of four stroke widths from the joint.

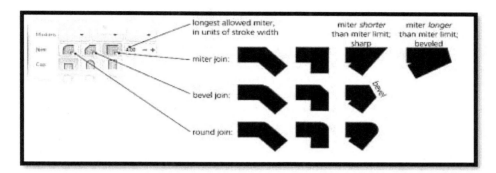

As can be seen in the image below, the artistic effect of switching between different stroke join settings is likely most readily apparent when it comes to text objects that have been stroked.

Stroke Joins in SVG

Miter, bevel, and round are the three possible values that may be assigned to the stroke-line join CSS property, which is responsible for controlling the joins in SVG. There is a distinct property called stroke-miter limit which is where the miter limit is saved.

Caps

An open path must be able to draw the ends of the stroke to function properly. There are three options available here as well, which are fairly comparable to the three types of joins: It is possible to have butt, round, or square stroke caps.

- **Butt cap:** Using this, the stroke is cut bluntly, perpendicular to the direction of the stroke, and directly at the end node of the path.

82

- **Round cap**: This adds a semicircular blob that rounds the end of the stroke seamlessly.
- **Square cap:** Adds a half-square blob to the end of the stroke.

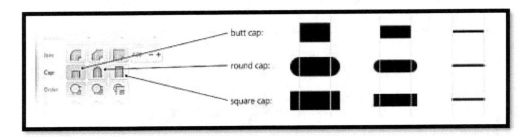

In addition to adding a cap that is half the width of the stroke to each end, round and square caps both make an open path longer by the whole width of the path. The path is precisely the same length as the distance between its end nodes, but only when butt caps are used, which is practically the same thing as saying no caps at all. The effect of join and cap options is only noticeable on strokes that are sufficiently wide or when zoomed in; for strokes that display at only two or three screen pixels, they make very little difference visually (with the possible exception of lengthy miters).

Stroke Caps in SVG

Butt, round, or square are the three possible values that may be assigned to the stroke-linecap property in SVG. This property is responsible for controlling the stroke caps of a path.

Dash Patterns

It is not necessary for a stroke to completely go from one end of a path to the other. You can stroke a path with a regular pattern of dashes that are separated by empty intervals of any length when they are used with SVG. You can construct new dash patterns for your benefit if you are familiar with the CSS syntax that corresponds to them. If this is not the case, select one of the several predetermined patterns that are contained within the Fill and Stroke window.

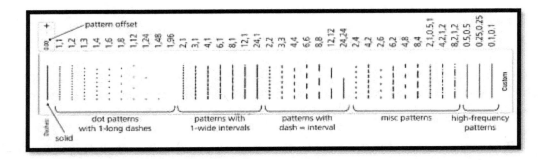

All dash patterns are specified in terms of stroke width, which means that the pattern scales up or down proportionally when you make your stroke broader or narrower. Each dash design is defined in terms of stroke width.

The following are some of the preset patterns, which are listed in roughly descending order from the most popular.

1. **Dotted Patterns**:
   - These consist of dots that are stroked segments whose length equals the stroke width.
   - The intervals between dots range from 1 to 48 stroke widths.
2. **Patterns with Long Dashes**:
   - These patterns have long dashes with intervals of single-stroke width.
   - The lengths of the long dashes range from 1 to 24 stroke widths.
3. **Patterns with Equal Dash and Interval Lengths**:
   - Dash and interval lengths are equal, ranging from 2 to 24 stroke widths.
4. **Patterns with Varying Dash and Interval Widths**:
   - Dash and interval widths vary, including combinations like 2 and 4, 4 and 2, 2 and 6, and so on, up to 8 stroke widths.
5. **Patterns with Long Dash Followed by Short One**:
   - These patterns feature a long dash followed by a short one.
6. **Patterns with Equal Dash and Interval Lengths Shorter Than Stroke Width**:
   - Dash and interval lengths are equal but shorter than the stroke width.
   - These patterns range from 0.5 down to 0.1 stroke widths, providing finer control over the appearance.
7. **Custom Option**:
   - Contrary to its name, the "Custom" option doesn't offer visual editing.
   - It presents a seemingly random pattern that can only be edited in the CSS editor, providing advanced customization options beyond the predefined patterns.

The Pattern offset field, which is located next to the dash pattern picker, gives you the ability to move the previously selected pattern down the path by a certain distance (again, measured in stroke width units). For instance, if you want your path to begin with an interval but you are using a pattern that consists of two dashes and two intervals, you may shift it by two.

Dashes in SVG

When using SVG, the stroke-dash array property is where the dash pattern of a stroke is provided. In addition to accepting values of none (a solid line), it may also accept a list of values that are separated by commas, with each odd value representing the length of a dash and each even value representing the length of an interval. An example of a stroke-dash array specification might be as follows: A dash of length 2 is followed by an interval of length 1, which is then followed by a small dash of 0.5 and another interval of 1 (all lengths are in the units of stroke width). This sequence follows a dash of length 2 that is followed by an interval of length 1. Within the group element that has the **id="dashes"** attribute, the list of the predefined dash patterns that are displayed in the **Fill and Stroke** dialog is saved in the preferences.xml file that you have. Adding, removing, or altering the patterns that are accessible through the Inkscape user interface may be accomplished by changing the children of this element. It should be noted that dashes are also affected by stroke caps. The round or square caps will be applied to both ends of each dash if you have a path that is specified to utilize circular or square caps. As a consequence of this, the length of each dash will significantly increase by one full stroke width in comparison to its length when the default butt caps are used. As an illustration, the **1,1 dash** pattern with round caps loses all of its intervals; the round caps of consecutive dashes, which are each 0.5 stroke widths in length, now contact each other, as the image below depicts.

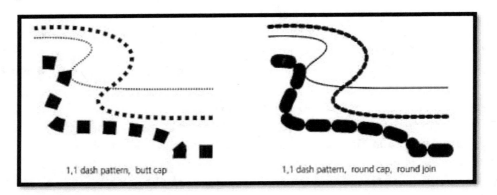

1,1 dash pattern, butt cap   1,1 dash pattern, round cap, round join

To generate a pattern of round dots that follow a path, you will need to employ a dash pattern that has zero-length dashes and round caps. This is because of the result of the previous sentence. Since Inkscape does not provide a list of such a pattern in the Fill and Stroke panel, you will be required to manually construct it. First, you will need to apply a pattern to your path that has the interval length that you want. After that, using the Selectors and CSS dialog, you will need to edit the stroke-dash array property of your path to set its dash length (first value) to 0. A pattern like this will, of course, render the path entirely invisible if it does not contain round or square caps. This is the reason why it is not included in the standard patterns; keep in mind that the default option for caps is butt. Dot patterns with very wide spacing, such as 1,48, may be used to quickly create a random dispersion of dots, which is an intriguing application of these patterns. Use the Pencil tool to create a doodle that resembles a spiral, and then apply a 1,48 dash pattern to it. This will transform the doodle into a cloud of dots that appear to be disconnected.

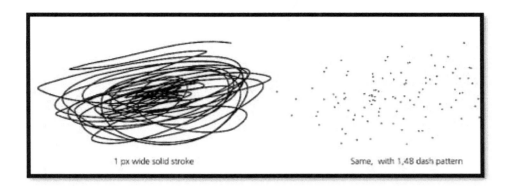

1 px wide solid stroke   Same, with 1,48 dash pattern

Additionally, the regularity of dash patterns works well with spirals, which are similarly regular shapes but consist of twists that get gradually longer and longer. Enchanting patterns may be created by the interaction of dashes that are evenly spaced apart and paths that progressively veer off course.

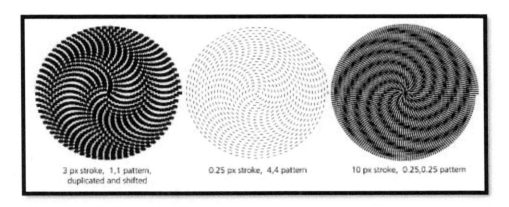

3 px stroke, 1,1 pattern,   0.25 px stroke, 4,4 pattern   10 px stroke, 0.25,0.25 pattern
duplicated and shifted

Markers

Markers are arbitrary objects (or even groups of objects) that are attached to a path and displayed as part of that path at (some of) its nodes. Markers may also be applied to groups of objects. The creation of arrowheads in flowcharts and diagrams is the most popular application of markers currently in use. Within a path, there are three distinct sorts of markers that might be present: on the start node, on the intermediate (mid) nodes, and the end node. Each copy of the marker is positioned at the node and rotated in such a way that it follows the path that is situated at this particular node. When you want to scale all of the markers on a path, you just need to make your strokes narrower or broader. The size of markers is proportional to the width of the stroke. Within the Fill and Stroke dialog, the Stroke style tab has three drop-down menus that allow you to select start, mid, and finish markers for the paths that you have selected.

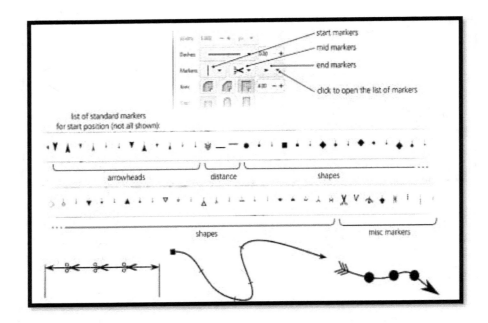

In other words, you are free to use any marker in any place. These three lists display all of the identical markers; however, the sample thumbnails show them applied to the beginning, middle, and end of a horizontal straight-line path. This allows you to get a sense of how the marker will appear on the real path. Let's look at what markers are in Inkscape's stock list.

Arrowheads

There are two distinct sorts of arrowheads: *one is fashioned like a dart and has two straight lines at the rear, while the other is delta-shaped and has a concave circular arc at the back of the arrow.* Generally speaking, there are three sizes available for each type of arrowhead: large, medium, and tiny. These sizes are not absolute values but rather related to the stroke width. Also, there are two orientations for each size: **start and end**. For instance, if you want your arrowheads to point away from the path, you should select one that has a start orientation as the start marker and one that has an end orientation as the end marker. If you get this wrong, the arrowheads on your arrows will point inward from the sides of the path. You can select the same end-orientation arrowhead for all three points (start, mid, and end) on your path. This will ensure that all of the arrowheads on your path point in the same direction, which is toward the end of the path. If you need to reverse a path, you may do it by selecting **Path > Reverse** from the menu.

Arrow tails

It is only possible to purchase an arrow tail marker in a single size (which corresponds to the size of the huge arrowheads) and in a single orientation (which makes sense as an end marker—that is, pointing toward the beginning of the path).

Distance measurement markers

Markers for measuring distance are nothing more than arrowheads with straight lines added at the points that are perpendicular to the arrowheads. The first orientation is for a start marker, while the second orientation is for an end marker. Geometric shapes have both orientations.

Geometric shapes

Round dots, squares, diamonds (squares rotated by 45 degrees), equilateral triangles, straight line stops, and full and empty half-circle markings are some of the geometric shape markers that are included in this collection. Variants that are hollow and solid black make up the majority of them. As is the case with arrowheads, these markers are available in three sizes: big, medium, and tiny. Additionally, some of them have start and end orientations. However, in the case of symmetric markers like diamonds, the only difference between the orientations is the location of the marker to its node. Different variations of triangle markers, such as those used at the beginning and the finish, can be utilized as arrowhead shapes.

Misc markers

Some fancy markers are available, the most notable of which are the scissors (which may be assigned to mid markers to produce a conventional "cut-off line") and the "infinite line" ellipsis ends. These markers will be added to the top of the drop-down marker choices, which will be segregated from the stock Inkscape markers that are located below them. If your document already employs certain markers of its own, these markers will be added. If you want to remove markers from a path, select the empty line that is at the very top of the list.

Markers in SVG

The process of assigning a marker to a path causes Inkscape to insert a copy of the marker into the document's defs and then to make the path refer to the marker that is located in the defs. When you use the **File > Clean Up Document** command, you may delete markers that you no longer use anywhere in the document. The list of markers that is displayed above the separator in the marker menus is simply the same as the list of markers that are contained in the defs.

Coloring Markers

As a result of the fact that connection lines in flowcharts and diagrams are often black, the stock markers that are provided by Inkscape are either completely black or black with white infill. On the other hand, if you had a blue or red connection line, you would generally want the arrowhead on that line to be blue or red as well. After assigning a marker to a path, Inkscape will automatically recolor the marker so that it is the same color as the stroke of the path. This is the default behavior. Whenever you alter the color of a path's stroke using markers, the markers associated with that path are also changed. This particular color-matching is not the behavior that is typical in SVG; rather, it is something that Inkscape performs to be helpful. When you change the color of a stroke, Inkscape will automatically produce a copy of each assigned marker, re-paint it with the new color, and then reassign it to the path. This happens behind the scenes. It is because of this that the copies of the markers that you have used that are of various colors will be displayed at the top of the lists in Fill and Stroke. If you recall correctly, the lists in Fill and Stroke list the custom markers of the document first, followed by the standard markers. The good news is that you can disable this feature by going to **Preferences > Behavior > Marker**. If you do not like this behavior, you can disable it.

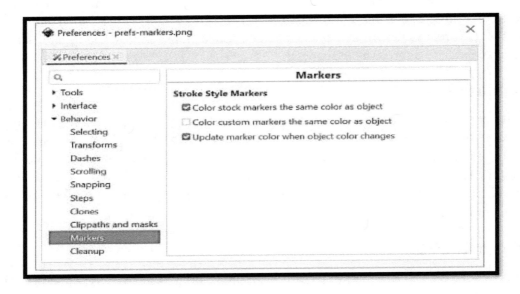

For example, if you wish to utilize a path simply as an unseen thread for a rosary of markers, meaning that you want to show the markers but conceal the stroke itself, you should deactivate automatic marker coloring. This is one of the reasons why you should disable automatic marker coloring. Before you can accomplish this, you must first assign the markers to a stroked path, and then you must remove the stroke (for instance, by middle-clicking the stroke swatch in the style indicator that you have selected). This will provide you with what you require, which is visible markers on an invisible path if you have previously ensured that the Update marker color when object color changes setting was turned off. When the strokes of the markers and the markers themselves have distinct colors, the sequence in which they are rendered is another factor that needs consideration. The stroke is painted first by default, which means that if it is different from its markers, it will only show through from behind the markers if they are transparent. A relatively recent development in Inkscape is the ability to automatically color markers. Before the availability of this feature, the only method to accomplish this task was to go to **Extensions > Modify Path > Color Markers** setting. This addon is still accessible, and it might be helpful in some situations since it provides some more options. Not only can you paint markers to match the object with it, but you can also change the colors of the fill and stroke, insert alpha optionally, or just offer your colors for the fill and stroke.

Creating New Markers

A marker doesn't need to be a single object that is simply painted with a single color. To put it another way, everything that Inkscape is capable of drawing may be used as a marker on a path. It can be composed of any number of objects, whether they are grouped or not, and it can have any paint, opacity, or even blur properties. Amazing compositions may be created by applying such complicated markers to paths that have a large number of additional nodes. Let's have a look at the process of making markers out of old-fashioned objects. In most cases, all that is required is to select the object or objects in question and then select **Objects to Marker** from the options presented by the **Object menu**. However, under the **Stroke style** tab of **Fill and Stroke**, you will see your new marker at the top section of the list of markers (just before the stock markers). This is because the selected objects will disappear. It is possible that to refresh the marker list, you will need to exit and then reopen the Fill and Stroke panel.

While Inkscape is in the process of constructing a new marker, it assumes that the original objects are positioned in the correct orientation on a horizontal path that extends from left to right. For instance, if you have a new arrowhead that you wish to utilize as an end marker, you need first make it point horizontally to the right before transforming it into a marker. When you modify the stroke width, the user-created marker will scale up and down in the same way that regular markers do. Each stroke will have a width of one pixel, which will correspond to its initial size, which is the size of the object that you have transformed into a marker. The point that will be positioned on the node to which a particular marker is attached is referred to as the anchor point for that marked marker. When you create a new marker in Inkscape, the anchor point is determined by the transformation fixed point of the object that was recently picked as the first object. According to the default configuration, the fixed point is located in the middle of the bounding box of the object. This indicates that the newly formed marker will be centered around the node itself. The new marker will make contact with the node that is located by the corner of the object if you move the fixed point to one of the corners of the object.

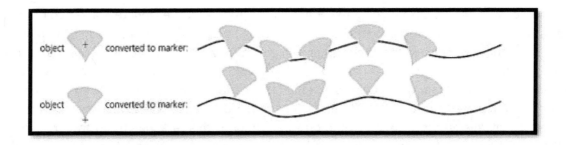

Can you perform the opposite operation and turn a path marker into an object (for instance, edit it and turn it back into a marker)? Can you do this? Unfortunately, this will result in the destruction of the path that the marker was applied to; thus, it is recommended that you create a duplicate of the path before proceeding. Choose the **Stroke to Path** command from the **Path** menu. Not only does it transform the stroke into a full path, but it also groups the converted path with objects that reflect the markers that were present in the original path. Remove the group, select one of the previous markers, rotate it so that it is oriented in the default orientation, and make any required edits. Please take note that you can transform a clone into a marker and then proceed to edit the original object while its marker clones are being updated in real time.

Advanced Markers

When compared to the user interface of Inkscape, SVG markers offer a few more helpful options that are not currently accessible. It is necessary to utilize the Selectors and CSS dialog in conjunction with Inkscape's XML Editor to make any changes to them. Release both of them. When using Selectors and CSS, you may choose an object by using markers. Once you have identified the marker property that you are interested in (marker-start, marker-mid, or marker-end), click the green arrow that is located at the right end of the line that contains that property. This will cause the XML Editor to scroll until it reaches the svg:marker element that your object is utilizing.

The following is a list of the characteristics that may be modified with this element:

- By default, markers shift their orientation such that they are aligned with the direction of the path. Remove the orient="auto" property from your marker if you want it to always have the same orientation, regardless of how the path proceeds at this moment in time.
- Adding the property markerUnits with the value userSpaceOnUse is the way to go if you do not want the marker to scale up and down whenever the stroke width is altered.

Rendering Order

As you have seen, a single solid object, and not a group of objects, may nonetheless have up to three unique components: its fill, its stroke, and its markers. The only question that has not been answered is the sequence in which these fundamental components should be rendered. SVG has its style property that regulates this situation since it is not possible to simply rearrange them in the same way that you would with individual objects that are part of a group. One of the six values that reflect all of the potential orderings (bottom to top) of the three components can be assigned to this property, which can be edited under the Stroke style tab of the Fill and Stroke tool.

- fill, stroke, markers (the default)
- stroke, fill, markers
- fill, markers, stroke
- markers, fill, stroke
- stroke, markers, fill
- markers, stroke, fill

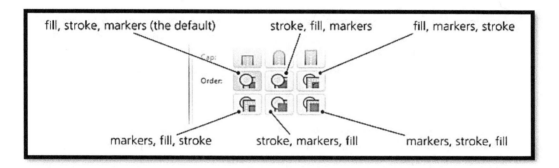

Stroke Always Centered on Path

Paint strokes can be entirely painted on the inside or outside of the path in Adobe Illustrator. This option is available to editors. In SVG, this is not feasible; stroke is always centered on the path (although this may change in future versions of SVG to provide for this possibility). When the fill is placed on top of the stroke, it moves up to the line of the path that the stroke is centered on. When the fill is opaque, the visual outcome of placing it on top of the stroke is almost precisely the same as if the stroke were half its width. This is because the blend is opaque.

CHAPTER 8
UNDERSTANDING PATHS AND NODES

Introduction to Paths

Within the realm of vector graphics, paths in Inkscape are the fundamental components that are utilized for the creation of shapes, lines, and curves. The contours, shapes, and trajectories of objects are defined by them, which enables exact control and manipulation of the objects. Node and segment are the two primary components that make up a path. Nodes are points that identify the corners or curvature of a path, and segments are the lines that link these nodes. Segments can be straight or curved, depending on the direction of the path. The shape or trajectory that is represented by the path is formed by the combination of the nodes and the segments.

There are several distinct sorts of nodes:

- **Corner Nodes:** The corner nodes are responsible for producing acute angles in the path, which results in noticeable shifts in the direction of travel.
- **Smooth Nodes**: Smooth nodes are responsible for producing transitions between segments that are smooth and curved. This enables continuous curves to be created without abrupt shifts.
- **Symmetric Nodes**: Symmetric nodes ensure that the curvature is symmetrical in both directions by maintaining equal control handles on both sides of the node.
- **Auto-smooth Nodes**: These nodes automatically change the curvature of nearby segments while maintaining a smooth transition. They help to ensure that the transition is seamless.

Using a wide variety of tools and methods, paths may be produced and altered in Inkscape, including the following:

- **Drawing Tools:** Inkscape provides a variety of drawing tools, including the Pen tool, the Bezier tool, and the Pencil tool. Each of these tools is designed to do a certain task and requires a particular level of accuracy.
- **Node Editing**: The Node tool enables direct editing of individual nodes, allowing alterations to be made to their location, type, and curvature to modify the shape of the path.
- **Path Effects:** Additional tools and effects that may be applied to paths to accomplish particular outcomes include placing text along a path, producing spirals, and applying pattern effects.

By employing Boolean operations, paths can be merged, intersected, or changed in the following ways:

- **Union** is a function that will combine several paths into a single shape by merging the areas that overlap between them.

- In the **difference operation**, one path is subtracted from another path, and the overlapping piece of the second path is removed from the first path.
- The **intersection** only keeps the region that is shared by numerous paths that overlap with one another.
- **Exclusion**: This function eliminates the intersecting regions that are shared by several paths, leaving just the sections that do not possess overlap.

Through the use of the **Fill and Stroke** dialog, it is possible to adjust the properties that are associated with paths in Inkscape. These attributes include **strokes (outlines) and fills (interiors).** This makes it possible to alter properties such as color, opacity, width, and style to produce the visual effect that is wanted. In general, paths are extremely adaptable and powerful tools in Inkscape. They provide the flexibility and accuracy that is required to produce elaborate designs, intricate shapes, and precise drawings with ease and creativity.

Editing with the Node Tool

As a result of the **Edit Paths by Nodes** tool, which we will refer to from this point forward as just the **Node** tool, we are fortunate enough to have the ability to create nearly any shape that we choose in Inkscape. To edit our shapes, however, we must first transform them from objects into paths. Once we have paths, we can edit them node by node. This is a prerequisite for editing our shapes. As a first step, let's go ahead and select our glass by using the Node tool that is located in the Toolbar section. The glass will be ungrouped by hitting the **Ctrl key, the Shift key, and the G** key, or by choosing **Object > Ungroup**, and then selecting the glass rectangle object. It is important to mention that we still own our corner rounding handles, which are properties of the object. We can edit all of the nodes rather than just the object properties when we convert from **Object to Path**. To accomplish this, we just click the **Object to Path** button that is located in the Tool control bar.

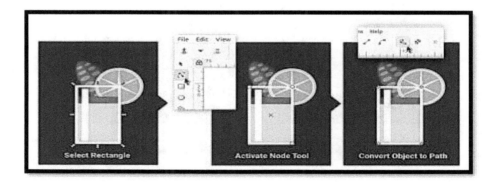

To adjust the size of the bottom of our glass, we now have four corner nodes that we can click and drag to change their size. From the middle of the glass, we would want to resize the bottom of the glass and distribute the liquid in an even manner on both sides of the glass. Either by first choosing the glass rectangle and the liquid rectangle, then pressing Shift and selecting, or by dragging and selecting a box around the bottom nodes, we can accomplish this desired result. We are provided with scale-transform handles, which allow us to adjust the size of the line that connects the nodes. In the same way that we did when we were resizing shapes, we can resize from the center by holding down the Shift key. Additionally, we can narrow the base of our glass from both sides at the same time.

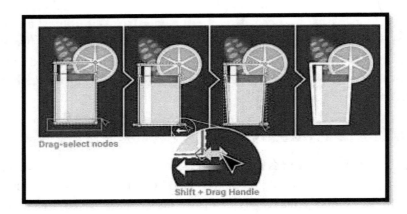

If the handles that allow you to resize are not visible, check to confirm that the **Show Transform Handles** option is turned on.

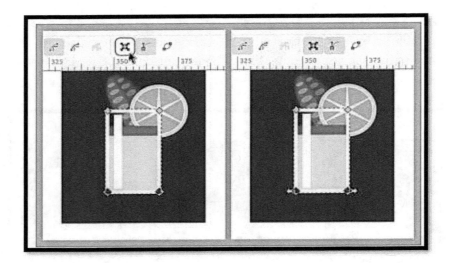

Additionally, you can click the nodes a second time to obtain the rotation handles, which will enable you to rotate the selection as you are doing so. This is not something that we will be using, but it is important to keep in mind in case you find yourself in need of it!

Adding and removing nodes

If we want more than four nodes, what should we do? When you are working with the Node tool in Inkscape, you can easily add and remove nodes by just double-clicking the path. You will now have another node to move about as a result of this.

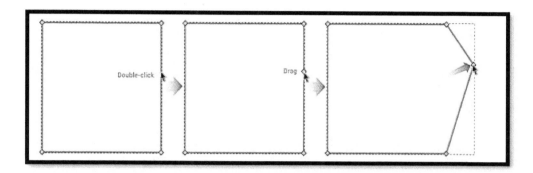

Maximize your efficiency in node manipulation with the powerful node tools located in the Tool control bar. Simply start by selecting a line segment with a single click. Once selected, you can take advantage of the "Insert New Nodes into Line Segment" button, also referred to as the "Add Node" button (marked with a + symbol). This intuitive feature automatically adds a node at the midpoint of the selected segment, precisely halfway between its two end nodes. But the convenience doesn't stop there! Click the button again to swiftly add center nodes to any two selected line segments, and repeat the process as needed. With these streamlined tools at your fingertips, node manipulation becomes a breeze, allowing you to focus more on your creative vision and less on tedious tasks.

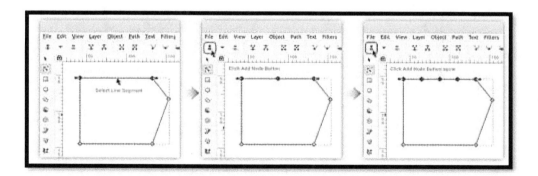

The removal of nodes is identically simple. Use the **Delete Nodes** button, press the **Ctrl key** and **the X** key (which is the typical shortcut for **Cut**), or touch the **Delete key**. All you need to do is select the node or nodes that you want to eliminate.

The picture that follows illustrates the outcome of removing a corner node:

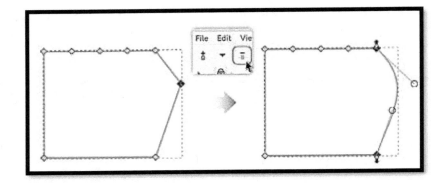

You might be wondering why Inkscape created a curve rather than just deleting the node and restoring the vertical straight line at this point. Inkscape will, by default, make an effort to maintain the general shape even when you destroy nodes by default. In the future, we will see additional examples of how the **Trace Bitmap** tool may be used to smooth out lumpy geometry or lengthy curves with an excessive number of nodes. The outcome is quite valuable for solving these problems. For the time being, if you want your straight line restored, you may do so by tapping the button that says "**Make Selected Segments Lines**." At the time of this writing, we are in the process of replacing this button with the more descriptive "**Straighten Lines**" button.

The outcome of the procedure on our select curve is seen in the image below:

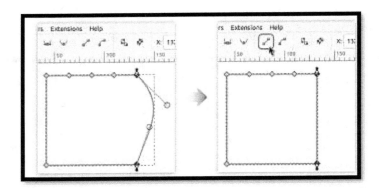

It is important to take note that the curve handles vanish completely every time we do this. If you choose to regain them, you need to click the button that is situated exactly adjacent to the **Straighten Line** button, which is shaped like a curve. This is the **Make Selected Segments Curves** button. To add insult to injury, however, that is not what it does. It does nothing more than add back the curve handles; it does not alter the line in any way. This is the reason why in the future it will be referred to as the **Add Curve Handles** button. The majority of the time, you won't even

97

actually require this button, which is a fortunate condition. Simply click and drag any straight line into the desired curve shape, and you will have the desired curve.

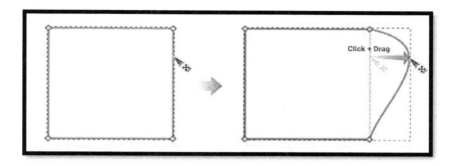

However, what exactly are those curve handles in the first place? Is it possible to construct a curve that is through a node completely smooth? Let's delve a little more into that, shall we?

Curve handles and node types

During the process of erasing that node, we were given our first glimpse of what a curve seems to be. Inkscape's curves are Bezier curves, and they are constructed from **one or more curve handles**, which are also referred to as **control points**. By clicking and dragging a curve handle, you can exercise precise control over the degree to which your curve leans in one direction or another. When many lines are linked to the same node, we have control over how the handles relate to each other, as well as control over the degree to which the curve that encompasses the node is smooth. Every time we want a smooth curve, we don't have to manually insert curve handles since Inkscape offers several node types that help produce different sorts of curves. This eliminates the need for us to manually place curve handles. Within the Tool control bar, we can select the kind of node that we want by choosing nodes and then clicking on the type of node that we want. **The following image provides a visual representation of the many types of nodes and the buttons on the Tool control bar that correspond to them:**

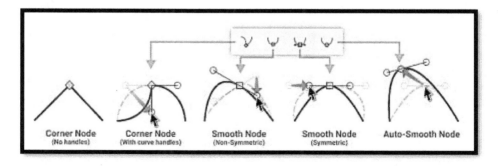

98

As can be seen, we have a wide variety of options, each of which is utilized for the creation of a distinct variety of curves. The Corner node is represented by a little gray diamond and may or may not contain curve handles (depending on the circumstances). If you add curve handles, you will have the ability to freely move the handle on each side of the node, which will result in the formation of a sharp corner. We have the option of selecting any of the two **Smooth** node options to obtain smoother options. The initial configuration is non-symmetric, which means that the handles will remain parallel to one another, but they will be located at different distances from the node on both sides. **Smooth Node Symmetric**, on the other hand, replicates the distance that you drag, which results in both handles having the same extent of length. A little gray circle represents the **Auto-Smooth** node, which is the final option available to you. Using the auto smooth feature, you may just drag around the node itself rather than the handles, and Inkscape will automatically construct smooth geometry wherever you move it. When you grasp the handle of the **Smooth** node, the node is immediately changed into a non-symmetric **Smooth node**. This not only allows you to modify the curve to your liking, but it also maintains the curve that you had previously.

Breaking and joining lines

In certain circumstances, we can find it necessary to break our closed path to make a gap in the shape. Take, for instance, the glass that we have. We may get to the conclusion that we don't want the top of our glass to have a stroke, for instance. We can select the top line of the glass and then utilize the "**Delete Segment between Two Non-endpoint Nodes**" button, which we will refer to as the "**Remove Line**" button from this point forward. As may be seen in the **following illustration, this eliminates not just the line but also the stroke that was located at the top:**

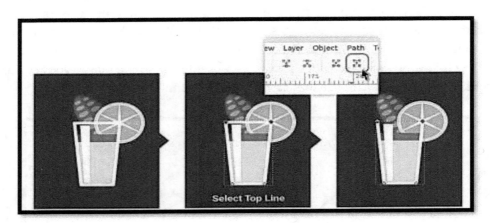

In the same vein, we can re-add it by clicking the **Join Selected End Nodes with a New Segment** button, which is also referred to as the **Add Line** button. This button is located just to the left of the **Remove Line** button. One thing that you could see is that the fill of the object might or might

99

not be affected by splitting the shape open in this manner. This is contingent upon the specific sections of the line that are disconnected. I normally do not advocate assigning a fill to a broken path because Inkscape needs to guess which parts to join when the closed shape is broken. Instead, I propose selecting a closed shape just behind the stroke as a distinct object, like we did when we made the fluids to fill our glass. This is because Inkscape has to guess which **sections to link. The image that follows illustrates some of how the fill-in shape might go awry, depending on how the lines are broken:**

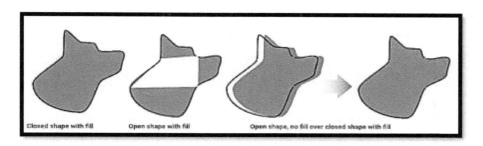

In addition to providing you with full control over the shape of the fill, ensuring that all filled shapes are closed will spare you a great deal of potential hassles that are associated with filling fills. In the absence of a line to close the gap, Inkscape is only able to attempt to connect with a straight fill. This is typically not what we want, and it causes a mess, particularly when we are attempting to utilize them in boolean operations. At this point, let's go with the process of designing custom shapes, but this time we will begin from scratch!

Drawing lines and shapes from scratch

We don't need to begin with any shapes at all. Inkscape will automatically link the points on the canvas that we click on with lines when we use the **Bezier Curve tool**. All we have to do is click in numerous locations on the canvas. Not only that, but we may finish a closed shape by clicking on the same node that we began with. Whenever you move the mouse over the first node, you will see that it will be highlighted in red. This is to signify that clicking on the node will cause the shape to collapse entirely.

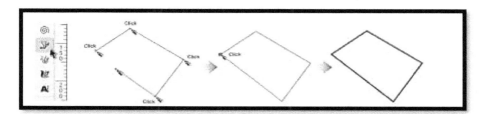

When we press the Enter key, Inkscape will finish the shape at the location where we clicked the last time, allowing us to create an open shape. If you misplace a node, you do not have to wait until a later time to correct it. By using the Backspace key, we can undo the most recent node that we clicked on. Inkscape will continue to delete nodes until there are no more nodes left, regardless of how many times you hit the **Backspace** button. With this method, we can easily create a polygon with straight edges; but, what if we wish to incorporate some curves into the design? We have the option of clicking and dragging out a curve rather than clicking the next node into existence.

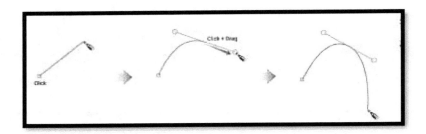

While we are now discussing open shapes, let us also discuss line styles so that we may make our lines appear exactly how we want them to.

Line styles

To this point, we have been essentially just embracing the notion that our lines are solid and do not have any breaks unless we break them manually. This is the case even though they cut off suddenly. On the other hand, it is possible to design our lines in such a way that the ends are rounded or square-capped, and our corners might be rounded, sharp, or chamfered. Through the **Stroke Style** option, we can do this. The Stroke width value may be accessed by clicking on it in the Fill and Stroke Indicator section, which is located in the bottom-left corner of the screen. This will allow us to enter this menu. The Stroke Style tab in the Fill and Stroke dialog will appear as a result of this action.

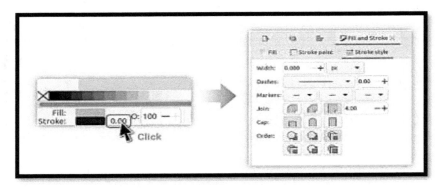

Let's focus on how our corners look first. You can see the **Join** field, which controls whether our corners are sharp, rounded, or beveled, based on whichever option is toggled on.

As you can see in *the image below*, with the Join and Cap fields, we can choose the following:

- **No cap**: This causes the line to come to a halt at the node
- **Round cap**: This cap is used to finish the line with a rounded end cap.
- **Square cap:** This cap is used to finish the line with a square cap, although it is slightly longer than the line (this is useful for eliminating minor gaps by overlapping).

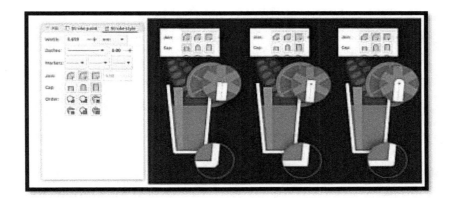

The option to transform our solid line into a dashed line is also available to us, in addition to the addition of caps. As can be seen in the image below, the **Dashes** dropdown menu allows us to select from a variety of presets, in addition to choosing **Custom**:

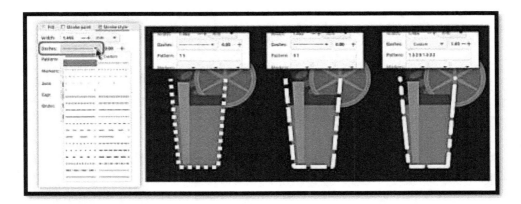

It is important to take note of the fact that when we select one of these options, a **Pattern field** emerges showing numbers that are separated by spaces. These numbers reflect the rhythm of the dashes and gaps. Although they appear to be enigmatic at first glance, the numbers in this box simply reflect the length of each dash and the space that follows it. In addition, you have the option of entering a decimal number, such as 1.5, to enhance the distance between your dashes. When working with rounded end caps, which tend to contact each other slightly at a gap value of 1, this comes in extremely helpful. For the same reason, perhaps you want your round-capped design to include round dots. It is possible to input a value of 1, however, the result will be a dashed line that is one length long and has end caps applied to it. If you enter a value of zero, you will only receive the rounded end caps (and hence a complete circle), and you will also receive your dots. When you add to it a value of 1.5 for a gap, it creates a good separation between them. You must use spaces to visually differentiate the numbers in your pattern. **The following development of values is depicted in the image below:**

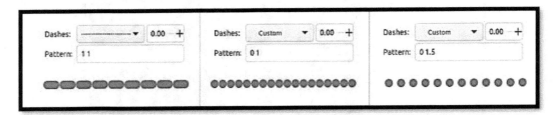

As you can see, we can achieve a variety of effects by utilizing both regular and irregular spacing combinations. However, there are occasions when we would like there to be custom shapes at the ends and corners of our lines. Let's imagine, for instance, that we would want to construct an arrow. The interface for picking the start, finish, and midway markers of our open shapes is depicted in the image below. Inkscape refers to these shapes as **Markers**. The following are **some of the options that are available to pick from:**

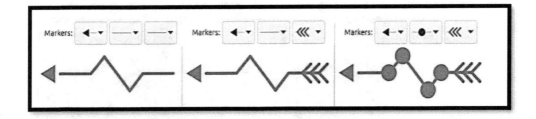

With Inkscape version 1.2, we cannot only select from a collection of attractive preset markers, but we can also edit those markers on Canvas, which is a feature that is quite helpful. You should know that the size of the marker in Inkscape is determined by the stroke width through the default settings. If you discover that you want some more precise control over the scale of the marker, we may select the **Edit on Canvas** option. This may be sufficient in certain situations, but if you find that you want further control, we can do so.

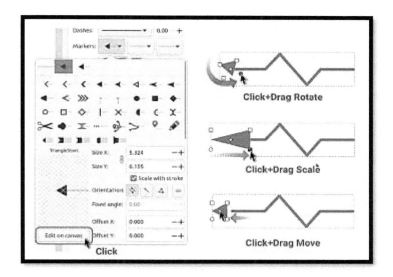

Altering the scale and rotation in the same manner that we do with normal shapes is something that we can perform for the middle and end markers as well. When we make changes to the **values on the canvas, the options and values that are displayed in the boxes will also change. Even though most of them are self-explanatory, here is what they do for your convenience:**

- **Size X and Size Y:** These dimensions determine the scale of the marker in both the horizontal and vertical directions. The origin, which is the small diamond that we grasp to move the marker around and which appears in the middle of the marker when we are editing on canvas, is used to compute this. An outward calculation is performed from the origin.
- **Scale with stroke**: This option will make an effort to automatically scale the marker head whenever you increase the width of the stroke. When you desire a thicker or thinner line, you won't have to manually modify the size of your markers because this eliminates the need to do so.
- **Orientation**: This has four buttons that control the direction of the line and markers:
  - ○ **Orient along path, reversing at the start**: This default setting ensures that the start marker is oriented forward and aligned with the front of the line (the end).
  - ○ **Orient along the path**: Similar to the first option, but both the start and end markers face forward, aligned with the line direction.
  - ○ **Fixed specified angle**: The third toggle in the row fixes the marker at the angle specified in the Fixed angle field, rather than having the marker follow the direction of the line.
  - ○ **Flip marker horizontally**: The last button in this row horizontally flips the marker.
- **Fixed Angle**: If the Fixed specified angle toggle is not active, this option will be grayed out. The angle at which the marker will be turned is determined by this setting. While we are

working on the canvas, this is automatically generated whenever we drag the rotation handle.

- **Offset X** and **Offset Y**: By selecting the Offset X and Offset Y options, you may move the marker farther from the beginning of the line or the end of the line, accordingly. When we move the marker using the diamond handle that is located in the middle of the canvas while we are working on the canvas, they are automatically populated.

Below the drop-down menus for the markers are a series of buttons that are a little bit confusing and appear a little bit like a question from an intelligence exam. Listed below are the many **Draw Order** options. When Inkscape produces a shape for us, it must decide whether to put the shape fill on top of the stroke or beneath the stroke. In addition, we have markers, which further complicates the situation. Should they be placed on top of the stroke or the fill, or should they be drawn beneath it? What is the proper order for them to be drawn? The image **that follows illustrates some different options for this Order, as well as the effects that these options have on the appearance of our shape:**

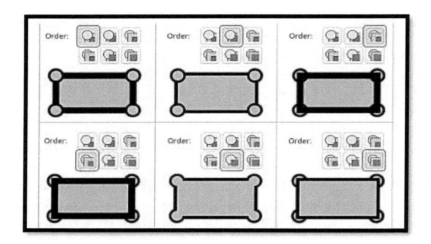

According to what you can see, the sequence in which we draw produces a significant impact on the appearance of our shape. While you are working, it is important to keep this specific point in mind. Two additional tools allow us to create custom shapes, and it is important to describe them before we get into actual practice.

Classical drawing tools

Sometimes, we would want to be able to select a tool, much like we would a pencil, and have Inkscape create a line down the path as we draw it. This would be a convenient feature. Two of Inkscape's tools are capable of doing this. In the first place, there is the **Freehand Drawing** tool, which is denoted by a pencil icon and can be found just beneath the **Bezier Curve** tool that we discussed before. Rather than clicking and dragging around the canvas, we may just click and drag and Inkscape will create a line that follows the path that we drag. It will stop drawing when we stop dragging and let go of the control button. By utilizing the **Smoothness** field that is situated inside the Tool control bar, we can exercise control over the smoothness of this path. **As can be seen in the image that follows, the smoothness of our line increases in proportion to the value of our smoothing parameter:**

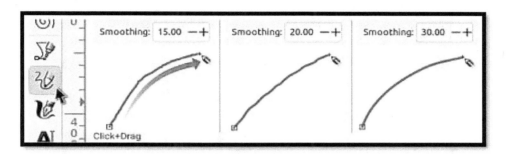

It is important to keep in mind that to view the result that came before, you must have the **Stroke color** and **Thickness** set, as well as the **Fill** set to **zero**. Because this was drawn using a mouse, we should anticipate that the line will be a little wavy as a consequence of this, and we may thus increase the smoothing to compensate for this. Using a graphics tablet is yet another way that may be utilized to get a smoother line. Specifically, this is a gadget that consists of a pen for drawing as well as a surface made of plastic that can detect where you are drawing. The pressure that you apply is also registered by it, which allows it to imitate the pressure that would be applied by a real pen, pencil, or paintbrush. Not only will this result in a far smoother line, but it will also make it possible for us to utilize the button labeled "**Use pressure input,**" **which, if we press it more forcefully, will result in a line that is thicker than before, as seen in the image below:**

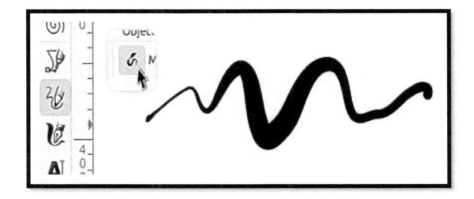

This will create a filled shape rather than a line; but, if we select our freshly created squiggle and activate the **Node tool**, we will notice that it is still simply a line with some cool additional handles that allow us to modify the thickness at various points along our line. In the program, Inkscape,

106

this particular line that has thickness handles is referred to as a **Powerstroke**. It is **possible to raise or reduce the line thickness by clicking and dragging one of these handles in either direction, as seen in the image below:**

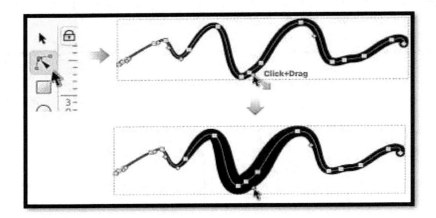

We could use this method to create all of our lines, but there is also the possibility that we could just want Inkscape to create full shapes for us rather than elegant strokes. To accomplish this, the **Calligraphy Brush** tool is utilized. It is true that drawing using this tool only results in the creation of filled shapes, as we can observe after drawing a squiggle in the same manner as **mentioned earlier. The squiggle and nodes that ended up being made using the Calligraphy Brush tool are displayed in the image that can be found below:**

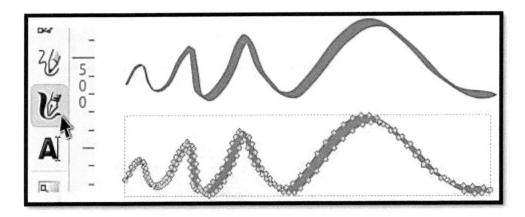

It is important to take note that the shape of the brush automatically generates a calligraphy pen effect that is flattened.

There are a large number of presets that may make a variety of shapes, including:

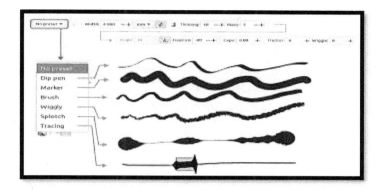

Through the selection of one of these presets, the settings in the Tool control bar will be altered to produce the desired appearance of the brush. Regrettably, modifying these variables will not result in the preset being altered; but, you can create your own presets by modifying the values to something that you prefer and then pressing the **Add or Edit Calligraphic Profile** button, which is located just to the right of the **Preset** dropdown menu. Enter the name of your preset into the box that appears when you click the button. Your modifications will be added to the list of presets that are called by that name.

Advanced curves and line options

We are almost finished with our tour of the Node tool and the custom shape tools that go along with it. On the other hand, there are a few additional types of curves and lines that we need to investigate. For now, let's return to the Bezier Curve tool and take a look at some of the various sorts of curves and lines that are available. The image that follows displays the Mode buttons, **which include four other types of curves and lines (the first of which is the Bezier Curve tool, which is enabled by default):**

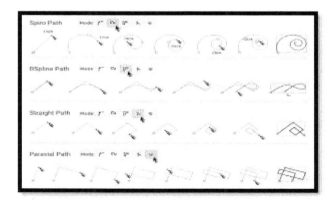

Your ability to create a variety of curves and lines automatically is made possible by the various modes, as shown in the illustration:

- **Spiro Path**: This feature enables you to create a flawless spiro curve just by clicking around (there is no need to drag). The usage of flowery flourishes, which are frequently employed in graphic design, is a perfect application for this.
- **BSpline Path**: An alternative form of curve is known as a BSpline Path, and it is distinguished by the fact that it uses points rather than handles to identify the curves. In some cases, this can be easier to deal with than Bezier curves, because it always results in lines that are connected smoothly.
- **Straight Path**: If you do not want your lines to curve in any way, you may find that the Straight Path option is useful. The click-and-drag curve options are disabled, and only straight lines are permitted to be drawn.
- **The Paraxial Path:** This is an intriguing one to consider. The starting angle is determined by the first line and each line that comes after it is a 90-degree angle from the one that came before it.

The **Bezier Curve tool** and the **Freehand Drawing tool** both accommodate these settings in their respective tools.

Making brush strokes with Stroke Shape

If you are not one of the fortunate individuals who have the financial means or the time to get a drawing tablet, there are still a few options that make life with a mouse somewhat less difficult. To be more specific, we may use **Stroke Shape** to create strokes that gradually widen. The first thing we should do is make use of the **freehand tool** and examine the **Shape** drop-down menu. **Using the different options that are present inside the stroke, the following image illustrates the type of stroke that may be obtained:**

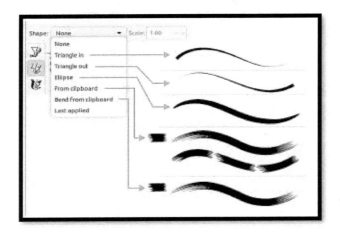

In the same way that we saw before with **Powerstroke**, these options provide you the ability to resize the stroke while maintaining the general shape of the emulated brush stroke. To produce the appearance of the most recent object that was copied, the last two options, which are referred to as **from clipboard** and **Bend from clipboard**, apply two distinct Path effects. To put it another way, you first copy a shape that you wish to use as your brush, and then you select one of the two options at the clipboard location. The texture of the object that was cloned will be reflected in the subsequent brushstrokes that you make. Since it has a Pattern Along Path effect in addition to a great deal of additional capabilities, such as **Repeat and Repeat stretch**, the **From clipboard option** is the one that I like out of the two available options for the clipboard. While drawing with our **Bezier Curve** tool, we can access these same options through the **Shape** dropdown.

CHAPTER 9
ADDING TEXT TO YOUR DESIGNS

Any text that you add to an Inkscape drawing will, as you would expect from a vector editor, continue to be completely editable as text at any point, regardless of the style, filters, or transformations that you apply to it. The Text tool is responsible for the creation and modification of text objects. It gives you the ability to write or remove words, wrap text into columns (either manually or automatically), apply style to text spans, modify kerning and spacing, and a variety of other options.

Since it is not very easy to manage big volumes of text, Inkscape does not compete with word processors or desktop publishing applications. On the other hand, Inkscape does not provide any tools for structural formatting, such as style libraries or automated headers. As an alternative, Inkscape is a visual design tool that will provide you with comprehensive and exact control over every glyph, word, and paragraph, and it will do so without surrendering the ability to edit text in the majority of occurrences.

Installing new fonts

As every designer is well aware, it is necessary to have a comprehensive font library for creative purposes. If you are restricted in the fonts that you may choose from, you can quickly add fonts to Inkscape to provide yourself with additional options.

Add Fonts to Inkscape
Quick Steps

1. Download the font folder
2. Unzip the folder
3. Open the font by double-clicking
4. Click on Install
5. Restart Inkscape

For the most part, I obtained all of my typefaces from Google's extensive font website, which can be found at **https://fonts.google.com/.** The reason for this is that Google takes great care in selecting the greatest free and open fonts, which may be used in a professional setting anywhere without the need to pay license fees. In addition, the SIL Open Font License, which includes all of these typefaces, guarantees that you will be able to use, edit, and expand the character set in accordance with your requirements.

Using the Text Tool in Inkscape

Just like the other tools that we have covered up to this point, the **Text tool** can be found in the Tool control bar on the left side of the screen. After activating it, we are presented with a little cross cursor that has the letter **A** next to it. At this point, we can click anywhere on the canvas to begin creating text. With Inkscape, we have access to a flashing cursor, which is something you are probably already acquainted with from other writing tools. If this blinking cursor is displayed, all that is required of us is to write out our text on the keyboard.

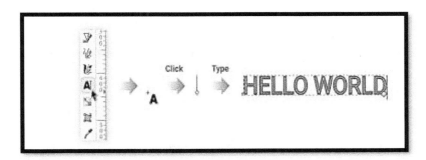

Note that Inkscape has, by default, made our text the same color for **Fill and Stroke** that we were using previously in our other shapes. This is something that you should take note of. We would prefer the text to be black for the time being, therefore we can easily make the fill black **by clicking on the black swatch at the bottom of the window, then pressing Shift and clicking on the red X swatch to unset the stroke color, as seen in the image below (you can also do this in the Fill and Stroke dialog if you have it up):**

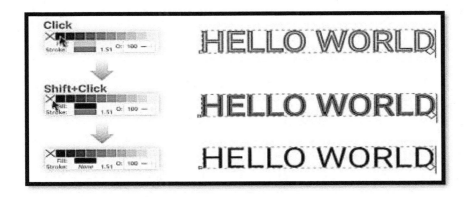

To add more text to a line below, we may do the same action as we would in other text editing apps by pressing the **Enter** key. There may be situations when we would like the text to automatically wrap around to the following line at a particular place. You may have observed the small diamond handle that is located in the bottom right corner of our text. This handle is

responsible for controlling the wrapping; all you have to do is move it to modify the wrapping limit:

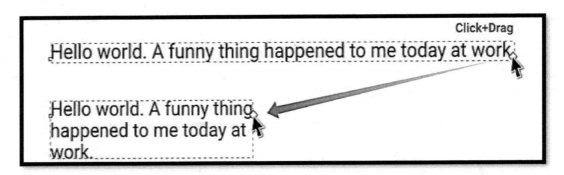

Before we begin typing, it would be helpful if we could first determine the wrapping area and the borders of a paragraph. This works very well. To do this, we can easily create a rectangle on the canvas by clicking and dragging the **Text tool**. This will allow our text to flow inside the rectangle. When we type, it will then wrap the sentences to that rectangle, which will be the result.

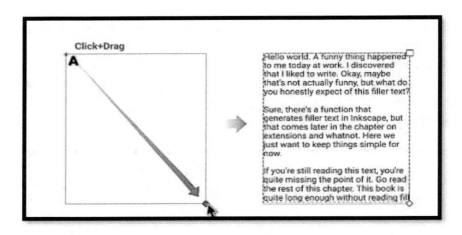

Take note that you may adjust the size of the text box at any moment by moving the handle located in the bottom-right corner. As for the top-right handle, what exactly does it do? A margin will be added to the text if you click and move it. You will notice this when you do so. These margins are applied uniformly on all edges of the text box, and they are particularly helpful for creating some padding around the text that you are displaying. It is possible that the text will not be able to fit inside the text box when it is of a size that is too large. The **Font Size** dropdown menu that is located in the Tool control bar allows you to make adjustments to the size of the text. If you want to use a custom value, you may either use the values that are in the dropdown menu or you can just click in the box and put it in.

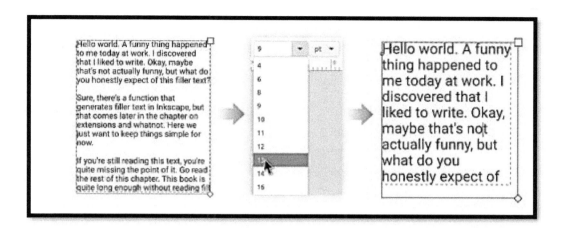

We noticed that when we suddenly changed the font size from **9 to 13**, our text was cut off at the bottom, and our text box went red. This occurred when we increased the font size. This is because Inkscape is alerting us to the fact that part of the text at the bottom of the page is being removed. This fragment of text is referred to as **overflow**. To retrieve it, all that is required of us is to adjust the dimensions of our text box so that it is compatible with the diamond handle located in the bottom right corner. Inkscape will change the color of the box back to blue if there is no longer any text that is overflowing. It is also important to notice that the drop-down menu that is located just to the right of the **Font Size box** allows you to modify the units of measurement.

What I do most of the time is simply utilize the default, which are points or points. Assuming that you want your font size to function like that of a word processor like **Microsoft Word or LibreOffice Writer**, this is the default setting for a document that is measured in **millimeters or inches**. However, if you want a greater degree of accuracy in terms of size control over your typefaces, you may convert these measurements to millimeters or inches. To format our text, the Tool control bar contains a wide variety of options, one of which is **Font Size**. We have a Font Family dropdown that begins at the far-left side of the bar. This dropdown will provide previews of all of the fonts that you have installed on your machine. Because of this, selecting a new font at a glance is a quick and simple process. On occasion, however, we would like to be able to preview the font that is now being used in our document with text that we have previously entered. To accomplish this, we may alter the font of the text that is now being shown by clicking on the **Font Family** box and then using the up and down arrow keys on the keyboard.

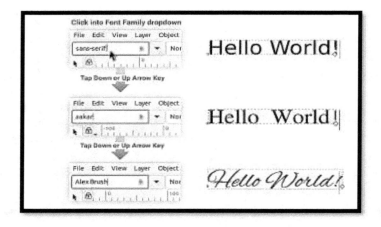

If you are aware of the name of the font that you intend to employ, you may also utilize the dropdown menu as a search bar. By simply erasing the contents and beginning to type, Inkscape will automatically reduce the number of font options available to you as you type. The **Font Family** dropdown has one cooler feature, and that is the small button that is located on the right-hand side of the field and has the appearance of a page. By clicking on this little button, you will select all of the text on the canvas that is of the same font as the one that is specified in the field. Because of this feature, it is quite simple to change the fonts that are used in all of the text boxes in your document. **The image that follows illustrates this procedure, beginning with a single text box that has been selected:**

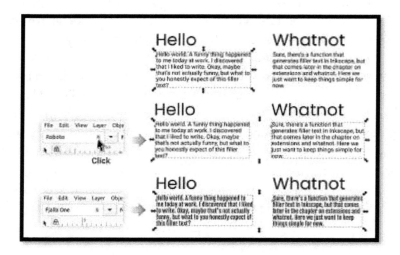

In the sample that came before, you should have seen that the title and the paragraphs are two separate text objects. In most cases, I opt to keep the titles distinct from one another since doing so makes it simpler to alter the typeface on other objects. The **Font Style** dropdown is located in the Tool control bar, right next to the Font Family dropdown. The font you have selected may contain one, two, or even a large number of styles, such as **bold, italic, italic bold**, and so on. **One sample of each of the Roboto font's styles is displayed in the image below:**

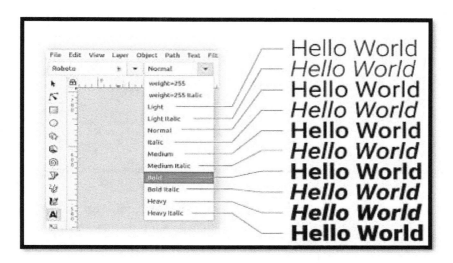

In addition to being useful for titles, this is also useful for highlighting particular words inside our paragraphs or sentences. To this point, we have altered the font for the entire text object; but, if we highlight certain words when editing, we can alter the style of those words without impacting the rest of the text. To bold or italicize text, we even have two useful hotkeys. The shortcuts for them are, respectively, **Ctrl + B and Ctrl + I.** Selecting text may be accomplished in one of two ways: either by holding down the Shift key while using the forward or back arrow keys to highlight the text or by clicking and dragging the mouse cursor over the word while editing the text. **After that, we have the option of selecting a new Font Style from the drop-down menu and then pressing the Ctrl key and B to make it bold, or Ctrl key and I to make it italic:**

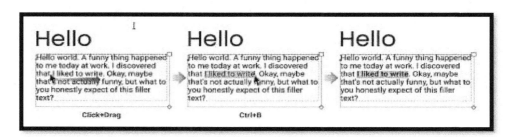

We are also able to alter the **Font Family** and the color of the text that is selected in the same manner. To do so, simply select the text that you want to modify and click on a color swatch, just as you would with any other object. The inclusion of your titles within the same text object as your paragraphs is, of course, within the realm of possibility thanks to this. On the other hand, I strongly advise you against doing this since it will make it more difficult to alter the typefaces in the future. This is because if you alter the font for the text object, the font style will be applied to everything regardless of whether or not you have a particular section of text **selected. It is possible to see how to change the font for a whole text block by looking at the image below:**

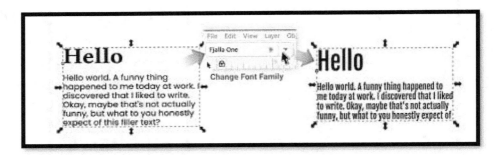

This leads us to the next item in the Tool control bar for the Text tool, which is the Baseline Spacing field as it is now displayed. By default, the units for this are set to the same units as the document; however, in this particular instance, we would like to modify those units to lines rather than physical units. This is because certain fonts are higher or shorter than others, and even if we have **mm**, for instance, when we change our Font Family, we will have to manually modify the spacing to accommodate the height of the new font. Rather than doing that, we would want to have Inkscape determine the height of our font and then use that measurement to determine the distance between the baselines. This simple approach will, in the majority of instances, save us from having to recreate our spacing if we change fonts. A change in our **spacing to lines, with a line spacing of 1.50, will have the following effect, as seen in the image below:**

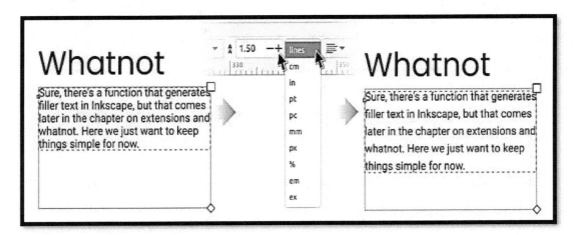

Many of us may be able to recall the requirement that the text in essays for academic research papers be written in a font size of **12 points** and double-spaced. We can accomplish this by defining the units as lines, which effectively enables us to do the following: we can set the spacing to **2.0 lines**, and we have our double spacing. Now, we can consistently space our lines as we see fit; however, what if we do not want the text to be left-aligned by default? It's possible that we would want a proper alignment for our paragraphs, either in the center or on the right. And with that, we have arrived at the next dropdown menu for Text Alignment. This **image illustrates the outcomes that occur when the Text Alignment setting is changed to one of the following options:**

Left

This paragraph is aligned Left. It's the default and generally speaking works the best for most situations where you have a lot of text to wrap around. It's the easiest to read, as the words are all spaced evenly and each line begins at the same position on the left.

Center

This paragraph is Center aligned. This is generally for smaller amounts of informational text where style is more important than readability. As you can see, it's a bit harder to read this vs the Left aligned paragraph. Use sparingly in consideration for your readers!

Right

This paragraph is aligned Right. This alignment is really only useful for short descriptive text of a picture or strong visual element on the right hand side of it. It would look quite silly without one, and is much harder to read than left-aligned text.

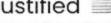

Justified

This paragraph is Justified. Not morally speaking, but rather the text is automatically spaced so that the text fills the horizontal space and makes a sharp edge on the left side of the paragraphs. This style is best where there are multiple columns of text side-by side, as in this example.

This paragraph is Justified. Not morally speaking, but rather the text is automatically spaced so that the text fills the horizontal space and makes a sharp edge on the left side of the paragraphs. This style is best where there are multiple columns of text side-by side, as in this example.

This paragraph is Justified. Not morally speaking, but rather the text is automatically spaced so that the text fills the horizontal space and makes a sharp edge on the left side of the paragraphs. This style is best where there are multiple columns of text side-by side, as in this example.

When utilizing flowing text (text in a box), the **Justified** alignment is the sole option available at the time of this writing. This is something that should be taken into consideration. Consequently, if you discover that it is grayed out, you may simply click and drag a box using the Text tool, and then copy and paste the text of your paragraph into it. The option to select **Justified** is then available to you. That is all well and good for horizontal text alignment; however, what if we want to take a portion of the text and make it superscript or subscript? That is, to make it seem smaller and slightly above or below the end of the text that came before it? For instance, we could wish to take the number **2910** and represent it as 29 raised to the tenth power. The baseline and font size for only the ten could be edited, but Inkscape has these cool buttons that do it for you. I would recommend using these.

To use the tool, just select the number 10, and then click either the Superscript or Subscript button located in the Tool control bar:

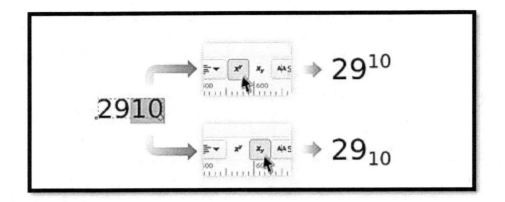

You may still make use of the superscript option even if you are not interested in mathematics. For instance, you can use it to make the thin fifth superscript. However, there are instances when you might desire a great deal more control over the spacing and location of individual characters. This is a good feature. Due to this reason, Inkscape version 1.2 has arranged the remaining options into a popover that is titled "**Spacing**."

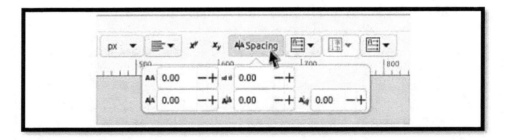

Character spacing is the first component in this box. Changing this value will result in a change to the spacing between all of the characters in the text, as demonstrated subsequently:

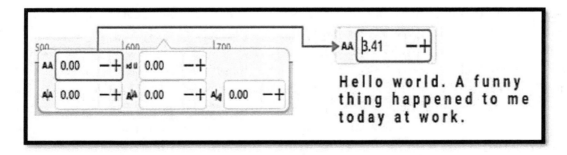

Similarly, the box that is directly to the right of the character spacing regulates the amount of space that exists between words, as illustrated below:

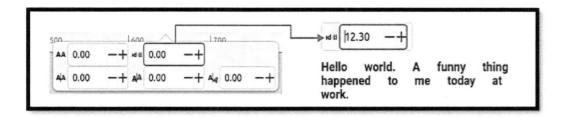

Within the next row of options in the **Spacing popover**, we have Horizontal Kerning, which may either raise or reduce the distance that separates two letters. This option is located on the far-left side of the row. **This is shown in the image below:**

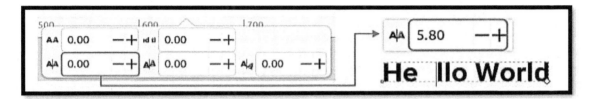

Take note that when you select **Path > Remove Manual Kerns,** you will have the option to undo **or erase this manual letter spacing. Between the same two characters, we can regulate Vertical Kerning, which is located one field to the right:**

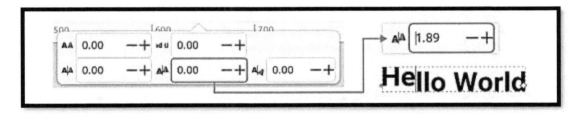

A question that you could be asking yourself at this time is, "**Why on earth would I use these options**?" When it comes to typography and graphic design, some elements, such as line spacing and letter kerning, are extremely significant to generate a headline that seems more professional or a paragraph that has an airier atmosphere. There are certain letters that, when placed next to one another, do not appear to be very attractive. Let's take the example of letter kerning; the spaces that exist between particular letter combinations might give the impression that they are either too far apart or too close together.

Take for instance the headline that is presented below:

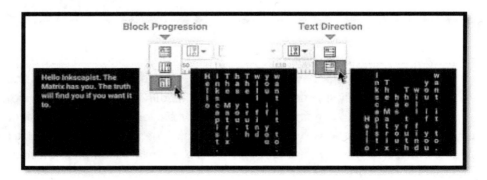

tap alt + left arrow key (three times)

World → World → World

It appears like the gap between the W and the o is just a little bit wider than it is between the other letters when you look at them carefully. It is almost as if the W is a little bit afraid of the o, and as a result, it is standing a little bit further away from where it was before. It is possible that this does not matter as much in the headline of a web post; nevertheless, when you are designing a logo for a company, these minor details are crucial. Not only do they contribute to the perception of the brand's quality, but they also contribute to the quality of your talent as a designer. The flashing text cursor is moved between the W and the o, the Alt key is held down, and the left arrow key is tapped a few times (in this particular instance, three times is sufficient) to get the o a little bit closer to the *W*. Take note of the fact that this results in the distinction between the letters in *World* appearing to be more uniform. Lastly, we will discuss the **Block Progression, Glyph Orientation, and Text Direction** dropdowns that are located in the Tool control bar for the Text tool. These are the three options that are the final ones to be discussed. Latin and Germanic-based languages (like **English**) are examples of languages that do not write or read from left to right. These are the languages that benefit the most from the utilization of other character sets. Nevertheless, this does not imply that we cannot have some fun with them in any manner, shape, or form. As an illustration, the following image demonstrates how we **may achieve a text effect that is similar to one that can be found in the film The Matrix by utilizing a different mix of these three potential options:**

With this, we have completed our investigation of the **Text tool** options that are located in the Tool control bar. From this point forward, character kerning in single-line text is only accessible if it is not wrapped. If you want kerning in your titles, you will be required to refrain from utilizing the handle for wrapping text in a single line and instead make use of the Enter key to create additional lines. To edit text, the Tool control bar provides a handy method to access the most often used options; however, there is also a separate dialog for this purpose that has other options that are worth examining. So, let's go on to the next step, which is to investigate the **Text and Font** dialog box in Inkscape to see what other amazing options it offers for us to experiment with.

Font collections

If you have thousands of fonts on your system, you might want to select a subset of your favorites to classify based on what you are doing. This is because there are thousands of fonts on your system. Therefore, the makers of Inkscape have once again bestowed upon us a brand-new feature that is included in Inkscape 1.3, and that is the capability to create Font collections. If you click the **font** folder icon located in the far-right corner of the Tool control bar (when the Text tool is chosen, of course), you will be presented with a popover that displays all of your Font collections along with a checkbox next to each inclusion. By selecting these boxes, you will **be able to conceal all of the other fonts from the Font Family dropdown menu, as demonstrated in the pre-and post-image diagram below.**

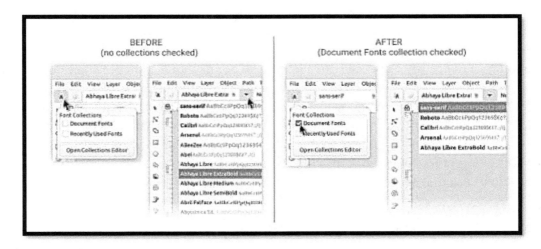

Therefore, Inkscape displays all of our fonts when there are no collections that are checked. However, if we check one or more collections, Inkscape will conceal all fonts except for those that are included in the collections that we have selected. **Pay attention to the fact that Inkscape provides us with a few collections to begin with by default:**

- **Document Fonts**: This collection is automatically populated with the fonts that you are presently using in your document.

122

- **Recently Used Fonts:** Inkscape will automatically fill this collection with fonts that you have recently used across all of your Inkscape projects, not just the ones that are now being used in this document.

In the popover, the final option is the button labeled "**Open Collection Editor.**" Clicking this button will bring up the **Font Collections** window, as seen in the following image.

Here, we can add our collections by clicking the button that has a plus sign on it and then giving the collection a name. After that, we can add fonts to our new collection by simply dragging and dropping fonts from the left side of the screen, which is located under **All Fonts – Font Family**, directly into our new collection. In the image, you can see that I have created a folder that I have named "**Favorites,**" and I have filled it with some of the typefaces that I think are my favorites. Additionally, Inkscape will automatically save these font collections for you, ensuring that your collections will be accessible in any projects that you create using Inkscape. To delete a collection, you must first click the red X button that is located after the collection's name.

The Text and Font dialog

To open the **Text and Font** dialog, simply choose **Text and Font...,** which is the first entry in the **Text** menu at the top of the screen. This will ensure that the dialog is displayed. When you open it, you will see that the Tool control bar contains a lot of the same elements that we have seen in the past when we were using the Text tool. Take note, however, that there is a preview located at the bottom of the page. Not only are we able to examine a variety of samples of different fonts, but we also receive good visual examples of each of the font weights.

When we call up this dialog and have a text object selected, the following are the visual representations that appear in the image below:

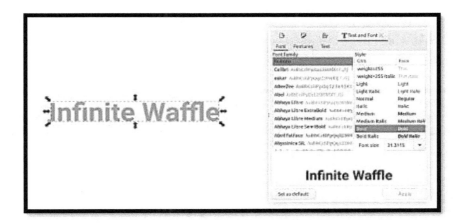

When we alter the **Font family, Font size, or Font style** option, however, our text object on the canvas does not instantaneously change. This is in contrast to the Tool control bar, which modifies the font instantly. As an alternative, it only modifies the preview. This may come in handy in some circumstances in which you just want to view what is accessible without having any impact on the text object. All you need to do is click the **Apply** button at the bottom of the page after you are satisfied with the preview. It is also possible to click the **Set as Default** button, which is located next to the **Apply** button. When you do this, Inkscape will automatically use the font you selected along with all of the other options that you selected as the default when producing new text. **Font, Features, and Text** are the three tabs that are located at the very top of the **Text and Font** window. Considering that we have just examined the Font tab, the **next one that we will investigate is the Features tab. As can be seen in the following image, this tab displays growing lists of checkboxes for font options that are arranged into categories:**

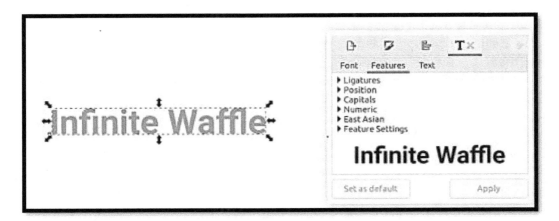

It will become apparent to you as you go through these that some of them are grayed out. This is because not all typefaces come with the same set of options embedded inside them. A good illustration of this would be the use of ligatures, which are specialized glyphs (letter symbols) that are used to replace two characters that would otherwise run into one another or be too **close together. The following image demonstrates ligatures that have been activated and deactivated for the typeface known as Abril Fatface:**

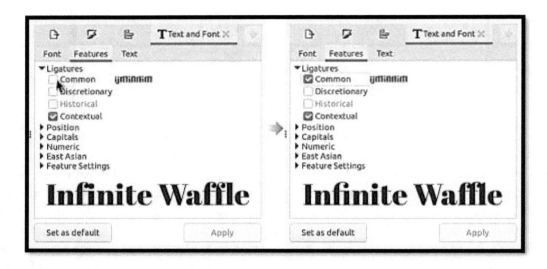

When you look attentively, you will notice that the dot of the i overlaps the f when the two characters are placed next to each other. When ligatures are enabled in Inkscape, the character collision is replaced with an attractive character from the world of science fiction. When it comes to the ***ffl in Waffle***, this is the same. The replacement of three characters with a single linked character transforms what would otherwise be characters that are either too far apart or too close together into a more beautiful whole. These unique ligatures are letters that were produced by hand and developed by the person who created the typeface. The incorporation of these ligatures within the characters is frequently a defining characteristic of a typeface that has been developed by a professional. Common ligatures are activated by default in Inkscape; however, you can disable them by simply unchecking the **Common checkbox** under the **Common** option. Additionally, several fonts come with **Discretionary, Historical, and Contextual** ligature glyph sets, all of which may be activated and deactivated in this section as well, provided that they are accessible. The next category of features is called **Position**. Are you familiar with the toggles for the **subscript and superscript?** Several typefaces feature specialized characters for it. In this section, you can turn them on and off by selecting either the **Subscript or Superscript** radio button that is located under the **Situation category**. On the other hand, this is only supported by a small number of fonts, which is why it is convenient that Inkscape will generate them for you by using the toggles indicated above in the Tool control bar.

The next category is **capitals**, and this particular category is particularly helpful for typefaces that provide it. Every character that you input is transformed into a unique, small-caps character produced specifically for you.

The following image depicts the many option options:

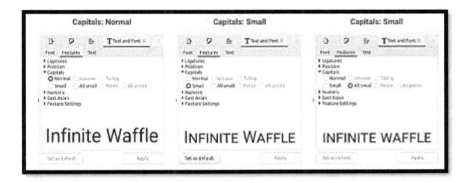

Take note of the fact that it gives the **Roboto Regular** typeface a more professional appearance. Indeed, it is almost as if a new typeface is concealed within it! This takes us to the **Numerical category**, which is composed of typefaces that offer specialized formatting options for numerical values. As can be seen in the image on the left, we can switch from the default **number style to the old-style number glyphs that are similar to the elegant numerals that are found on homes or to a portion of an address:**

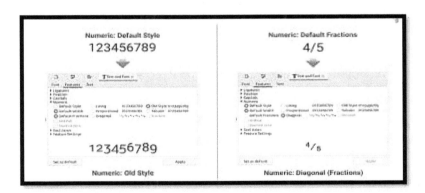

In addition, we have the option of selecting a different format for fractions that we type out as 4/5. With the modification of the **Default fraction**, the addition of **superscript and subscript** to the left and right sides of our slash is automatically performed, as seen in the image on the right. Although the **East Asian** category has aspects that are pertinent to font glyphs for East Asian languages, I was not at all familiar with East Asian language font glyphs at the time that this article was written. We will be lenient with them and get directly to the category that I consider to be the most enjoyable, which is the **Feature Settings**. This is a catch-all for anything special that the font maker decided to put into the font. Perhaps it irked the designer that they couldn't incorporate a curly-style (also known as a **looptail**) "g" character into the default font. Consequently, they concealed it within the Features section, patiently awaiting the discovery by individuals like you and me. In the image below, various features are displayed for the same Roboto Regular font we've been utilizing, featuring the coveted looptail "**g**".

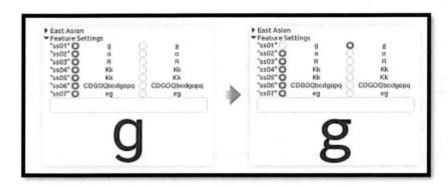

On the bottom of the **Feature Settings** page, there is a box that you might have seen. Here is where you should enter the settings for various characteristics that are associated with the **Cascading Style Sheets (CSS).**

Understanding variable fonts

Up until this point, we have seen some secret font options that changed particular glyphs in the font with other ones. However, there is a class of font that allows you to change a great deal more features of the letter shape. First, let's take a look at **Decovar24,** which is one of the most intriguing options. The following image illustrates the effects that may be achieved by adjusting **the settings of a few of the several variable font sliders that are located at the bottom of the Font tab of the Text & Font dialog:**

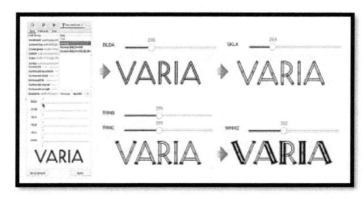

As of the time this article was written, there are still only about one hundred decent variable fonts available. When changeable fonts become more widely used in other graphics apps, you may anticipate seeing an increase in the number of available options. You should go discover your favorites and experiment with them in Inkscape. Many of them provide a basic set of options, such as sliders for tilt, character width, boldness, or thinness. I encourage you to go find them and play around with them.

Text on a curve

As far as font style on a straight line is concerned, we have surely investigated a wide variety of options. Sometimes, however, we would like to bend our text around the perimeter of an object, such as a circle or even just a curve. This is something that we would like to do. As an illustration, we would want to incorporate some text into a wave-like line so that it flows with the curve of the line rather than the conventional baseline, which is rigidly straight. We can accomplish this by first creating a path with a wavy line, then selecting both the text and the **path that we have created, and then selecting Path > Put on Path. This procedure results in text that has a curved baseline, which can be seen in the image below:**

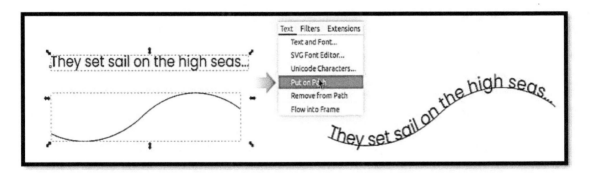

It is important to keep in mind that changing the text relocates it away from the curve. In most cases, I either move the line rather than the text (the text follows the line), or I group them and move the group rather than the text or the line. This is done to prevent this from occurring. It is most likely that you do not want that curved line to be seen as much as possible. Getting rid of the stroke color is the method that I consistently use to conceal it. Since it is fully invisible, the challenge that emerges is how to select it to edit it at a later time. This may be accomplished in two different ways. There are two ways to select the invisible line: the first is to drag a selection box around it. Utilizing the **Outline Overlay View** mode may also be accomplished by selecting **View > Display Mode > Outline Overlay** from the display mode menu. You can see that this puts graphical overlays on all of the concealed material, which allows you to select and edit the curving line that is not apparent to the naked eye.

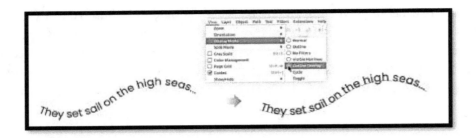

To switch back to **Normal Display Mode**, it's **View** > **Display Mode** > **Normal**: When it comes to putting text on a path, this way is quite effective. In addition, we can use the same method to put text on shape objects so that we can do the same thing.

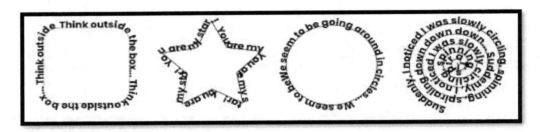

To further control which side of the shape (inside or exterior) the text flows, you may either flip the shape horizontally or vertically, or you can turn the shape into a path by selecting **Path > Object to Path**, and then selecting **Path > Reverse**. Both of these options allow you to choose which side of the shape the text flows on. You will note that the letters are a little bit more crowded together as a result of being on the inside of the circle when you do that, therefore you will need to modify the letter spacing to provide a more comfortable reading experience.

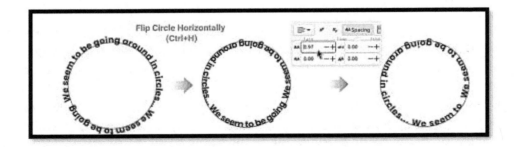

During the practice session, we are going to do a little bit more circular text since there are certain secrets to getting it perfect from the beginning. At this point, we have sufficient knowledge about wrapping text around shapes, and we can go to the next step, which is flowing text through shapes!

Flowing paragraphs into shapes

Text should be allowed to flow through shapes other than the conventional rectangle shape at times. Thankfully, Inkscape is capable of doing this with ease! The process consists of creating a block of text and one or more shapes, selecting all of them, and then selecting **Text > Flow into Frame**. As an illustration, we will begin with a block of text and four hexagons as our starting point. To select the text object, all that is required of us is to click on it. After that, we will use the Shift key and click on each shape in the sequence that we want our text to flow through. This procedure is illustrated in the image below, which shows the hexagons being sequentially added to the selection. After that, selecting **Text > Flow into Frame allows the text to flow through the shapes in the sequence the shapes were clicked:**

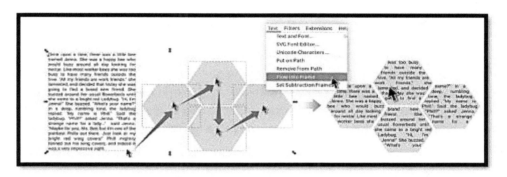

After selecting our text and double-clicking (or switching to the Text tool) to edit it, we are presented with a handle that allows us to alter the margins. This is similar to the text boxes that we made before. It is possible that we would like for the text to flow around a shape rather than through it for certain situations. This is also something that can be done easily with Inkscape. Select the text object you want to flow around, as well as the shape you want it to revolve around, and then select **Text > Set Subtraction Frames from the menu. After that, the text will flow around the shape, as can be seen in the following example:**

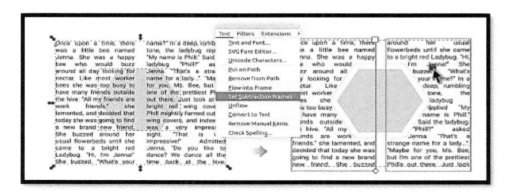

It is important to keep in mind that for this to function correctly, you will need to have flowed text between two rectangle shapes, just like we did with the hexagons. I would like to bring to your attention the fact that when we edit the text, we now receive two handles: one for the text margins, and another for the **Set Subtraction Frames** margin. You should also be aware that you can unfollow your text at any point by clicking the text object and selecting **Text > Unflow** from the menu that appears. By doing so, the text that has been flowing will be converted back into a single line of text. At this point, we have covered most of the text options, and we have undoubtedly gained a great deal of knowledge regarding how to make your text appear just as you want it to. Nevertheless, before we go on to the practice session, we will briefly go over a few text-related tools that are the proverbial frosting on the cake when it comes to dealing with text in Inkscape.

Check spelling and other handy tools

Although we have practically exhausted all of the entries in the Text menu, we will discuss something that you will most likely want to make use of every time you use text in Inkscape: **Text > Check Spelling**! It is not surprising that this causes the **Check Spelling** dialog to appear. **Press the Start button, which is located in the bottom right corner of the dialog box, to begin the spell check. If Inkscape discovers something, it will call attention to the word by highlighting it with a red box:**

At this point, you have the option of either selecting the word you want to modify or editing it using the **Text tool** or selecting one of the terms that are shown in the **Suggestions**: box and then clicking the **Accept** button to make the change and proceed. There is also the possibility that you will conclude that the name **Phill** is the proper spelling of the ladybug's name. In this case, you will be able to press the Ignore button, which will move you to the next word without you having to worry about it again for the remainder of the spell-checking procedure. Similarly, **Ignore Once** will disregard the spelling of the word for the first time, but it will continue to inform you that the name is Phil the next time it discovers your peculiar spelling of the name. You could wish to add the double-*l spelling of Phil* to the dictionary; depending on how obstinate you are, so that

Inkscape will never again annoy you by telling you that it is wrong. Should this be the case, you may choose to hit the **Add** button instead, and Inkscape will not worry you about the spelling of Phill throughout any of the subsequent spelling checks. The **Stop button** allows you to halt the spell-checking process at any moment, which is another helpful feature. The **Language dropdown** menu, which displays all of the language dictionaries that you have installed on your device, is the final step. Therefore, if you have more than one, you can swap languages at that location. Before we go on to the next step and begin practicing, it is important to point out that the Extensions menu (**Extensions > Text**) has additional Text tools that were not previously mentioned. **You should be aware of the following, which is a brief selection of the most useful ones:**

- **Change Case:** Perhaps you would like to change all of your lowercase letters to capital one's before sending them. You could wish to avoid using capital letters altogether, or you might want to use a blend of the two. Because it is more convenient for you to avoid manually retyping everything, these tools automatically change the letter case, whether it be capital or lowercase. The only thing you need to do is select the text that you want to change to the selected case, and then select one of the options from the menu that is located under **Extensions > Text > Change Case**.
- **Convert to Braille** By selecting this option, your text will be converted into Braille dots, which may be raised and read by visually impaired individuals using just their touch.
- **Hershey Text**: If you are cutting out your text with a router, this function will change the font that is currently being used to one that is composed of lines that are composed of router paths. If none of it makes any sense to you, feel free to disregard it. It is a function that is used for engraving text by specialists.
- **Lorem Ipsum**: This function, which is also known as Lipsum text, just fills your textbox with an infinite amount of meaningless text that seems to be entered words. If you want to check how your paragraphs seem but don't want to make up short stories, this is a handy tool to have.
- **Merge**: This is a tool that merges two or more text objects that have been selected to create a new text object that contains the text of both sources. If you are unable to observe the outcome immediately, search the page and the desk for the newly created text object.
- **Replace Font**: This tool will replace one font with another, and it will do so by going through all of your text objects (or only the one you have selected, if you check the box for that option). If you have used more than one font within a text object and you want to replace one of them without altering the remainder of the text, this is a valuable tool to have.

Split Text is a tool that allows you to divide your text into lines, words, and other categories. Quite a few new text objects are produced by it. Utilizing this tool allows you to create word clouds from text without having to manually write each word.

CHAPTER 10
VECTORIZING WITH TRACE BITMAP

What is Trace Bitmap?

Trace Bitmap is a tool in Inkscape that enables you to transform raster images (such as JPEGs, PNGs, or BMPs) into vector graphics. This function will allow you to create vector graphics. By employing a technique known as "*image tracing" or "vectorization*," Inkscape performs an analysis of the raster image and generates a vector representation that corresponds to the image based on the visual features that it contains. Picture yourself taking a snapshot and then changing it into a stunning illustration that is made up of scalable paths and shapes. That is the miracle that is "**Trace Bitmap**." It gives designers, artists, and creators the ability to give their raster images a fresh lease of life, which opens up a whole new universe of creative possibilities. Users can make use of the benefits of vector-based editing within Inkscape by transforming raster images into vector graphics. Without being constrained by predetermined resolutions or pixelation, they can handle, edit, and polish their images with a high degree of accuracy. To add insult to injury, vectorized images are extremely versatile and adaptable, making them suited for a broad variety of uses across both print and digital media. Essentially, "**Trace Bitmap**" is a manifestation of the transformational potential of technology. It enables artists to break through the barriers that exist between raster and vector graphics, enabling them to release their creativity in ways that are unexpected and thrilling.

Getting Started with Trace Bitmap

Step 1: Click on an image to select it

Before you can begin the process of tracing your image, you will first need to ensure that you have it chosen. This will allow the program to determine what it is that it should trace. To select your image, you just only click on it. It is important to bear in mind that **Trace Bitmap is only capable of working with pixel-based images**. Your attempt to trace a vector path will not be successful if you make this attempt.

Step 2: Open the Trace Bitmap menu by pressing Shift+Alt+B

If you are using Windows or Linux, use **Shift+Alt+B** on your keyboard to enter the Trace Bitmap menu. If you are using a Mac, press **Shift+Option+B**. All of these commands should be performed while your image is chosen. It can also be located via the menu system by navigating to **Path > Trace Bitmap**

Step 3: Choose the desired mode for your tracing

After it has been launched, the Trace Bitmap menu will appear as a dockable menu on the right-hand side of your screen. It should appear something like this, with a window that displays a **preview of the vector tracing capabilities of the image that you have selected:**

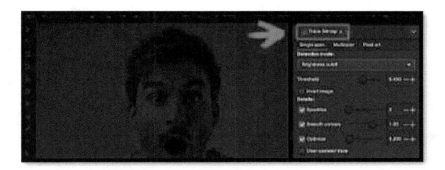

There will be three distinct tabs presented to you at the very top of the menu. These modes are known as tracing modes, and it is essential to be familiar with them since they will affect the kind of tracing that the software creates.

There are three modes:
1. **Single Scan**
2. **Multicolor**
3. **Pixel Art**

Let's have a look at what each does so you can decide which type of tracing you'd like to make. The image that follows illustrates the locations in Trace Bitmap where the three different tracing modes may be accessible. The selection of each tab will result in the display of a set of parameters that are specific to the mode being selected.

134

Single Scan

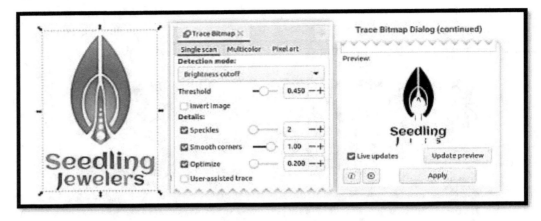

By using the Single Scan option, you will be able to generate a single monotone tracing of your image that is completely black. To select what components of the image should be traced, it makes use of areas of contrast in the image. The Single Scan mode will include other modes that reflect alternative approaches that the program will use to trace your image. These modes may be found within the options menu of the Single Scan mode.

A few examples of these are:

- **Brightness Cutoff**
- **Edge Detection**
- **Color Quantization**
- **Autotrace**
- **Centerline**

By selecting the **Single scan** option and adjusting the **Detection mode to Brightness cutoff**, we can obtain a black-and-white preview at the bottom of the dialog box. It is important to take note that a portion of the preview is missing since our logo bitmap is colored with gradients. This is because the **Brightness cutoff** makes use of the **Threshold** value to ascertain the appropriate location for the brightness cutoff. Smaller numbers that are closer to **0.0** will only catch the darkest parts of the image, whereas values that are closer to **1.0** will record colors that are brighter and lighter. It is recommended that we raise our threshold to a higher number because there are components of our logo that are lighter in color and do not display in the preview window. When you drag the **Threshold** slider, the preview will immediately update itself if the **Live Updates** box is checked. This is something to keep in mind. You can see that increasing the value to around **0.8** fills in the lighter parts of the image that are missing in the preview.

This is seen in the image that falls below.

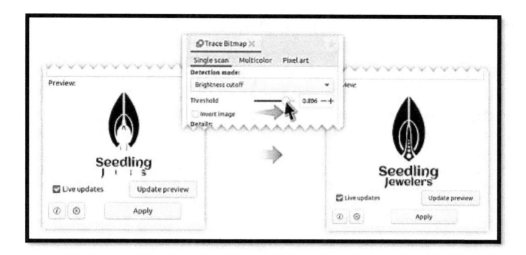

If you click the Apply button, the image will be traced to vector paths that are contained within a single object that is filled with black and is located above the original image. It is important to note that this does not remove the original image that is below. You have the option of keeping this image for future auto-tracing or using the eyedropper tool to sample colors from it while you are recoloring the logo.

A few additional options can be found under the Threshold section of the Brightness cutoff detection mode. These options are as follows:

- **Invert image**: By checking this box, the single scan trace is inverted, causing the black regions to become white and the white parts to become black. Repeatedly turning this on and off will allow you to observe the outcomes. When you wish to capture the brighter portions of the bitmap rather than the darker ones, it is beneficial to have this tool.
- **Speckles**: If you select this option, the trace will no longer contain any speckles, which are very small shapes. When the value of the slider is increased, proportionately larger shapes will be eliminated from the selection. If you are tracing a grainy texture that is extremely detailed and you want to catch all of the small areas, you should uncheck this option.
- **Smooth corners**: This option allows you to select the degree to which the edges will be smooth. To achieve a more angular result, reduce this value and try again if you find that you are obtaining an excessive amount of rounding in areas where there should be sharp edges.
- **Optimize**: Inkscape may attempt to build an excessive number of nodes with an excessive amount of detail while it is tracing images with a higher resolution. Improve the efficiency of your efforts to cut down on the number of nodes that are produced by the trace. Whenever the value is increased, the number of nodes that are formed to trace the shape will decrease.

The results may get a little mushy if this value is pushed up too much; thus, unless you want it, I suggest leaving it at the default setting, which is somewhat near to 0. If the process of tracing anything causes Inkscape to crash or takes an excessive amount of time, raising this number could be helpful for systems that have less memory.

- **User-assisted trace**: This option makes use of a method known as **Simple Interactive Object eXtraction (SIOX)** to divide a single region of the bitmap into its parts. Want to trace a white puppy out of a dark backdrop image? To use the user-assisted trace feature, just draw a vector shape over the dog, select both the vector shape and the image, and tick the **User-assisted trace** checkbox. Following the addition of the new trace, Inkscape will update the preview.

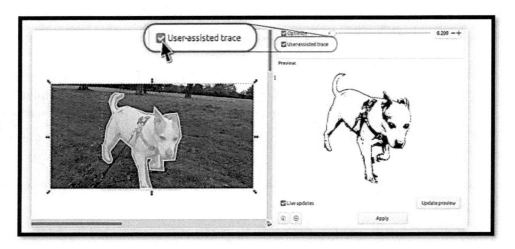

Note that the **Update Preview** button is located to the far right of the **Live Updates** checkbox. This is an important feature. If the preview generation process is taking a considerable amount of time, you can choose to leave the **Live Updates** option unchecked and instead make use of the **Update Preview** button to update the preview only when it is required. Similarly, if the trace process takes an excessive amount of time, you may immediately cancel it by pressing the **x** button that is located to the left of the **Apply** button. Within the **Detection mode** dropdown, other options may be utilized for a variety of single-scan tracings that include a wide range of possibilities. **Edge Detection** is a technique that locates the outside of objects and creates a filled vector shape based solely on the edge. Based on the number of colors you have selected; **Color Quantization** will select opposing colors from your bitmap and assign them alternating black-and-white values. This process is called "**color quantization.**" The colors in the bitmap are averaged by **Autotrace**, which then attempts to choose the most appropriate shape and color for the vector trace that is produced.

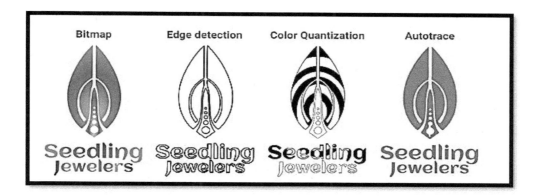

As a consequence of the trace, the options have, up until this point, produced closed and full shapes. **Centerline trace** is the only option available in the dropdown menu. This is to trace items like maps and line drawings into single vector lines that are not filled in and are not closed shut. After tracing, you can edit the stroke thickness without having to deal with all of the other geometry that is included in the other options. This is a highly handy feature. On a line map of the United States, the image below depicts the outcomes of a **Brightness cutoff** trace against a **Centerline tracing.**

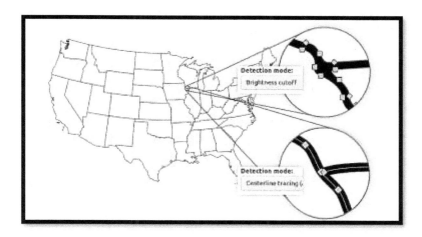

Multicolor

By using the multicolor mode, you will be able to make vector tracings of the image that you have picked in full color.

Within the Single Scan mode, there are some different options from which to pick, including the following:

- **Brightness Steps**: This option takes into account the colors present in your image to produce a vector tracing that gradually increases in brightness.
- **Colors**: This option produces vector tracings that encompass the whole color spectrum. On the tracing, you can either increase or reduce the amount of colors that are utilized to make it simpler or more intricate.
- **Grays**: This mode produces tracings in grayscale, which is sometimes referred to as black and white.
- **Autotrace**: This mode functions similarly to the Colors mode; however, it takes a while to process because it renders more information than the Colors mode does.

As you can see, the options on the **multicolor** tab attempt to create distinct vector shapes by blending colors that are similar in the bitmap. At the time of this writing, the number of scans, which is the default value, is eight. This value controls the number of distinct color objects that Inkscape will generate.

When this value is increased, our gradients will appear to be smoother; nevertheless, this will need the creation of a greater number of shapes. Even more unfortunate is the fact that when you zoom in on all of these flat shapes, you will notice that the vector images that are produced have borders and little gaps. Consequently, in a general sense, we will want to maintain the **Scans value** at the lowest possible level.

To trace a logo that has gradients, it is quite probable that we will want to perform our tracing in the Single scan tab, and then manually apply the gradients using the Gradient tool. Let's take a second look at the **multicolor** options, this time with the **Color** detection mode because this will provide us with the best results and the most amount of control over the appearance of the colors and shapes. When we click the **Stack and Remove** background checkbox options, the image below shows that the results are different from the other one.

It is important to note that if we select the **Stack checkbox** option, Inkscape will stack the components one on top of the other rather than making cuts for the shapes that are being layered on top of each other. We also have the option of selecting the **Remove background** checkbox, which will determine whether or not the background color, which is white in this instance, will be included as a shape in the group of stacked objects that are produced. The usage of **Stack** has the benefit of preventing us from noticing any minor gaps in the logo when we zoom in. This is because the logo is constructed like that of a layer cake rather than utilizing puzzle pieces. Zooming in on the difference between the two outcomes is depicted in the image that may be found below.

Photographs can also be used to perform this trace. It is recommended that you save often while you are tracing complex images, since this process may take a significant amount of time and result in the creation of hundreds of thousands of nodes in the objects that are created! Using the Smooth checkbox and sliders will help you minimize the number of nodes in the graph. You also have the option of selecting the objects that you have traced and selecting Path > Simplify. This will make an effort to decrease the number of nodes that are present in the shapes. After tracing a duck photo, I removed the backdrop to simplify the process before beginning the trace. The outcomes of this process are seen in the image below.

Pixel Art

The last tracing mode available in the Trace Bitmap menu is called Pixel Art, and it is designed for tracing little icons that demand precise details:

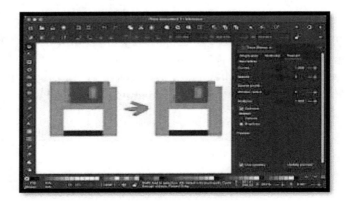

You may have already caught on to the fact that the tracings that are produced by Trace Bitmap are not always precise or clear. As an illustration, it has a propensity to round corners and smooth edges to an excessive degree. If you are tracing anything that is more intricate and requires higher precision, this may provide a difficulty. The Pixel Art mode is what you need to use at this point. A drawback is that this option will produce more exact tracings of the image that you have picked; however, there is a catch. It is advised that this mode be used only on tiny images (such as icons) that are no larger than 100 by 100 pixels because it requires a significant amount of processing power from the central processing unit.

The Pixel Art mode is comprised of two basic modes, which are as follows:

- The first mode is called **Voroni**, and it generates a tracing that is made up of a large number of very small vector boxes that are each colored differently.
- Secondly, the **B-Spline**s mode is responsible for the generation of a tracing that is composed of bigger vector shapes.

To reiterate, there are sliders for the parameters that may be altered below, allowing you to customize the tracing to your preferences. After you have determined that the preview of your tracing is satisfactory, you may produce it by pressing the **Apply** button, and then you will be finished.

Using the Fill Bucket tool to trace bitmap parts

Imagine for a moment that we would want to create a great logo by using portions of our duck head. We can make an effort to automatically trace it using **Trace Bitmap** and then remove the parts that are not being utilized. Alternatively, we could just use the **Fill Bucket** tool to selectively collect shapes. Additionally, we can obtain shapes from a region of color regardless of how bright or dark the region is by using this approach. For instance, we may trace portions of our duck's head by selecting the Fill Bucket tool and then clicking and dragging over the sections of color that we want to preserve. If we repeat this process numerous times, we will be able to construct a far more compelling graphic than we would have otherwise obtained. **This procedure of clicking and dragging iteratively is depicted in the image below;**

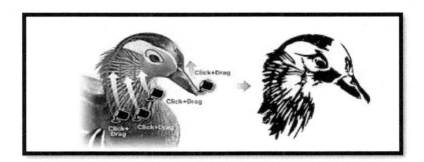

It is important to note that once the **Fill Bucket** tool is active, the tool controls bar, much like the tool controls bar for the other Inkscape tools, provides options for the tool. When the **threshold value** is increased, more colors that are similar will be captured more quickly. This is especially beneficial when single-clicking a region (as opposed to clicking and dragging), as Inkscape will utilize the color that is right under the mouse click to create a shape. If the threshold value is higher, then a greater amount of money will be added to that particular region. There is also the option to utilize the **Grow/shrink by** value function to obtain a bit more globby expansion region; however, this will result in the trace losing its sharpness and accuracy. It is more beneficial to utilize this option when coloring comics with the **Fill Bucket tool** since it reduces the likelihood of white gaps between neighboring regions.

The difference that occurs when we attempt to color in some of the feathers in our illustration duck head trace is seen in the image below.

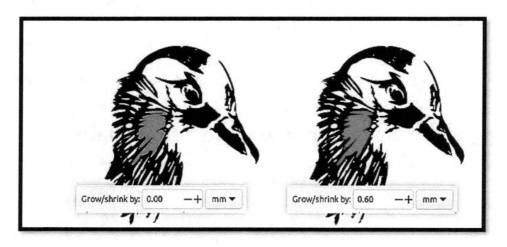

There are rare circumstances in which the **Fill Bucket** tool will be unable to locate a closed shape to fill in. This is because the shapes have minor gaps that allow the fill area to flow over into the canvas region. By using the **Close Gaps** selection, you may instruct the **Fill Bucket** tool to disregard these very insignificant gaps. Additionally, you can select the size of your gaps from the options of **None, Small, Medium, or Large**. The Fill Bucket tool has been utilized in the Fill by: Visible Colors mode while we have been working up to this point. Other options that enable you to isolate distinct sections by different criteria are available through the Fill by dropdown that is located at the far left of the tool controls bar. These options include the **Red, Green, and Blue** color channels, as well as **Lightness, Hue, Saturation,** and even **Alpha** (transparency) for PNG images. It is important to note that these options are available.

CHAPTER 11
USING LAYERS

About Layers

There is a method of organizing and compartmentalizing your artwork that is known as layers. Layers provide you with the ability to divide the components of your artwork into distinct areas. Following that, the stacking orders can be altered to allow for the reorganization of these portions and their positioning above and below one another. The management of intricate designs and artwork that has a great deal of moving elements is simplified as a result of this process. Additionally, layers provide you the ability to lock layers so that you are unable to make any changes to them and adjust the visibility of layers. Additionally, you can alter the blend mode of a layer, as well as the opacity and blur effect of an entire layer. It would be helpful if we went over all of it in greater detail. We will begin by discussing the operation of layers in Inkscape, and then we will proceed to discuss all of the features and subtleties.

- To access the Layers menu in Inkscape, navigate to: **Layers > Layers**
- Alternatively, you can access it using the keyboard shortcut: **Control + Shift + L**
- The **Layers** menu will be opened as a dockable menu on the right-hand side of your screen:

Layers are a method of segmenting and arranging your artwork, as was previously mentioned. When you create a new document in Inkscape, it will automatically consist of one layer, which will typically be referred to as **"Layer 1."** In the absence of any further instructions, each piece that you produce will be positioned on that respective layer.

Working Example

A working illustration of how layers function and the reasons why they can be advantageous is provided in the following excerpt. **Through the utilization of layers, the following design was constructed:**

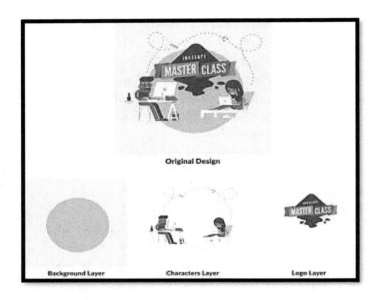

As depicted above, the design consists of three primary segments:

1. **Logo**
2. **Characters**
3. **Background**

These three sections each feature a variety of design components inside their respective sections. The order in which the layers are stacked on your canvas is determined by the order in which the elements are arranged. Therefore, all of the items that are included within the "**Logo**" layer will be positioned above all of the elements that are contained within the layers that are underneath it. This is because the "**Logo**" layer is located at the top of the order in the Layers menu. When it comes to working with layers in Inkscape, there are a few different methods that you may use to manipulate them.

How to Add New Layers

The process of adding a new layer in Inkscape is as simple as clicking **the addition sign (+)** located in the lower-left corner of the Layers menu.

This will bring up a new dialog box that will ask you to select a name for the layer you are working on. You will be able to select the name of your new layer as well as its position from this point. You are free to give it whatever name you wish because the name you select will only be used for your reference and will not have any effect on the way the program operates. Another option is to leave the default name for the time being and then return to change it at a later time. **In addition, you will be invited to select a Position for the new layer you have created. There are three options available:**

- **Above current**: this will place the new layer above whatever layer you currently have selected.
- **Below current**: this will place the new layer below whatever layer you currently have selected.
- **As a sublayer of current**: this will make the new layer into a sublayer of the layer you currently have selected.

In essence, sublayers are layers that are contained within layers. In a minute, we will discuss that specific topic. After clicking the **Add button**, you should be able to see that the new layer has been added to the index of the **Layers** command. After you have picked that layer, any objects that you create will be positioned on top of it. The objects may also be moved from one layer to another by simply copying and pasting them from one layer to another. Simply click on the layer you want to continue working on to select it. This will allow you to stay on the original layer.

How to Remove Layers

If you ever decide that you would like to get rid of your layer, you can do so by choosing it and then clicking the **minus sign (–)** that is located toward the bottom left corner of the screen.

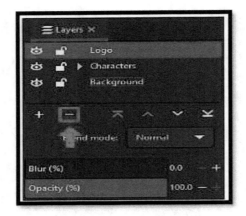

By doing so, the layer will be completely removed. Be aware that if you delete layers in Inkscape, **you will also be deleting the contents of that layer.** This is something that should be taken into consideration. Consequently, check to see that there are no significant components on that layer that you would like to maintain.

How to Rearrange Layers

In this lesson, we will discuss how to alter the order in which your layers are stacked. Changing the order of a layer may be accomplished by simply clicking and dragging it over or below another layer. This is one method for rearranging layers. The difficulty with utilizing this method, however, is that if you place the layer right on top of another layer, you will be adding it as a sublayer rather than merely shifting its position in the stacking order. This is a problem since it is not a straightforward process. Because of the frequency with which this occurs by mistake, it is strongly suggested that you make use of the menu interface to reorganize your layers accordingly. **Towards the bottom of the Layers menu, you will see a series of arrow buttons:**

These buttons allow you to reorganize a layer that you have picked in the selection process. The layer is moved up one place in the order when the up arrow is used, and when the up arrow is combined with a line above it, the layer is moved to the first position in the order. Similarly, the down arrows do the same function. The down arrow will move the layer down one step, while the down arrow with a line under it will move the layer down to the bottom of the page.

How to Rename Layers

Simply double-clicking the name or label of the layer is all that is required of you if you ever decide that you would like to rename a layer. After that, you will be allowed to enter a new name. Another option is to right-click the layer and selects the **Rename Layer** option from the context menu.

Layer Visibility

You will see an eyeball icon to the far left of each layer, placed next to each layer:

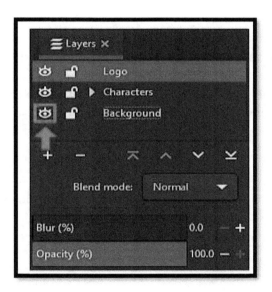

A symbol that represents the visibility of a layer is shown here. When you click it, the visibility of your layer will be briefly disabled. By clicking it once again, you will be able to restore the visibility. Please take notice that this is **only a temporary situation**. There is no need to worry about the pieces being removed from your screen because you have not truly eliminated them. As of right now, you have rendered them momentarily invisible. The usage of this may be quite beneficial when dealing with intricate designs that have a great deal of layered components. By temporarily turning off the visibility of a layer, you will be able to begin working on other layers without the layer being in the way of your progress.

Layer Locks

To the right of the visibility switch, you will see a little lock icon:

The lock for the layer is represented by this icon. If you enable it, the layer will be locked, which means that you will be unable to select, edit, move, or add to any of the items of that layer. This will restore the elements' ability to be edited after it is disabled. It should be brought to your attention that, similar to the layer visibility function, this is simply a temporary feature. You can find the lock option to be helpful in situations when you wish to concentrate on other aspects of your artwork while simultaneously ensuring that you do not inadvertently change other layers while you are doing so. The layer(s) in question must be locked for this to be feasible.

Sublayers

The ability to arrange your work even more is made possible by sublayers, which are layers that are contained within layers. **You can see that I utilized a sublayer for the "Characters" layer, which is represented by an arrow icon, in the example that is presented below:**

The contents of the Characters layer were segmented with the help of the sublayer using this particular context. This layer is made up of the two characters, but it also includes the squiggly line that is located above the two characters for further visual interest. As a means of maintaining a higher level of organization on that particular layer, the wavy line was positioned on a sublayer. Simply select an existing layer and then click the addition (+) symbol to add a new layer. This will add a new layer to the existing layer. Make your selection from the **Position prompt** by selecting **"As a sublayer of current."** Simply clicking and dragging an existing layer on top of another layer that you want to nestle it within will allow you to make that layer a sublayer of the layer that you currently have.

Layer Features

Now that we have covered the fundamental capabilities of Inkscape layers, let's have a look at some of the extra options that are available through this menu.

Blur

Once you reach the bottom of the Layers menu, you will see an option to blur the image. This enables you to add a Gaussian blur to the whole layer that you have selected, regardless of which layer it is. The blur option in the **Fill & Stroke** menu operates in a manner that is quite comparable to this. The only difference is that this option applies the blur to all of the objects that are included within a layer, as opposed to applying it to a single object.

Opacity

It is expected that you will find an additional option for modifying the Opacity of a layer directly beneath the Blur facility. With the use of this slider, you may choose to make a whole layer, along with all of its contents, partially translucent. The opacity of the layer may be altered by simply clicking and dragging it. Similar to the Blur function, the Opacity feature applies the changes to the whole layer. This is in contrast to the Fill & Stroke option, which only applied the changes to a specific object that was selected.

Blend Modes

Blend Modes, which are sometimes referred to as "layer modes" in certain instances, are a method of altering the look of a layer such that it depends on how the composition of that layer interacts with that of another layer. At the very bottom of the Layers menu, you will find a dropdown menu that allows you to change the Blend Mode of a layer.
The available blend modes in Inkscape are:
- **Normal** (no change)
- **Multiply**

- **Screen**
- **Darken**
- **Overlay**
- **Color Dodge**
- **Color Burn**
- **Hard Light**
- **Soft Light**
- **Difference**
- **Exclusion**
- **Hue**
- **Saturation**
- **Color**
- **Luminosity**

The makeup of the layers that are influenced by each of these blend types causes the outcome to be different for each of these modes. You should try out a few of them to get a feel for how they operate. It should be brought to your attention that blend modes are often designated for environments that are pixel-based and the editing of photographs. Having them accessible in Inkscape is unquestionably beneficial; yet, in a vector context, they serve a far more limited role than they do in Photoshop.

Cloning layers

Selecting the layer to be cloned and then selecting **Edit > Clone > Create Clone**, just as we did previously, is all that is required to produce a clone of the layer. The image that follows demonstrates that we obtain a new clone object that is located outside of our layer and is referred to as use176. This object can be renamed to anything more memorable, such as a **raccoon clone** if we so like.

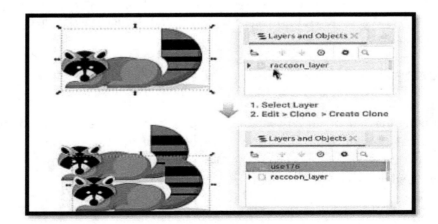

However, there is a catch: to obtain that additional security, we will have to forego the ability to resize our original. This is because the instant we group a layer to enlarge the original without resizing the clones, we leave the layer open to the possibility of being picked on canvas and ungrouped. On the other hand, there is a solution that allows us to temporarily group **raccoon_layer**, resize it, and then ungroup it once more without having any impact on the clones created.

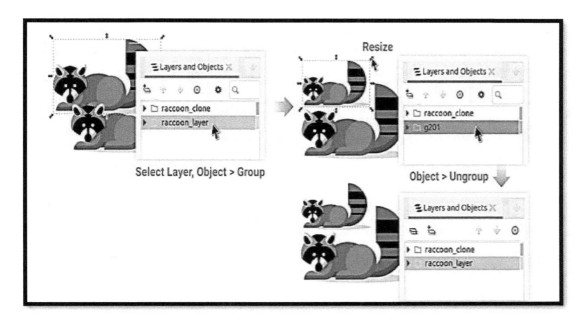

As a last point of interest, it is also possible to clone, group, and ungroup a layer or object directly within the Layer and Objects dialog by right-clicking the entry and selecting the relevant action from the context menu. This is similar to how you can do it over the canvas.

CHAPTER 12
MORE ON SHAPES

Automatic Shape Alignment in Inkscape

The Align and Distribute dialog

I would like to bring to your notice the **Align and Distribute** dialog, which can be accessed by **selecting Object > Align and Distribute or by using the magic combination of Ctrl + Shift + A on your keyboard, as demonstrated in the image below:**

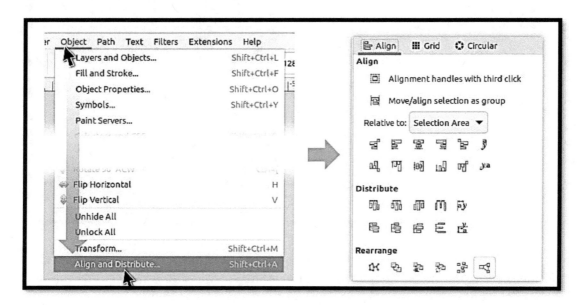

Here, we have a lot of options, but if you look closely at each of the icons, you will notice that they accomplish exactly what they say. For example, the **Align section** aligns all of the selected shapes together, and the **Distribute section** equalizes the distances between shapes in a variety of different ways.

Let's start with the Align section and see some practical examples.

Take for example that you own a building and a few window washers. You would want to position the window washers so that they are aligned with the side of the building. This would prevent them from hanging out over the street and posing a threat to people in a manner that is contrary to the laws of gravity.

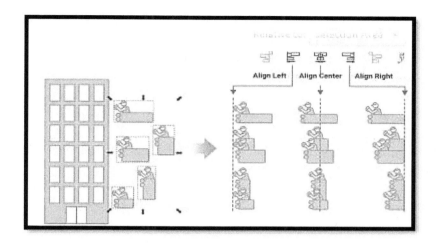

The **Align Left** option, as you can see, provides us with the outcomes that we desire, with all washers giving the impression that they are washing the same surface. However, we are currently facing a new challenge: the area is rather congested. In an ideal scenario, we would want to distribute our window cleaners in such a way that they have sufficient space to work and do not become irritated with each other's elevator boxes, which are very peculiar in shape. To accomplish this, we will be utilizing the **Distribute buttons**; but, before we can make good use of these buttons, we will first need to make more room in our selection by retracting the bottom cleaner a little bit farther down. Unlike the **Align options**, the **Distribute** options always utilize the selection area to calculate the spacing. This is something that you should be aware of. Consequently, if we do not make any efforts to generate additional room, our washers will continue to be cranky and squeezed together, although in an equal manner. In the image that follows, we begin by lowering the bottom window washer, and then we proceed to display the outcomes of our different distribution activities on our selection:

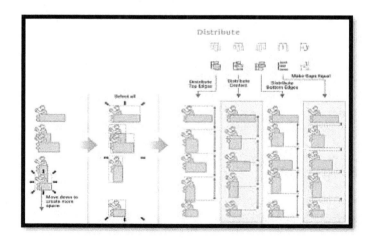

Make Gaps Equal, the final option, yields the best results, as can be seen, as it ensures that each washer receives the same amount of headroom. You might also note that this also gives the most visually beautiful results, to the point that you can typically forget about all of the other options and simply try this one first. These are the aesthetically pleasant outcomes. After that, if the outcomes aren't quite how you would like them to be for your situation, you may try out the other options until you find the ones that you like. Although the other rows of options for **Align and Distribute** are concerned with horizontal alignment and distribution, the effect is the same regardless of whatever row you choose. It is highly recommended that you select the **Make Gaps Equal** option 99 percent of the time. You also have the option of using the **Align horizontal** option, after which you may vertically position a single object to properly center it within another object. Make sure that the dropdown menu labeled "**Relative to:**" is set to "**Last Selected.**" **An illustration of how to use this approach to align a smaller circle to the center of a bigger circle is shown in the image below:**

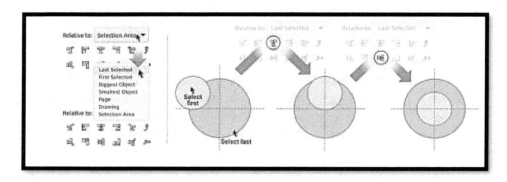

The Relative to: dropdown menu contains other options, as you will see. If we had picked the enormous circle first, we may have achieved the same results using **Biggest Object or First Selected.** On the other hand, I typically keep this set to the **Last Selected** option because it is the most straightforward item to manage. So, here's why. Even if the object you wish to align to was not the most recent one to be picked, you may still remove it from the selection by pressing Shift and clicking on it again. You can then press Shift and click once more to add it back to the selection, making it the most recent object to be selected. Because of this simple little technique, the **Last Selected option** is the most adaptable, and it is a decent default for the majority of projects. **Page** is another tool that I recommend using to align everything to the middle of the page in a natural way.

Text object alignment

Even though we will proceed to explore the text in greater depth when we talk about the Text tool, it is important to be aware that there are certain unique options available for text objects.

You can observe that these alignment options align various text objects following the baseline of the text by looking at the image provided below:

This is because there are characters that fall below this line, and the majority of the time, it is the baseline of the text that we want to align with, rather than the lowest point of a lowercase letter y, for example. **The image that follows illustrates the distinction between aligning using the standard bottom alignment button and using the text baseline alignment option:**

The whole thing functions rather nicely. If, on the other hand, certain capabilities allowed us to align our shapes on the canvas, wouldn't that be nice? Considering that we have handles that allow us to rotate and resize... How come we can't align with the handles as well? The short answer is that we can!

On Canvas Alignment

It is possible that you would like to align objects on the canvas rather than clicking on the several buttons that are designated for alignment. The **On Canvas Alignment** tool is available in Inkscape versions 1.0 and above, which is a wonderful development.

You can turn this tool on and off by using the toggle switch, which is represented in the image below:

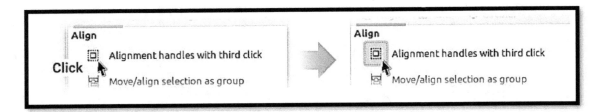

The On Canvas Alignment tool adds one more mode to the Selection tool:

1. Click once to get the **Resize** handles.
2. Click twice to get the **Rotate** handles.
3. That third click will now get you **Alignment** handles!

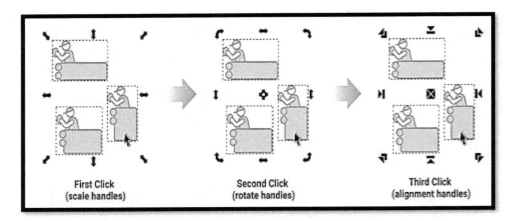

| First Click (scale handles) | Second Click (rotate handles) | Third Click (alignment handles) |

The objects that are selected are aligned to the side of the selection that is picked when you click on a handle, as you would anticipate. To align left, click left, and to align right, click right. It should come as no surprise that the top and bottom are also obvious, but what about the middle? When you click the middle icon, it will automatically align to the center in a horizontal direction; however, you could want to align it in a vertical direction. To accomplish this, you need just click while holding down the **Shift key**. Isn't it neat? In situations where you have a lot of alignment to do, this comes in quite helpful. Additionally, the Shift key performs the same functions as the other alignment handles, namely, it aligns the objects that are located on the opposite side of the selection. Consider the scenario in which your window washers are hanging over your building rather than being positioned on the side of the structure.

The image that follows illustrates what occurs when you hold down the Shift key while clicking the right alignment handle to align them with the outside of the structure, as they should exist:

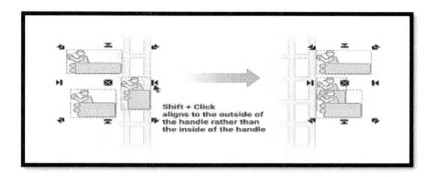

As soon as you get the hang of utilizing it, you will come to question how you ever managed to get by without it. However, it is one more click in the select/rotate/align chain, so it is also great to be able to toggle it off when you are not using it. This will allow you to avoid making additional clicks when you are resizing and rotating the image.

Rearranging options

There is a mystery row of icons that are fairly confusing and are located below the Alignment icons. These icons are used to rearrange our objects. Because they can be useful for switching things around, let's take a quick look at some of the options by examining some instances from the actual world. Consider the fact that you have created some aesthetically pleasing logos for a customer. To make it simple for them to choose their favorite among the group, you have done them the courtesy of numbering them, as can be seen in the image that is located on the left side of this particular page. However, after all of that counting and meticulous alignment of each succeeding number into the top left of each sample box, you realize that you have overlooked a number! You are going to have to go back and remember everything when you get to this point, right?

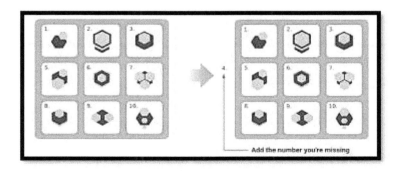

158

We failed to remember the number 4. It would be preferable for us to move everything over to one and get rid of our ten instead. Well, our friend, the **Rearrange by Selection Order** option is here to help us. The only thing that remains for us to do is to put the number that we failed to notice someplace on the canvas (as seen on the right side of the image above), select each number that we want to move in the opposite order, and then click the "**Rearrange by Selection Order!**" button. It is easy to see how this may save us a significant amount of time, depending on the number of items that we have numbered for ourselves.

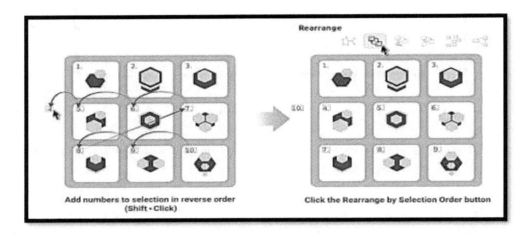

When it comes to reorganizing, the other options are slightly less beneficial. Having said that, let's go over them together for completeness.

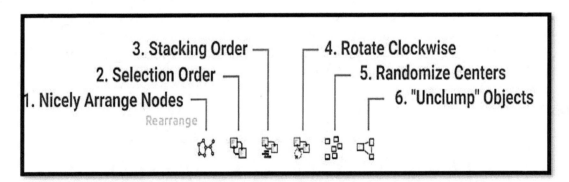

We will briefly discuss each and what you might potentially use them for:

1. **Nicely Arrange Nodes**: This button takes a selected diagram network that was created with the Connector tool and makes your diagrams appear great without giving you the need to manually move all of the elements around.

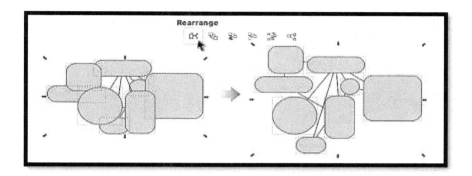

2. Selection order: This is the same one that we just used to renumber our logos, thus this is certainly the same one. Click this button once you have selected your numbers in the opposite order. Simply said, this is the only one that you will most likely require frequently because it is both easy and effective.

3. Stacking Order: Inkscape can establish the order in which to rearrange your shapes by using the current stacking order of your shapes. You can modify the order by rearranging elements in the **Layers and Objects** dialog, as well as by sliding shapes on top of or below one another. This is made possible by the **Stacking Order** organization style.

4. Exchange around Center: We could have also utilized this one to fix our numbering problem, as our error happened at the beginning of the second row, which was a favorable location for us to make our mistake. This may save you some work if you have shapes that are oriented around a circle, a large square, or perhaps something else.

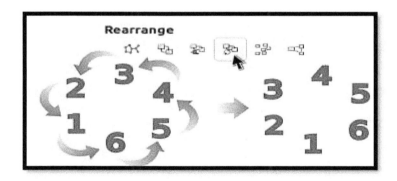

5. Randomise Centers: Perhaps we do not wish to take the time to reorganize our shapes. By selecting this option, you will also have the ability to effortlessly add some chaos to them. When you choose objects, hit the button labeled "**Randomize Centers**," and then watch as your objects move around in a manner that is not predetermined. After that, you may choose to equally spread them out in the **Remove Overlaps** area right below, entering figures for **H: and V:** (horizontal and vertical gaps, respectively), and then selecting the **Remove Overlaps** button to achieve a more satisfactory result.

160

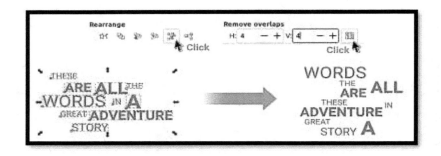

6. Unclump Objects: This tool does not unclump anything in the manner that you would most likely anticipate. To my knowledge, I have never once been successful in getting it to unclump overlapping or close objects satisfactorily. The purpose of this function is to make an effort to get a distance that is equal between the centers of the objects that you have picked by moving them around. Using the portion that allows you to remove overlaps is a much better option. As a result, the conclusion that can be drawn from this is that the option that gives you the most degree of direct influence over the outcomes is the **Selection Order** option, which is the obvious winner of the **Rearrange** beauty pageant set. When it comes to aligning the rows and columns of shapes, this is all well and good; however, what if we want to organize our shapes in rows and columns at the same time? We might have to do a great deal of alignment procedures to achieve the desired effect. Thank goodness, we don't have to do that! That will be handled for us by Inkscape.

Grid arranging shapes

The process of manually aligning objects to each other was something that we learned, but let's imagine we want to construct a grid out of all of the objects. Take this as an example: we would like to present a grid of items, which in this case would be coffee and snacks for one of those fashionable menus that are found in coffee shops. We want to spend more time selling coffee and less time organizing things, so we will utilize the Grid Arrange tab in Inkscape, which was formerly known as the **Arrange** dialog. As of Inkscape 1.1, the Grid arranges tab is now placed in the same **Align and Distribute** dialog that we have been using.

161

When you have all of your item graphics selected, you can use the **Grid tab** to set the number of **rows and columns** you want, the type of spacing between items (**equal height and equal width**), which point on the objects to align to (we will see why this is useful in a moment), and whether to **Set spacing** of the gaps between graphics to a specific measurement or **Fit into selection box**, which will save you from having to estimate the size of the gaps. What occurs when we manually set our spacing to 3 millimeters and apply the **Alignment** value to the center is depicted in the image below (on the left). Compared to what was there previously, it is far better; yet, the text titles of each item are not aligned. **To ensure that these graphics are aligned with the bottom, let's make sure that the alignment is set to the bottom:**

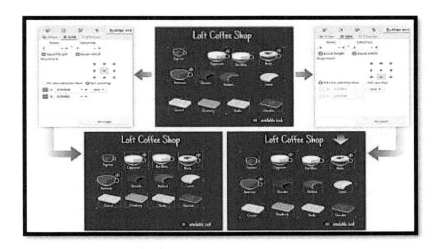

Additionally, the entire assortment of things is somewhat off to the right, which indicates that our guesses on the distance between graphics were incorrect. By checking the box next to the radio button labeled "**Fit into selection box**," we also spare ourselves some time spent re-estimating. As can be seen, the outcomes are far more favorable. There are just a few things (**Cappuccino and Strawberry**) that require manual adjustments, and they are the ones that have letters that are lower than the baseline of the text. After that, we are good to go! Grid layout is pretty helpful for dealing with a wide range of activities, and it will be of great use to us while we are creating using Inkscape. On the other hand, there are occasions when we would want their objects to be organized in a different manner, such as in a circle, for instance.

Circular arranging shapes

Grids are always a fantastic idea, but what about a circle being used instead? That may appear to be an unusual pattern to organize the majority of the time; but, let's assume you want to create a graphic version of a watch face or a clock. At the same time as you are arranging the numbers in a circle, you are also required to arrange all of the hour, minute, and maybe even second markers. That's a lot of arrangements to make! To proceed, let's navigate to the **Circular** tab under

162

the **Align and Distribute** dialog box. To begin, we may begin with a circle and 12 dashes for hour markers. We can then set **Anchor Point** to **Objects' bounding boxes** and select **the top center green dot (the center is the default). The top of each line will be fixed to the circle as a result of this:**

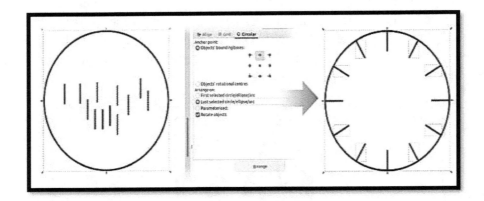

The **Arrange on:** options don't matter here since we only have one circle but say we want to arrange a bunch of small circles on our large circle. By using these options, Inkscape can determine which of the circles should be arranged. In most cases, I keep this option set to Last Selected since it is simple to determine which shape is the final one in the selection by simply deselecting it and then re-selecting it as a component of the selection. In conclusion, the **Rotate Objects** setting will mechanically rotate our lines so that they face inwards toward the center of the circle once it is activated. Because we don't want to find ourselves in an inverted position at six o'clock, we make sure to turn this off when we arrange our numbers in a circle, as you can see below. In addition to that, we will move **Anchor Point** to the center position:

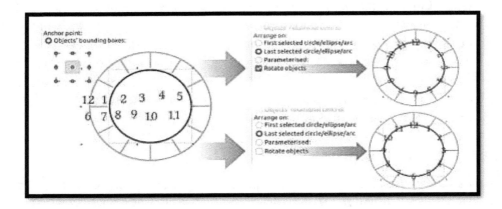

Take note that the ordering of the selections and the rotation of the circle both has a role in determining where the numbers begin and stop. Inkscape's circles begin and stop on the right-hand side by default, which is where the arc handles are located. This is something that we had observed while we were experimenting with ellipses and arcs. Because this is the point at which Inkscape will begin aligning our numbers, we need to rotate the circle 90 degrees anti-clockwise (counter-clockwise) to relocate the beginning of the circle to the top (**Object > Rotate 90 ACW**). The next step is to select the numbers in the sequence that we want them to appear, starting with the number 12, then moving on to the numbers 1, 2, 3, 4, 5, and so on. Therefore, if your numbers are not in the appropriate locations, you may have overlooked one of these procedures. At this point, we have discussed some helpful methods that may be used to automatically organize and align objects; thus, let's gain some more practice with an additional illustration. Because there are a great number of additional components included within this one, it will immediately become evident how beneficial it is for Inkscape to automatically align the objects for us.

Automatic spacing and alignment with Smart Snapping options

The snapping toggle has a little arrow next to it, and we can toggle on/off the alignment options.

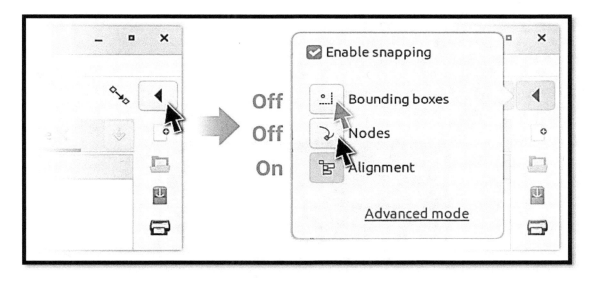

In a normal situation, we would just leave them toggled on; but, for the sake of demonstration, we would like to observe the effect of only the alignment options alone. The thing that we discovered is that when we have numerous shapes in a row, we can add more with the same spacing as the others. Inkscape will kindly identify this and offer snapping and alignment distances that match comparable gaps that it has detected.

The following image illustrates what occurs when we move a third rectangle to the right of two others and drag it closer to any of them:

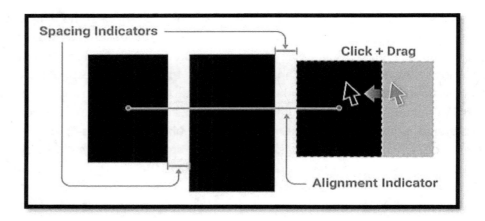

When these spacing and alignment indications show, you may let off the mouse drag to snap the shape to the location that the indicators suggest. In the Advanced options, there are two ticks: one to enable Object snapping, and another to enable Node snapping. Both of these checkboxes come in useful when you are working on custom shapes.

Your Personal Exercise

We are going to illustrate a glass of juice as a new item that will be added to the menu of the cool coffee shop. Our reliable new set of alignment tools, together with some straightforward shapes, will be utilized. In the image that follows, we can see the components that we need to create as well as how they will be assembled to form the final product.

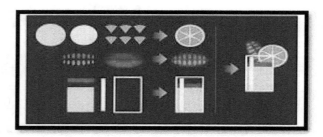

Let's get right into it!

1. Begin by using the **Circle and Ellipse** tool to create the circles and wedges that represent the lemon slices. Start by drawing a circle that is smaller than the beige circle, and then utilize the circle **Start** and **End** settings in the Tool Control bar to transform the circle into a wedge. This will allow you to create this wedge.
2. For the Start, enter **240**, and for the End, enter **300**.

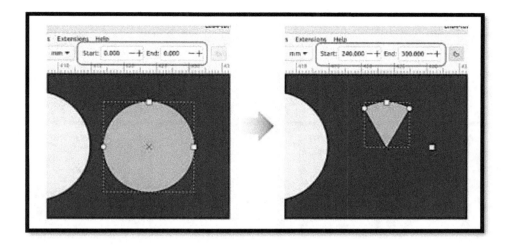

3. It is necessary to bring the rotating center up to the edge of the wedge before we can proceed with making duplicates of the wedge. Within the context of Step 5, this will make it possible for us to make use of the **circular** alignment dialog to rotate and align these segments into position.

4. While the **Select and Transform** tool is active, select the wedge, and then click once more to reveal the rotation handles and the rotation center handle. The rotating center handle should be dragged up to the top edge of the wedge.

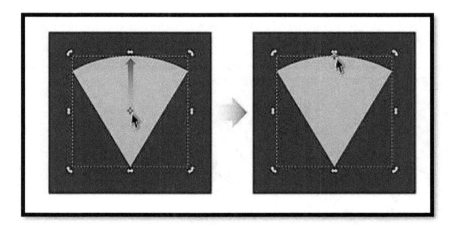

The wedge may now be duplicated, and you will be able to make five copies of it. The new copies will likewise have the same rotating center at the edge where we relocated it.

5. We are going to use the **Circular** tab in the **Align and Distribute** dialog (**Object > Align and Distribute)** now that we have all six wedges in our possession. The **Objects' rotating centers** and the **Last selected circle/ellipse/arc** radio buttons should be checked after you have picked all six of your wedges respectively.

166

6. Next, select all of your shapes by boxing them, and then press Shift and click to remove the circle from the selection. Once you have done that, click once more to re-select it so that it is the final circle that is chosen.

7. After you have clicked the **Arrange** button, all of your slices will be arranged in a lovely radial pattern around the circle.

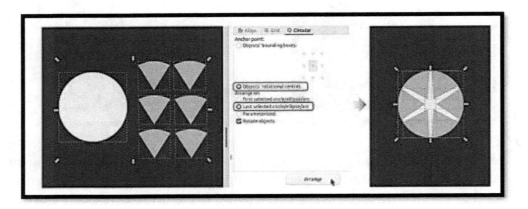

8. To remove the circle from the selection, hit the Shift key and then click in the middle of the circle. This would leave only the slices chosen. To line these slices with the two circles, we are going to group them by selecting **Object > Group** from the menu bar.

9. To finish the lemon, select the two circles and the group of slices, and then click the buttons in the **Align and Distribute** box that correspond to the vertical and horizontal alignment.

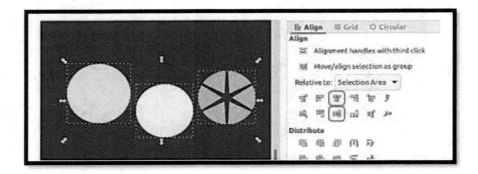

9. As a last step, you have the option of selecting **Object > Group** and grouping all of the ingredients to finish your image of lemon slices.

This will make it easy to move them later on. This is the combined effect, as shown in the image below:

11. As we go on to our leafy garnish, we will make some further ellipses, two half ellipses, and some little ovals.

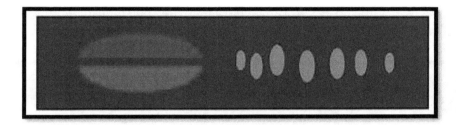

12. Let's make that leaf oval by drawing our elongated circle and setting the **Start** and **End** values like before. However, this time, we will just enter a value of **180** for **End**, leaving **Start** at **0**.

13. Making a copy of this oval by using the **Copy** command and then selecting **Edit > Paste in Place** (or hitting **Ctrl + Shift + V)** will result in a copy of the oval that is placed immediately on top of the original oval. After that, we can modify the **Start and End** values to **180 and 0**, respectively, which will result in the creation of the other half of our leaf and the assignment of a relatively darker fill to it. Both are depicted in the image that can be found below, with a variety of **Start and End** values:

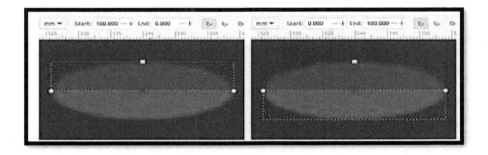

14 We would want the little ovals that make up the leaf details to be oriented to the bottom, and then we would like them to be uniformly spaced by leveling up the gaps first. Consequently, we need to select our row of ovals and then click the **Align bottom Edges** button. After that, we need

to click the **Distribute horizontally with even horizontal gaps** button. Finally, we need to group the ovals by selecting **Object > Group** or by pressing Ctrl + G.

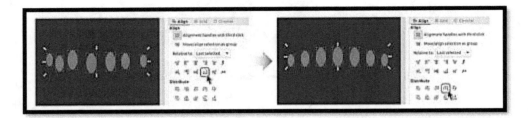

15. Because our top row is a mirror image of our bottom row, we will copy and paste it, and then we will use the V key to flip it vertically. Our leaf is the outcome of putting together the components, which we may then group.

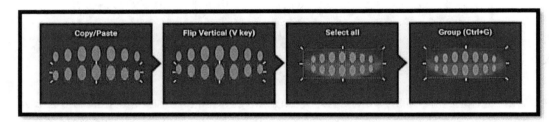

16. We are utilizing rectangles in the production of our glass. To have some experience with the **On-canvas alignment** option, let's turn it on and try utilizing it. Make sure that all of your rectangles are selected, and then use the third click button to activate the **alignment handles**.

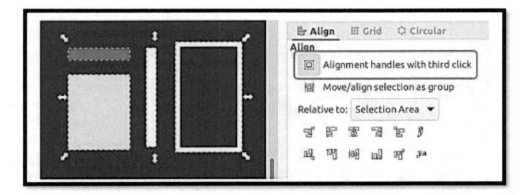

17. **When you activate this button, you will be able to obtain the alignment handles with the third click following:**
- Click one selects the shape(s).

- Click two changes handles to rotation.
- The third click gives us our on-canvas alignment handles.

18. After that, we may click the center alignment handle in the middle of the selection while holding down the Shift key (if you don't hold down the Shift key, it will align horizontally and automatically align itself). Through this process, the rectangles will be aligned vertically to the center.

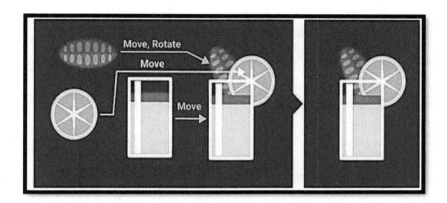

19. At this point, all that is left to do is put together our three drawings, which are the lemon, the leaf, and the glass, to create the delightful lemon-lime drink. This will be a lot simpler assignment for you to do if you are meticulous in grouping your objects. Simply put each component in its proper location, and the ultimate result will be determined by a single grouping of the three components.

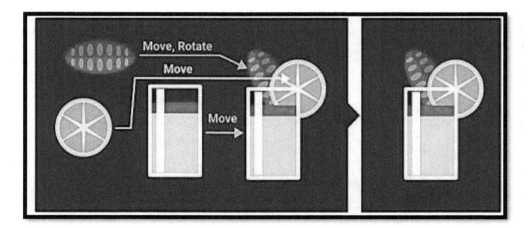

CHAPTER 13

MAKING USE OF CLIPS AND MASKS IN INKSCAPE

Through the use of clipping and masking, Inkscape provides strong tools that allow users to precisely control the visibility and look of objects.

- **Clipping** is a technique that includes using one object, which is referred to as the "clip-path," to determine the visibility of another object or group of objects by clipping. Clip paths, in their most basic form, perform the function of a stencil, selecting which aspects of the objects that lie underneath them will be seen and which will be concealed. When objects are clipped, they are limited to the shape or outline of the path that is being clipped.
- **Masking** is a technique that restricts the visibility of objects, much like clipping does, although it offers greater flexibility and complexity than clipping does. To put it simply, a mask in Inkscape is a grayscale image or object that is utilized to determine the transparency of another object. The sections of the mask that are darker make the regions of the masked object that correspond to them transparent, while the lighter areas continue to act as opaque.

As you can see in the image below, we can use our **Bezier Curve** tool to trace the periphery of this fetching mannequin and select both the shape and the picture. However, rather than selecting **Object > Clip > Set Clip** as we did in the past, we are going to right-click on the objects that we have selected and select **Set Clip** from the context menu that appears.

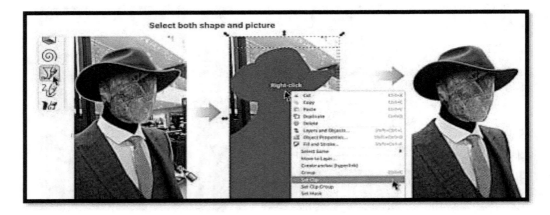

It is important to take note that the context menu has more clipping options; nevertheless, before we get too deep, let's investigate some cool tricks that can be accomplished with **Set Clip**. When you have your clipped object chosen and the Node tool is functioning, you will see that the Tool control bar contains an additional option for you to choose from. That's right, it's the one with the green line (although the color of the line could change depending on the theme you're using). This is the **Show Clipping Paths** option, and it does exactly what it says it would do: it displays the path that you first used to clip the photo. In addition to this, it provides you with nodes that you may use to edit that shape.

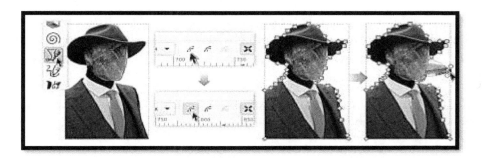

When we want to edit the object that is included within the clip, what should we do? This is quite great. With that being said, we could just right-click and select **Release Clip**, following which we would edit our photo and use **Set Clip** once more. However, this method may be a bit laborious when we are working with many objects, and it does not allow us to view the final product until after we have clipped it once more. However, there is a catch: Inkscape can apply clips to groups by itself! Consequently, Inkscape will convert our picture into a group consisting of a single object if we select it and then select **Object > Group (or press Ctrl + G).** After that, we can utilize the Set Clip function to select the group as well as the clipping shape. In the same way that it cut our initial photo, this will clip the group as well. There is not much that has changed at this point, except for the fact that we can now double-click within our group and move and resize our image within the clip to whatever we like. It is updated in real-time by Inkscape, which allows us to view the results right away.

Additionally, when we are within this clipped group, we can add shapes in the same manner as before, and they will likewise be contained within the clip. We can leave the group by either double-clicking on an area of blank canvas or by repeatedly hitting the Esc key. Both of these options are available to us. Inkscape will take the top shape and use it to clip all of the shapes that you have selected individually when you are clipping more than one shape at a time. However, this is not what you want in most cases because it generates a wide variety of shapes, each of which is clipped with a duplicate of its clip shape. Therefore, before you use Set Clip, I suggest that you first group the items. If you don't, working with the outcomes is just going to be more difficult overall. You can select **Edit > Preferences > Behavior > Clippaths** and **masks** and set the option to "**Put all clipped/masked objects into one group**." This provides you with the ability to always create a group for your clipped objects whenever you set a mask or clip, in addition to providing you with some other helpful options.

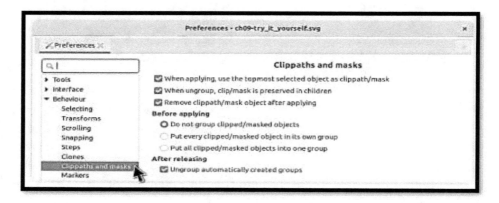

These options are particularly helpful for modifying the behavior of Inkscape when you set a clip or mask, and they are as follows:

- **When applying, use the topmost selected object as clip-path/mask**: After observing how Inkscape conceals the initial clipping shape to transform it into a clip or mask for underlying objects, we have seen how this happens when we set a clip or mask. If you would rather have a visible duplicate of this shape hanging around instead, ensure that this box is checked.
- **When ungroup, clip/mask is preserved in children**: Ungrouping a group that has been clipped will, in most cases, result in the removal of the clip. You can ungroup items with this option, but the objects will not be unclipped in the process.
- **Remove clip-path/mask object after applying**: Whenever we release a clip or a mask, Inkscape will often return us to the clipping shape that we had originally intended to use. If that is something that you do not desire, then you should check this box.
- **Before applying**: This is a list of options that Inkscape uses before deciding whether to set the clip or the mask. Currently, three options are available.

- **Do not group clipped/masked objects**: The default setting is this. When you clip or mask in Inkscape, the program does not automatically establish a group for this purpose.
    - **Put every clipped/masked object in its group**
    - **Put all clipped/masked objects into one group**

There may be times when we would want to maintain the shapes that we are using to clip the picture or objects rather than having them disappear when we utilize the **Set Clip** function. Inkscape includes a tool known as **Set Clip Group** that is specifically designed to accomplish this. Take, for instance, the scenario in which I wish to make a clip consisting of three circles.

To add more circles and other shapes to the clip, I would want to clip them to themselves rather than clipping them to a different shape. This would allow me to better organize the clip. In a normal situation, we would have to make a copy of those three circles, then group them, and last, you would have to utilize them as a clip shape over the three circles that were already grouped. Instead, we can take our three circles, right-click on them, and select the **Set Clip Group** option from the context menu. This enables us to click within the group and add more shapes (in this example, three smaller circles) within the clip, as can be seen in the image below.

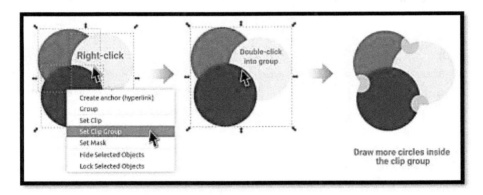

Clips inside clips

Perhaps you are thinking to yourself at this time, "Well, this is pretty cool... but is it possible for me to make a clip inside of a clip?" In response to your question, the answer is yes; it is possible to clip through another clip. On the other hand, when you do so, you will first need to make certain that the object that has been clipped is grouped to itself. If you do not do this, the only clipped shape that will be utilized for clipping and masking will be the topmost one, and all clipping shapes that are included within it will be removed. For example, consider a circle that has been clipped with a star and then clipped with a rectangle. The image that follows demonstrates that if we do not group the freshly clipped star circle, Inkscape will entirely discard the star clip when we attempt to clip it to the rectangle. This is something that you can observe for yourself. This problem is resolved by grouping the star circle to itself after it has been clipped, which provides us with the desired outcome.

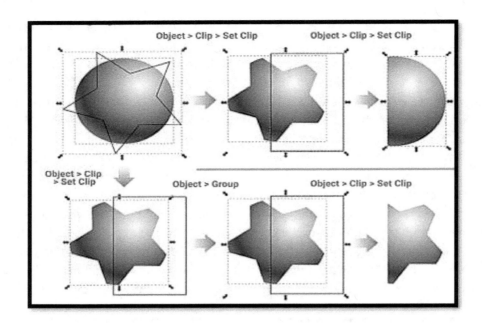

Naturally, if you have instructed Inkscape to automatically include your group in what is clipped by using the options that we discussed before, you will not need to carry out this additional grouping operation on your own. When you clip again, Inkscape will automatically group the shapes that you have already clipped. It is safe to say that this is the end of the narrative about clips in Inkscape. In a nutshell, the other shapes will be clipped to the geometric border of the vector shape that you employ, regardless of whether the vector shape is filled or empty. With that being said, it is possible that we would want to regulate the transparency of objects by using a color gradient or even an image rather than simply clipping them. This would be a more sophisticated approach.

How to mask with vector shapes and images

You can set the boundary cut-off of shapes when you use vector shapes using **Set Clip**. In a much more flexible manner, masks allow you to modify the transparency of the same shapes that you are working with. Say, for example, we have an illustration of a fish, and we'd like to make it half… I don't know… squirrel! Sure, why not? We'd like to gradually fade out the squirrel half into the fish half. To do this would ordinarily need a great deal of intricate gradients; however, we are lucky enough to be able to employ a straightforward black-to-white gradient shape as a mask to blend the squirrel into the fish.

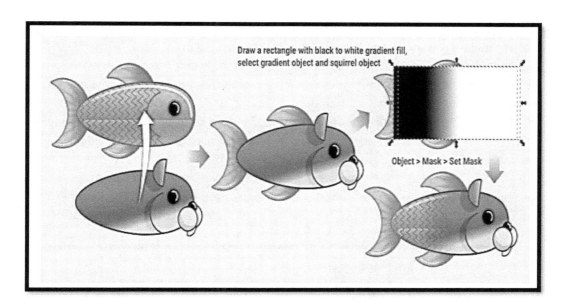

It is important to take note that the squirrel head is opaque in areas where the gradient is white, and the darker the gradient becomes, the more transparency we receive. This is the fundamental concept behind how masks function in Inkscape and a wide variety of other tools. The color of our masks and, consequently, the areas of transparency may be controlled by us through the utilization of radial and even mesh gradients, as is of course possible. Gradients are not the only restriction. We can perform our masking function with any object that possesses both bright and dark colors, including patterns and even images. Through the utilization of various objects as masks, we can accomplish a variety of outcomes, as seen in the image below.

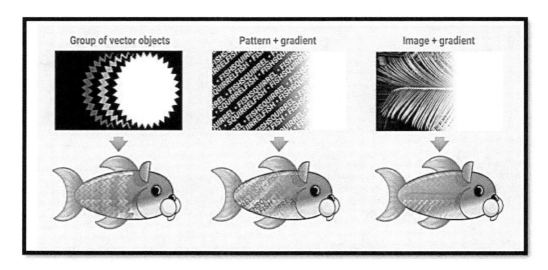

Isn't it very cool? It is possible to observe the amount of variety and detail that we can achieve by including an image such as that of a leaf in our mask while still maintaining our vector shapes. When vector shapes are involved, doing such things by hand would take an excessive amount of time. As a consequence, masking provides us with a wonderful option that allows us to get some very excellent outcomes with a small amount of effort. It is important to keep in mind that Inkscape handles transparent sections as if they were a dark color in the mask. This means that the transparent portions in the mask will be the transparent parts in the final product. Because of this, you can easily use a gradient mask that transitions from white to transparent and achieve the same effects as you would if you were going to use a gradient mask that transitions from white to black. Especially in situations where we want to blur-mask something, this comes in helpful. Making a white object, blurring it, and then using it as a mask is all that is required of us.

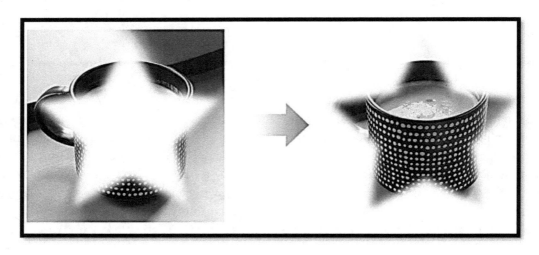

CHAPTER 14
CLONES AND SYMBOLS

It is only logical that the vector style of thinking about graphics would give rise to the concept of a clone, which is a connected replica of an object that automatically updates itself whenever the original modification is made. A clone is not an actual object; rather, it is only a command that says, **"Display a copy of the object here**." This command is stored in the document, which is not a material object. It is only in the memory of an SVG program like Inkscape that an actual object is formed, rather than the command, when the application displays the document. The usage of clones can be done for both aesthetic and practical purposes.

Having the opportunity to observe the live transformation of many objects while editing only one is an exhilarating experience that opens up a wide range of creative possibilities. In contrast, the utilization of clones rather than duplicates has the potential to reduce the size of an SVG document and make it show more quickly. It is natural for clones to have a variety of symmetric designs or patterns, as well as map symbols, repeating design components such as bullets or icons, and other similar features used repeatedly. Inkscape is one of the few vector editors that enables you to make live-connected copies of objects with the same level of simplicity and directness as it does.

Creating a Clone

You may clone a single object or several objects by selecting them and pressing the **Alt-D key** (or by going to **Edit > Clone > Create Clone).** The result that is displayed is precisely the same as the result that is apparent when duplicating **(Ctrl-D):** a copy of (each) chosen object is made and placed on top of the original. If you require a clone of many objects in their entirety, you should group them together and then clone the group. Of the utmost importance, a clone replicates the content of the original. If it is a clone of a path or shape, it will exactly recreate the original form, and it will update itself immediately if you edit the original using the **Node tool or the shape tool**.

The textual content of a clone of a text object is identical to that of the original text object, and it is also updated in real-time if the original text object is edited using the Text tool. In conclusion, if you clone a group, you will be able to access that group to add, delete, or edit objects that are contained inside the group, and the clone of the group will immediately update. It is not feasible to edit the content of a clone since it does not have any content of its own. This means that you cannot edit the content of a clone in any way, including editing nodes, changing text, or ungrouping it as long as it is still a clone.

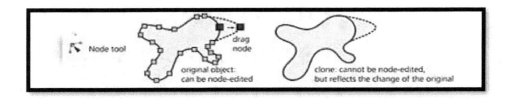

Then there are the transformations. Every one of the original's clones will behave in the same manner if you scale, rotate, or skew the original. On the other hand, if you just move the original object, the clone will not move by default (although that behavior can be changed, see below). When you select both the original and its clone, you can transform both of them together. This includes the ability to move, scale, rotate, or skew the original.

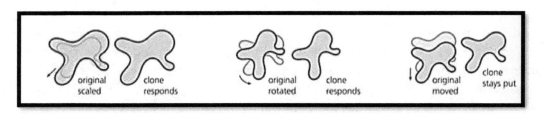

Additionally, you can move, scale, rotate, or skew the clone in a manner that is 100% independent of the original. The transform that is inherited from the original is applied on top of the transform that is applied by the clone on its own. For instance, if you squeeze a clone vertically and then rotate the original, the clone will be rotated and squeezed at the same time. However, the vertical squeeze will be applied to the shape after it has been rotated, which will result in a skew.

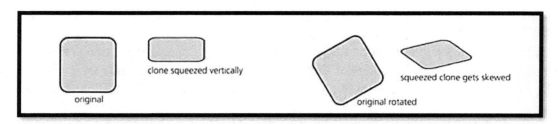

In addition, the style of the original is utilized in the creation of its clones. When you paint the original with a different color for the fill or stroke, all of the clones of the original will take on the same color at the same time. If, on the other hand, you attempt to paint a clone, it will simply refuse to change color and will continue to take on the appearance of the original. Exceptions to this rule are allowed, as you will see in the following paragraphs.

This table summarizes various things you can and cannot do on a clone and its original and how those changes affect one another:

	Move	Scale, rotate, skew	Node or shape edit	Style
Applied to original	does *not* affect clones (by default)	does affect clones	does affect clones	does affect clones
Applied to clone	is possible	is possible (on top of original's transformation)	is impossible	is impossible (unless unset in the original)

Cloning groups

A sheet of stickers is a good example to take into consideration. To edit the sticker, we could just copy and paste it into some new stickers and arrange them in an even manner throughout the page. However, we do not want to go to the trouble of rearranging everything before editing the sticker. By utilizing clones, we can have the task done for us. However, our stickers are likely constructed from more than one part of the object. Thankfully, Inkscape allows for the creation of cloning groups, which means that all that is required of us is to group all of our sticker elements, and then clone that group to clone the entire sticker along with all of its components. ***The image below* shows a sticker I've made of many different vector parts, which are grouped, cloned, and then arranged on a sheet.**

As you can see, going inside the group gives us the ability to edit several aspects of the original sticker, such as the gradient that I used for the tea color. As you can see, cloning a group may be a very time-efficient method of doing things! This method has been utilized over many years to create a large number of sticker sheets for use on commercial product packaging. But clones are capable of more than just that. Let's have a look at some of the other things that they are capable of doing, such as acting as masks and clips simultaneously.

Clones as clips and masks

When we use clones as clips and masks, we can exert a considerable lot of control over the appearance of our clip shapes. A mock-up of, for example, a t-shirt with a logo is something that I use very frequently. On both shirts, we would want to have the same logo, but one of the shirts is black, thus we do not have a white logo. To clip a white rectangle with some minor gradients that match the coloring of the black shirt, we may utilize a clone of the original black logo as a clip shape to clip the rectangle. Because our clone serves as a clip shape, modifying the original will also result in a change to the clip shape on the black shirt. This will save us from having to redo all of the work that was done in terms of duplication and clipping, as seen in the image below.

Additionally, we can add blurs and opacity to our clones, and then layer them to generate intriguing effects like shadows and glows. These effects will alter per the adjustments that are made to the original shape. On the other hand, there are situations when we would like to alter the fill and stroke properties of the clones. Since our original has a fill and stroke already allocated to the shapes, this is not something that can be done normally. By unsetting the original fill and stroke, on the other hand, we can modify the fill and stroke of a selected clone to anything we choose. By right-clicking the **Fill and Stroke** color indications and selecting either **unset fill or unset stroke**, the process of unsetting the fill and stroke is demonstrated in the image that can be found below. Following the jelly bean's transformation into a dark color, we will be able to clone, color, and edit the original jelly bean to modify the shape of all of the jelly beans simultaneously.

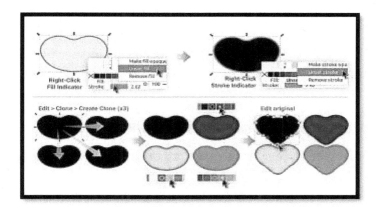

As an instance, this is pretty helpful, but it could be a little annoying at times. Jelly beans, after all, have a glossy appearance with various shadows and highlights. We are fortunate in that we are not restricted to cloning only a single object. The glossy reflection and shadow can be created, the objects can be grouped and cloned in the same way that we did with a single object, and the color of the beans can be altered. In addition, we can change the color of the shadow to a black gradient and the color of the reflection to a white gradient. Changing the color of the bean will not have any impact on the sections of our cloned group that are affected by the change. We are going to clone the bean shape that we have unset the fill and stroke on, and then we are going to utilize the clones to create reflections and shadows. First, we can group our unset bean base to itself and then build a clone of the group. Additionally, we can tint the clone red in the same way that we did previously. Because of this, we will be able to observe the effect of what we are doing on the black bean a little bit more clearly. The initial unset black bean may then have three shapes added to it: two gloss reflections and one shadow shape at the bottom with white and black-to-transparent gradients. These shapes can be added to the bean. The cloned red bean may then be copied and pasted, and the colors modified in the same manner as previously. This procedure is depicted in the attached image below.

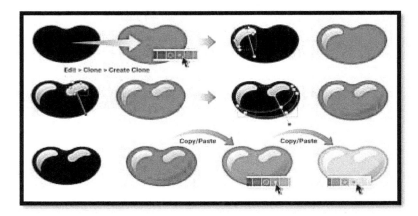

182

Pay attention to the fact that the white and black gradients on the new clones maintain their original color even after we change the color. The reason behind this is that the color of a clone only has an effect on strokes and fills that have not yet been specified before. A term that describes this effect is **inheritance**. It is given this moniker since the colors that you set on the clone are passed down to the unset shapes in the clone.

Managing clones using clones of clones

It will be necessary for us to have a reliable method of managing clones after we have reached increasingly complicated combinations of clones. If we change to ungroup or delete our original cloned object by accident, Inkscape will quietly unlink our clones, and we will lose the ability to make changes to all of them at the same time. Because of this, we will often group the original, place a rectangle behind it with a label, and then move it off the canvas so that it is not in the way of the primary design. You can see what this appears to be like in the image below.

As can be seen, the warning instructions and the box provide a quick overview of what is occurring, ensuring that there is never any uncertainty regarding what must be done (or if it should be done, in this particular instance). When we start producing clones of clones, this features an even greater degree of utility. Take, for instance, our logo symbol, logo name, and tagline; we will not always want them to be ordered in this manner, and depending on what we are developing, we may want to eliminate some elements of them. We would want a single modification to affect all of the components of our design, regardless of how we have them arranged. So, how exactly do we go about doing this? Clones of clones are the solution to this problem! The first thing that we do is split each component of our logo into its groups, then we name and box them, and last, we remove them from the canvas, just like we did previously. After that, we can click inside each box group, create a clone of each component of the original, and then combine those clones to create two new arrangements: a horizontal and a vertical version of our logo, as seen in the image below.

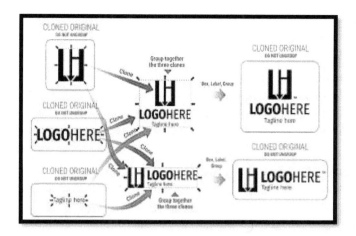

It is important to take note that we have incorporated a trademark sign (™) into each of our arrangements placed in various areas. If we had included them in the cloned objects that were first created, we would have been unable to change their position in the clone copies. As a result, it is simple to mix clone and non-clone shapes in this manner, and we can maintain the ability to edit any subsequent combinations by editing our initial clones. If we now edit the initial logo, the changes will be immediately applied to both the horizontal and vertical configurations. These modifications will then automatically propagate to clones that we make of the horizontal and vertical logo orientations as well. This will enable us to use these two arrangements throughout the entirety of our project without having to reassemble them each time we make a change to the original logo symbol, logotype, or tagline. The image that follows displays all of our off-canvas cloned groups as well as the many ways in which we may utilize them in various locations across our documents.

From the perspective of just this one project, this may appear to be a lot of labor for only a small amount of reward. It is to our good fortune that we grouped our objects before cloning them, which means that we may reuse this same file to automatically make mock-ups for any number of projects that may come along in the future. Simply copying and pasting the new logo into the existing group and removing the old logo is all that is required to accomplish this target. Although you will need to make some adjustments to the designs to accommodate the logo and branding of each new customer, the cloning and duplicating work has already been completed. When I take on a new customer, I always employ this method since it helps me avoid having to repeatedly perform the same repetitive tasks over and over again. This frees up more time for me to focus on the design work that needs to be done. I prefer to refer to this user-friendly and automated technique for creating mock-ups as a **supertemplate** as it is straightforward to use. We will indeed include the **supertemplate** in the filename when we save the file. This will allow me to locate it at a later time, create a copy of it, and use it for a completely other project that is of the same kind. In this particular instance, we will give this one the name **teeshirt_and_business_cards_supertemplate.svg.** Using a file browser to look for anything will become simple as a result of this!

Leveraging linked image files

There is an additional helpful method for reusing assets in our documents. Any modifications that are made to the source images will be mirrored in our document when we link them into it! We are offered some options for incorporating an image file, such as a photo, into our document when we import it into Inkscape by dragging and dropping it from our disk (or by selecting **File > Import**). The importing procedure and available options are depicted in the image below.

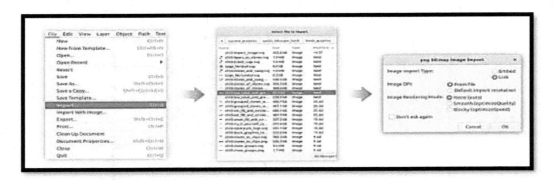

There is a wide variety of options available here; however, the **Embed and Link** options are the ones that are most relevant to our objectives today. If we select the **Embed** option, Inkscape will create a duplicate of the image and then insert it into our project. The image is saved within our document when we embed it, which increases the file size. On the other hand, if we do this, we won't have to maintain the original image file, which is a different file. However, this does come with a drawback: if we copy and paste this embedded image, each time we paste, it will embed an entirely new version of this image, which will cause our file size to constantly increase, even though the image itself remains the same! This may be circumvented in some different ways. It is possible to clone the image and then copy and paste the clones instead of copying and pasting the original image. Selecting **Link** rather than **Embed** during the import process is the alternative method, which results in even greater space savings. This has the additional benefit of allowing us to make modifications to the original image, for example in a photo-editing application like **GIMP or Photoshop**, and when we save the modified file over the original one, the modifications will be immediately updated in our Inkscape document. One of the drawbacks is that we have to retain the image in the same location it was in before so that Inkscape can locate and load it. There is also the option of storing the image in the same folder as the **.svg** file that you have saved, and Inkscape will be able to locate it in this manner. If Inkscape is unable to locate the image, it will display a large red circle and an **X** signs in its place, as demonstrated in the image that may be found below.

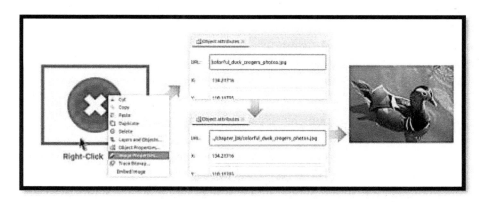

You always have the option to just put the file into the same folder as your saved **.svg** file and then re-open it in Inkscape if you feel that this represents an excessive amount of trouble. If Inkscape opens a file and discovers a broken file link, it will immediately look in the same folder as the **.svg** file. This will ensure that the proper file is located. Thereafter, Inkscape will automatically fix the broken link for you if it is present in the document. My linked files are often stored in the same folder as the **.svg** file because of this reason. In general, this is a good practice since it makes it simpler to locate your images in the future and allows you to reuse them in other aspects of your projects. This increases the likelihood that you will discover them together in the future. Note that you can alter your mind and embed the file at any moment you want by right-clicking the image and selecting the **Embed Image** option from the **Context** menu. This is something that should be taken into consideration. A second option that you will notice is the **Edit Externally** option, which will launch an image editor (the GIMP by default, provided you have it installed on your computer). When you save the original connected image in Inkscape, any modifications that you make to the original in GIMP will be mirrored in Inkscape.

Symbols

A symbol may be thought of as a collection of clones that are arranged in libraries for reuse. Inkscape's Object4Symbols dialog, which can be accessed by pressing Shift-Ctrl-Y, provides you with access to a variety of graphic symbol sets that are included in the program. Additionally, it allows you to develop and maintain your collections of custom symbols if you so want.

You should be able to get an idea of the types of objects that it could be a good idea to collect into a library by looking at the premade symbol sets that Inkscape provides:

- **AIGA (American Institute of Graphic Arts):** Urban signage, used mostly in airports: arrivals, customs, barber shops—very recognizable and very 1970s.
- **US National Park Service Map Symbols:** Campgrounds, guided trails, post offices—stylistically similar to AIGA symbols.
- **Flow chart shapes::** The conventional blocks of flow chart diagrams, such as storage, extract, merge, display, and so on.
- **Logic diagram symbols:** The AND gate, OR gate, NOT gate, and friends.
- **Word balloons:** Various shapes of word balloons to be used in comics.

To insert a symbol into your document, simply drag it from the dialog onto the canvas. The object you receive behaves similarly to a clone of something, although the status bar description indicates "**Symbol**". However, if you wish to edit this object, you can perform the same action as you would for a clone: navigate to **Edit > Clone > Unlink Clone.** (If your intention is solely to move, scale, or rotate the symbol, there's no need to unlink it.) Through the use of the search field within the Symbols dialog, it is possible to locate a symbol that has a certain word or phrase included in its description. Whether you want to search in the presently chosen symbol set or in all of them, the search is carried out in the following symbol sets: All of the symbol sets.

When you switch the dialog to **Current document (see the image below),** you will notice that it already has all of the symbols that you have added from the standard libraries, if there are any. There is also the possibility of adding your objects as symbols in this section: Click the Add Symbol button located in the lower-left corner of the screen after selecting an object. The original object can be removed from the list and a duplicate of the symbol can be substituted for it after the new symbol has been added to the list. The new symbol that you have produced will be added with the same dimensions and formatting that it had when you first made it.

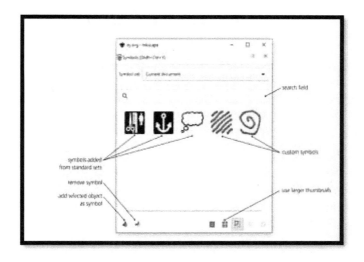

To remove a symbol from the document, you must first select it from the list and then utilize the button labeled "**Remove Symbol**." Once you have done this, a physical duplicate of the symbol will be put on the canvas, and all occurrences of this symbol will be transformed into clones of the visible object. Unfortunately, when you create a new symbol in Inkscape, it does not ask for a title; instead, it assigns it an unhelpful numeric name, and as a result, it cannot be searched by title. If you want to remedy this issue, you need first to set the **Title** in the **Object Properties** before you transform it into a symbol. If you want to share your custom symbol library with other documents, all you have to do is insert an SVG document that contains the symbols into the symbols folder of Inkscape. To accomplish this, navigate to the **Preferences page** of the **System menu** and click the **Open button** next to **User symbols**. Following that, your symbol set will be accessible in the Symbol set list, which is located under the name of the SVG file you have created.

CHAPTER 15
MAKING USE OF LIVE PATH EFFECTS

The non-destructive effects that are offered by the path effects, which are often referred to as Live Path Effects (LPEs), may be applied to paths to generate a wide variety of effects that would need a significant amount of effort to create manually. When we talk about generating shapes, editing photographs, and other similar things in graphic design, there are two different sorts of paths that we may follow to obtain what we want: **destructive and non-destructive**. It is possible to choose any of these paths. To put it another way, a **destructive workflow** is one in which, after we have made a change to a shape, that change is irreversible (except for a brief time during which the **Undo feature** is available).

For instance, when we subtract a square from a circle by using our Boolean operations (by picking **Path > Difference**), we create a new shape that is composed of nodes, lines, and curves. As a result, the circle and the square are eliminated to create the new shape, and they are no longer changeable at the individual level. We would be very much out of luck if we wished to move the square without altering the portions of the circle, considering the circumstances. After drawing a fresh circle and square, we should combine them once more in the same manner. This would be the best course of action. A **non-destructive** workflow is different; if we take that same circle and square, add a **Boolean path effect**, and set the effect to **Difference**, we can subtract the square and then later move it around separately, which then moves the hole in real-time as you drag it on the canvas (which is what makes it live), without affecting the geometry of the circle. Furthermore, because our square is still a rectangular object, we can round the corners, which in turn round the corners of our hole. This is an even better situation.

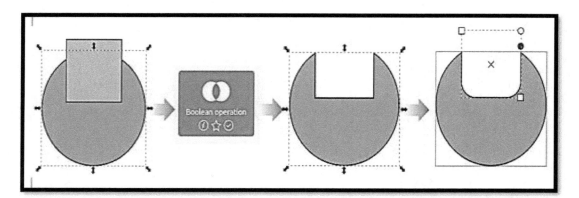

Additionally, we can switch from a **Difference** operation to any of the other Boolean operations at any time along the process. It is also possible to eliminate the path effect while still maintaining our original shapes. This is the reason why it is non-destructive; at any point in time, we can make

189

alterations without permanently altering our initial shapes! So, how do we manage this witchcraft? We start simply by selecting one of our objects and choosing **Path** > **Path Effects…**, which calls up the **Path Effects** dialog.

The Path Effects dialog

A dialog for Path Effects is provided by Inkscape, much like the majority of our other advanced capability products. When it is accessed, we will see a pretty simple interface that is similar to the Layers dialog, with the exception that it is devoid of any content. There is currently nothing to do in this location since there are no objects selected, and the controls are now grayed off. For the Add path effect control, which is represented by the plus sign in the bottom-left corner of the dialog, to become active, we must first select one object, and only one object. As soon as we click that button, we are greeted with a plethora of fantastic new tools that allow us to adjust our paths in a way that is not detrimental.

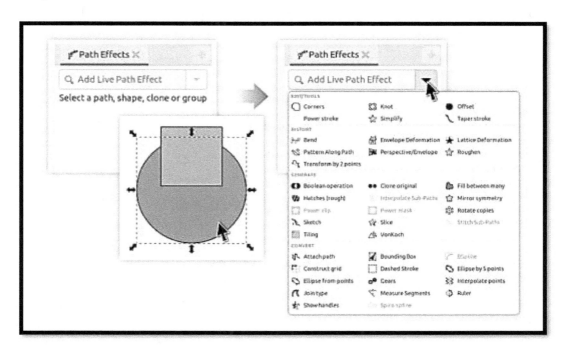

The shape we have chosen may undergo a variety of transformations, depending on the path effect that we select. For instance, adding a **Boolean operation** path effect to our circle does not immediately have any effect; all it does is add an entry to the **Path Effects** dialog and display the options for the **Boolean operation** path effect. Specifically, this is because we need to select and copy our square object to connect to it. After that, we select our circle once again, and then inside the **Path Effects** controls, we click the button that says "**Link to item**."

190

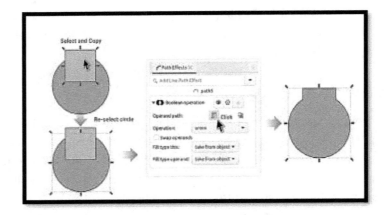

You can see that this has added the circle and square together. This is because, by default, the **Operation** type is set to **union** in the dropdown in the **Path Effects** dialog. As was noted earlier, you can select any other effect, such as **difference**, by modifying the value of this dropdown menu.

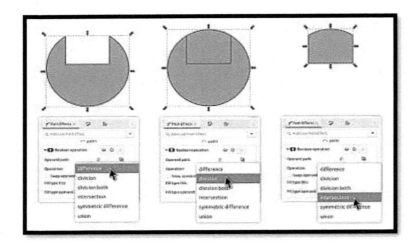

You will see that there are other options available for the **Boolean operation** path effect; however, we will not be discussing each one of them in this discussion.

Using Path Effects with single-path objects

So, it's true that Booleans are wonderful and everything, but what if we want to round the corners of a combination shape that we've previously created? It is to our good fortune that there is a wide range of path effects that apply to single-path objects and that enable us to do actions depending on the nodes. Consider the scenario in which our customer requested that we fashion a llama out of nothing more than rectangles for her Boxy Llama Coffee business. Following the completion of the task, she returns and expresses a desire to have some of those corners rounded.

To accomplish this on a corner-by-corner basis, we may take advantage of the **Corners** path effect. Using the same method as previously, we just select our boxy llama path and then add a Corners path effect by going to **Path > Path Effects** and selecting the **plus** button in the **Path Effects** dialog box. The path effect has introduced specific handles for us to pull out and round those corners, so this time we will select the **Nodes tool**, which will display them to us.

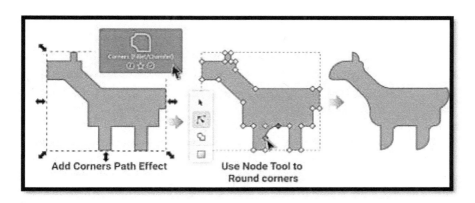

The llama continues to have a lovely and boxy appearance, but it now has a more designed appearance thanks to those wonderful, rounded edges. This is because we did not round all of the corners. To make use of this effect, we will need to transform our object into a path that is composed of nodes. This, however, is not the case with each path effect. While some are good with objects or even a group of objects, some require paths, while others are fine with objects. If anything is not functioning as effectively as you anticipate, you could want to begin by turning the object into a path. Take the **Bend** path effect as an example, for instance. Although we would want to utilize it to bend our headline text, Bend is only capable of working on paths at the time this article was written. Therefore, For Bend to have an effect, we need to turn our text object into a path by selecting **Path > Object to Path** from the menu.

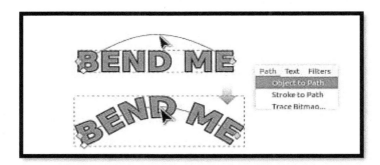

Now that we are familiar with a few different ways to apply path effects to single objects, what happens if our object is composed of more than one component? From the moment we select more than one object, we are unable to add a path effect to the selection. Despite this, we can apply a path effect to a single group of objects.

Using Path Effects with groups

You can only add a path effect to one selected object at a time, as was already stated. The **Path Effects** dialog's **Add Path effect** button will be grayed out if you select more than one. Some path effects, on the other hand, will work on a group of objects as if they were one. This can be seen in the **Rotate copies** path effect. That is, let's say you have a mouse eating cheese and you want to make that mouse into a circle of mice eating cheese. With the mouse parts all grouped, it's easy to add a path effect. Just select the group and scroll down until you find the **Rotate copies** path effect. Here are the results of what you did.

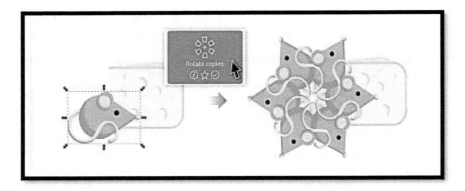

There are that many mice in this. They are mostly looking the wrong way, though, so they can't eat our cheese. They are turned around at a different point, which needs to be changed. Selecting the **Node** tool and adjusting the starting handle will allow us to accomplish this.

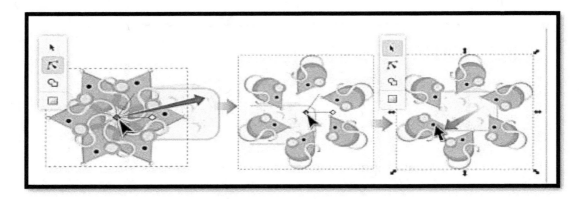

193

The Node tool gives you access to the on-canvas controls for path effects, just like the handles for rectangles and ellipses do for those special objects. The object group can also be edited by double-clicking on it. This is very helpful if we want to change something about the mice, like their attitude. To get into the mouse group, we just double-click on it. To change the shape of the eye, for example, we use the Node tool. Then, as you can see below, there are a bunch of happy mice eating some tasty cheese.

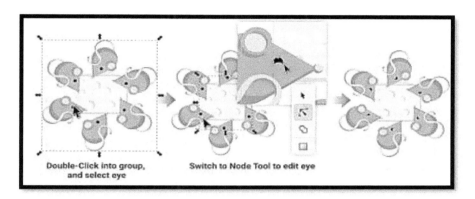

It's important to note that you can change things like the number of mice, whether the copies are reversed when the puzzle turns, and more. I like the Rotate copies path effect because it has these and other great features that make it great for quick sunburst-style rotating design work. This saves a lot of time, but what if we want to bend our ring of mice like we did with our text? It turns out that adding path effects makes this easy to do.

Stacking Path Effects

You may have seen that the **Layers and Objects** dialog box and the Path Effects dialog box look a lot alike. As we add effects, we can see that they all fit together the same way. In the case of our mice, we could add a **Bend path** effect to make the whole ring of mice that are munching bend.

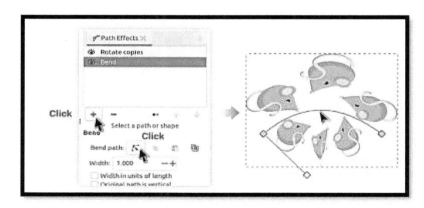

194

It's more likely that we'd only want to bend one mouse than the whole rotating group, though. We just need to move the Bend path effect above the Rotate copies path effect to make this happen. To make this easier, click on the little arrow on the left side of the bar to shrink Bend. Then, click and drag the handle on the right side to move the item to the top of the list. At the top of the Rotate copies line, there is a small colored dot that shows you where the Bend path effect will go when you let go of the mouse button. After that, we can bend each mouse separately.

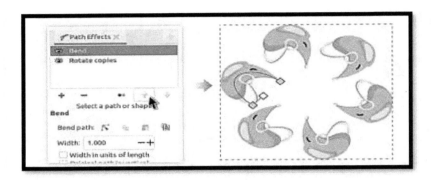

You can see that Inkscape uses the path effects from top to bottom, starting with the first effect and ending with the last effect at the bottom of the stack. This means that we can change the order of the path effects. We can get the effects we want with this very strong tool. Even though the effects are very different from our original, note how our original geometry is still changeable. This is what non-destructive processes in Inkscape can do for you.

Limitations of Path Effects

Path effects are always being worked on to make them better and add features that people **have asked for. Since new path effects are usually added with every update, these restrictions will probably be lifted in the future:**

- At the moment, path effects can only be used on one object at a time.
- Imported pixel or bitmap images will not be affected by path effects that change shape (such as bend, perspective, and so on).
- Objects that are text will not be affected by path effects that change the shape of text. The text object can be turned into a path by first choosing **Path > Object to Path**, which will work around this.
- When SVGs are put into web browsers, path effects will not show up.

You can add path effects to your geometry, though, by going to **Path > Object to Path**. This will add all of your path effects and give you geometry that you can then edit regularly. Plus, this works even better than watching an SVG in a web browser, since the object no longer has any path effects after the object-to-path conversion.

CHAPTER 16
WORKING WITH FILTERS AND EFFECTS

A lot of different bitmap processing algorithms can be used on the objects in your drawing with Inkscape filters. In the spirit of vectors, filters don't remove anything; you can always change the settings of any filter and still be able to edit the original vector object. Blurring, sharpening, changing colors, adding texture, distorting images in different ways, creating 3D effects like bevels, and many other things are all things that filters can do. As an example, when we move the **Blur scale** in the **Fill and Stroke** dialog box, we tell Inkscape to give the object a **Gaussian Blur** effect. We can be sure of this by seeing that the chosen object is now filtered in the status bar, as shown below.

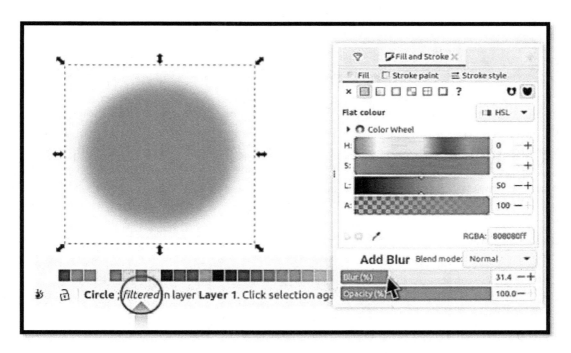

This is also how the **Blend** mode object works in the **Fill and** Stroke dialog box. What else can we do with filters? It turns out that it was a lot of things! A quick look at the **Filter** menu in the menu bar will show you a lot of different types of default filters that you can use. We can add a drop shadow to our chosen object or group by going to Filters > **Shadows and Glows > Drop Shadow**... for example. The image below shows how to give the squirrel a **Drop Shadow Filter**. The pop-up text box lets you set the filter's parameters. To see what you're doing, make sure the live sample box is checked. Then, hit the **Apply** button to see the changes take effect.

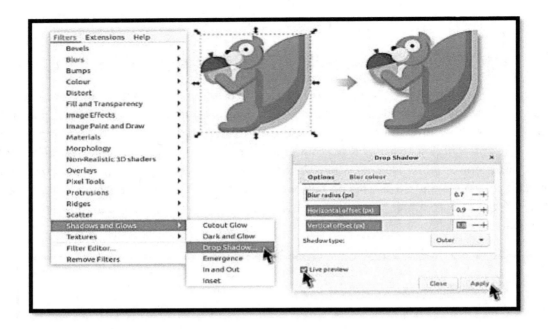

Changes to the squirrel graphic's objects will cause the drop shadow to update itself as you do so. In the case of complicated images, this can save time! Right now you might be wondering what the **Drop Shadow** effect does. To find out, we only need to go to **Filters > Filter Editor** and open the **Filter Editor** text box. This will show us what's inside the filter, and it lets us change things. The image below shows the Filter Editor dialog box with our carefully chosen squirrel picked. From the very top to the very bottom of the filter process, I've written what they are at each step.

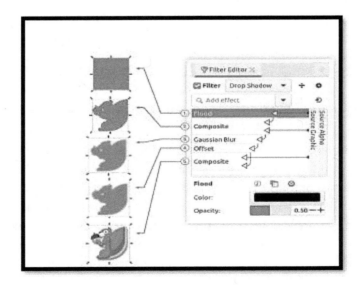

With all the lines going around and linking parts, this seems a bit hard to understand at first. As a top-down list of effects that can be used to make the drop shadow, this conversation starts to make more sense of what's going on.

Let's go through the parts of the Drop Shadow filter, starting at the top of the dialog:

- **Flood**: This effect takes the main graphic (in this case, the squirrel objects) and fills the whole graphic's rectangle area with a color. The bottom of the Filter Editor dialog, which displays details for the currently chosen effect, shows that the color is black and the opacity number is 50% in this case.
- **Composite**: Note the small line that comes from the Flood effect and the other that comes from the source image. This effect takes the original image and mixes it with the previous effect (Flood). This cuts the black rectangle into the shape of the squirrel.
- **Gaussian Blur**: According to its name, it blurs the results of the first two effects. It does this by following the line from the last effect in the recipe.
- **Offset**: This controls where our distorted shadow is in space compared to the original image. We can make the shadow go off-center in any direction we want.
- **Composite**: This just puts the real squirrel on top of the shade to finish the effect.

Note that we can choose **Filters > Remove Filters** or uncheck the Filter box at the top of the Filter Editor menu if we change our minds about that Drop Shadow filter. Don't worry if it's still not clear what's going on. We're about to get our hands dirty and use some of these parts to make our filter.

Creating custom filters

Let's say we want a filter that automatically shades the inside of one side of our shapes so they look 3D instead of 2D. Like a drop shadow. Beginning with a fresh file, we can draw a simple circle. Next, we can select the circle and go to **Filters > Filter Editor**. There is a blank place and a button that looks like a **plus sign (+)** at the top. When we click the + button and check the Filter box, we can see what the filter found. This gets rid of the circle, as you can see below!

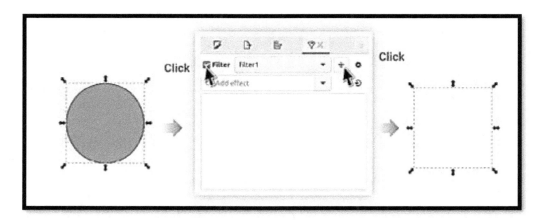

It makes sense, though, since we told Inkscape to filter the circle and give it nothing as a recipe. It then gives us nothing back! We could use this as a disappearing effect, but we already have **Object > Hide**. Now let's add our first effect. We select **Flood** from the list of options in the **Add Effect** dropdown menu. Right away, we see the same square we saw before. To add a second effect, we can click on the **Add Effect** menu again and choose **Composite** this time. This will combine our first circle with the other one. But nothing takes place. That's because both of the lines that go to **Composite** come from the **Flood** effect. This means that Inkscape is just putting two copies of the same square on top of each other. Instead, we need to link the first arrow to the source image. Using the image below as a guide, we click and drag the arrow's head to draw a line, then drag that line over the **Source Graphic** bar to join it.

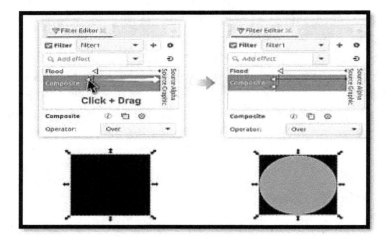

This has the effect of placing the original circle on top of the Flood square, as you can see. This will give our shadow some darkness. Now we add a Gaussian Blur effect in the same way we did with the first two effects. We also raise the Size number to 9.86 or something close. As the image below blurs, you can see that Inkscape makes the edges darker to fill in the blurred area.

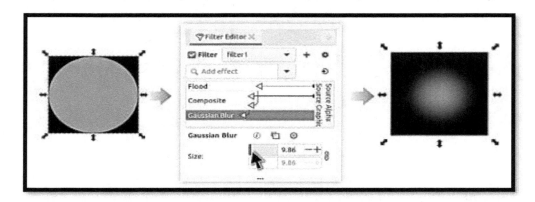

Now that we have a lot of black shade, we need to combine it with our original circle shape. To do this, we add a **Composite** effect like before, but this time we link the source graphic to the second input by clicking and dragging the second arrow to the **Source Graphic** bar. We will also change the **Operator** setting to "**In**" this time. This makes the shadow fit into the circle shape, as you can see below.

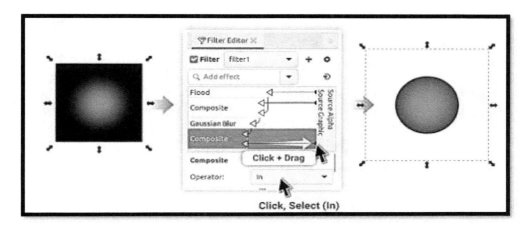

It now has a nice, even shadow all around, but we'd like to move our shadow to the lower right so that more of it is there. With a light source in the top left corner, this will make it look more like a ball. One way to do this is to put an **Offset effect** in front of the **Gaussian Blur** effect. We do the same thing again that we did in the **Layers and Objects** text box. Just add it like we did with the other effects and then click and drag the bar up until the drop indicator shows a line between the first Composite effect bar and the Gaussian Blur effect bar. Finally, we can adjust Delta X and Delta Y to put the shadow where we want it. The image below shows this process.

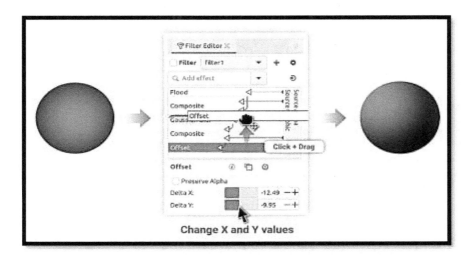

The question you may have now is why we didn't just use a radial blur. The real magic happens when we change the shape, though we could certainly get the same effect for a circle in that way. Watch the video below to see how the filter automatically changes our shadow when we change the shape of the circle!

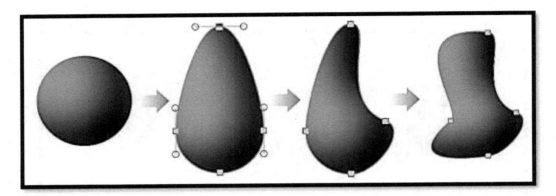

You can also change the object's fill color, and the filter will still work on top of it. Remember that to get the same effect in the past, we had to deal with complicated clone setups. To add our filter to any shape, we just need to open the **Filter Editor** menu, pick our filter as **filter1,** and check the **Filter box**. You can guess that we want to give our filter a name other than "filter1." To do that, click the dropdown menu next to filter1, double-click the name, and change it to 3D Shadow. Then, press the Enter key on your computer to apply, as shown below.

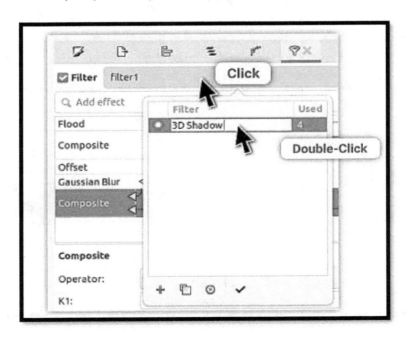

You can try out all the different effects in the **Add Effects** dropdown and the many preset categories in the filters menu. Just by looking into these options, you can learn a lot, like we did with the **Drop Shadow effect!**

Working with Extensions

Extensions are extra moves that were written by the Inkscape community but aren't part of the main code. They do many things, which we will talk about here. Extensions are different from filters in that they only change or add objects to your image once. Once you run an extension, the only way to get your original shape back to how it is to use the Edit > Undo option. These changes are destructive instead of the previous non-destructive changes. This is another reason why I think you should save your work before using an app. Because there are so many types of extensions, they are functionally grouped into groups, which you will see if you open the **Extensions** menu in Inkscape's menu bar.

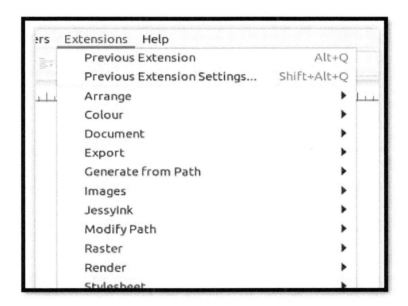

The groups are as follows:
- **Arrange**: This group of extensions allows you to rearrange the things you select like how the **Arrange** window works. **Deep Ungroup and Restack** are the only two additions available right now. Deep Ungroup does multiple ungroup moves at once, and Restack rearranges things in the Layers and Objects dialog based on where they are on the canvas.
- **Color**: This useful set of add-ons only works with vector shapes and lets you change the color and fill in how you might see them in photo-editing software. Some of the color changes you can make with these tools include **Greyscale, Desaturate, Negative, and HSL Adjust (Hue, Saturation, and Lightness).**

202

- **Document**: Extensions that have to do with the document. For example, DOC Info opens a text box with all the details about the document that you can copy and paste as text.
- **Export**: Add-ons that let you export to different file types that aren't available in the main file menu. For example, **Plot** lets you export a file that can be used on industrial cutting machines.
- **Generate From Path**: Extensions that take chosen object geometry and make more geometry based on it. For example, **Interpolate** takes two selected shapes, like a circle and a square, and adds shapes between them that transform the circle into a square.

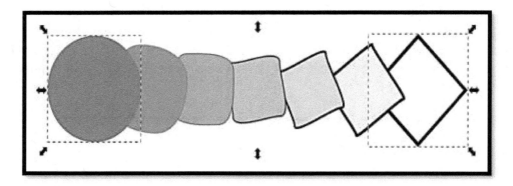

- **Images**: Add-ons for your document that work with chosen images. If you want to insert an image but choose to link to it instead, you can use the insert extension to do that. In the same way, Extract will make a linked image from an embedded image and save a copy of it in the same area as your document.
- **JessyInk**: This is a JavaScript tool that has add-ons that let you use Inkscape SVGs to make presentations.
- **Modify Path**: These extensions add modes to your geometry and transform the paths in particular ways. For instance, the **Add Node**s extension allows you to add nodes to your path in specific places. Some, like **Whirl**, try to twist your path around a center point.
- **Raster**: These add-ons work with bitmap images and give you photo effects like you might find in photo-editing software. You should save your work before using these actions because they can delete it. Keep in mind that if your image is tied to a document, these filters will embed it for you before you even use the filter.
- **Render**: This category has many useful items that make vector shapes. For example, **Extensions > Render > Barcode > QR Code** lets you make a QR code (those blocky codes you scan with your phone's camera), standard (Classic) barcodes for your inventory, or even calendars that you can print out!

There's lots of cool stuff in this. You should play with them all for a while to figure out which ones you like best. Knowing what your options are is half the fight, and you never know when they will save you a lot of money.

- **Stylesheet**: This will output **Cascading Style Sheets (CSS)** code for websites from objects on your canvas. Don't worry if you don't know what this is; it's a tool for web coders.
- **Text**: Yes, you got it! This group has tools that change or edit text. If you get a whole line in capital letters, **Sentence case** will make the first letter of each sentence capitalized and the rest lowercase, saving you from having to retype everything. Other nice options include the ability to change your text to all capital letters with **UPPERCASE**.

You can also use Lorem ipsum to fill a textbox with sample text that looks like a paragraph. Just don't forget to change the text before you print it! This is another area you should know about and look into after every big release. As this is written, a new tool called Increment is being added that will automatically number things. I like this one a lot because I number a lot of sample sheets for clients.

- **Typography**: This section has tools that let you work with SVG fonts and make your own. Graphic design has a whole field called "font making," and I think it's awesome that you can make your fonts in Inkscape!
- **Visualize Path**: Sometimes you need more details about the path you're working on. But what if you want to find the length of a curve or circle? You can see the width and height, but not the length. Measure Path, for example, will show a curve measurement for your chosen object or the distance around your circle. This category has exactly what you're looking for.
- **Web**: This has many tools for making things for websites. With **Interactive Mockup**, you can make presentations that are based on SVG that you can interact with. With Slicer, you can cut up your document and export the pieces as PNGs. You can also set JavaScript properties for custom scripts that are inserted in SVG. If none of that makes sense to you, dismiss this group as yet another set of tools for web developers.
- **Manage Extensions**: Can't find what you need? This opens a new browser window where you can look for, download, install, and make your own Inkscape add-ons. It uses ones that people have shared to **https://inkscape.org/** and that have been picked out by people who work on the Inkscape project.

CHAPTER 17

ALL ABOUT EXPORTING, DOCUMENT PROPERTIES, PAGES, AND PRINTING

The Document Properties dialog

Could it be that you haven't given enough thought to how big things are? How big is your canvas? What size are your shapes? Which numbers do you use to measure? A4 page sizes and mm units are things that come with Inkscape that we don't think about much. This works fine for most things. But what if you want to use inches or even screen pixels? The **Document Properties** window box lets us change these things and a lot more. We just go to **File > Document Properties** to bring it up...

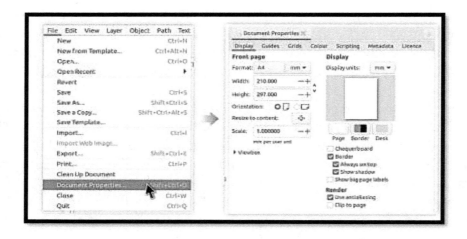

As you can see, there are numerous options, which are grouped into tabs. First, we'll look at the options on the **Display** tab. Take a look at these two sections. One is for the **Front page** and the other is for **Display**. Units can be changed with a dropdown menu in both columns. The usual unit is **mm**. Truly; I don't know why anyone would want to use two different units for Format and Display. I suggest that if you change one, you also change the other. Otherwise, you will have to spend a lot of time in the **Tool Control** bar moving between units as you work. What appears by default in most of Inkscape's layout is set by these options. So why should it matter what units show up? We don't know the exact size of the screen users are using when we're working on web graphics, for example. Having a general idea of the different screen sizes is possible with pixels. That's why I usually work with pixels for website images and video graphics themes and **mm** for almost everything else, just like most people outside of the US. If you want to, you can change to **inches**, but then you have to deal with 12 inches being equal to a foot and tiny bits of an inch. It gets confusing very quickly. The client can send measurements in inches, so you can set the file's starting size to inches. Then, you can change the measurement system by calling up **Document Properties**. There is a dropdown menu for the page size at the bottom of the **Front-page** column. Keep in mind that if you choose a US page size, this will change the page and display numbers to inches. Further down, some fields make it easy to change the document's height, width, and orientation. The link icon lets you resize proportionally based on its current size and the orientation changes the document's height and width to make it portrait or landscape. There's a helpful button below that says "**Resize to content**." This will make the document automatically resize so that everything on your painting fits on the page. Also, if you select objects and then choose **Edit > Resize Page to Selection** (or press **Shift + Ctrl + R**), you can change the size of the page to fit anywhere on your canvas. Although it's nice to have a button for it in the Document Properties window, I use this hotkey much more frequently than I do when opening the document properties. Scale is the next thing in this piece. I don't think you should change this number; it's only useful if you're bringing something that doesn't scale right compared to the original. People who use Inkscape can't see the user units, so changing them would cause scaling issues when saving and loading.

Another thing you should not pay any attention to is the **Viewbox** dropdown right below this. In a web browser, this sets the size of the SVG file's viewbox. The size of this area should match the page size unless you change it... We can change how the **Page area** looks by going to the Display column. Keep in mind that there is a sample of the canvas (also called **Desk**), the page, and page styles like the border (the thin line that goes around the canvas). Here are some parts of your document that you can change how they look. The **Chequerboard** choice might be the most useful. If you check this box, the parts of your document that are not opaque will be shown as a grid. This makes it easy to see what is not opaque and what is. If you are working on light-colored pictures that will be shown in black, you can also change the current page color to fit. The image below shows the **Display column** and what happens when you check this box and change the color of the page's background.

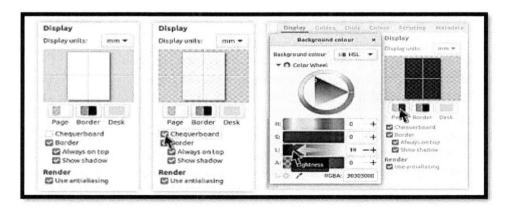

The **Color** tab has details about related color profiles. To put it simply, color profiles change the colors you see on your screen into colors that are close to matching on different outputs, like print (usually CMYK) and television (NTSC, PAL). Most current printers will happily change your sRGB PDFs (or even PNGs or JPEGs) to the CMYK profiles that work with their printers, so you don't need to change or worry about these settings. You can link the printer's color setting here, though, if it has one.

However, keep in mind that linking in a CMYK color profile does not automatically change RGB numbers to CMYK, and as of this writing, Inkscape does not allow this conversion either. If none of this makes sense to you, know that color profiles are a very technical part of printing and that the printer should most likely handle them. Video editing tools can easily change the normal sRGB color profile to the output formats needed, so there's no need to use the video color profiles at all. The image below shows how to link in a color profile. The **Available Color Profiles** dropdown menu lets you pick a color profile.

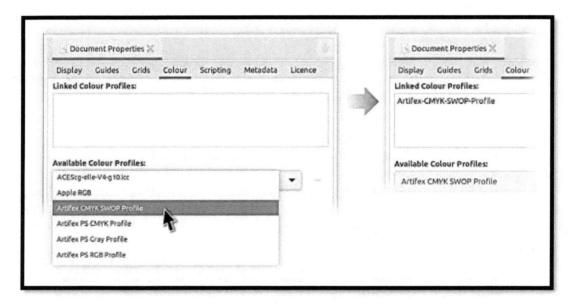

The next stop on our tour is the **Scripting** tab, which has tools for handling scripts that are linked to or inserted in your SVG file. A script is a piece of code that does something inside an SVG file when it's added to a webpage. These apps can be run in the web browser to make things like animations, interactions, and more. We'll move on to the **Metadata** tab since we're not going to learn how to write. But it's just a way to store information about the document, like the author, license, search keywords, and even a description. That sounds complicated. The image below shows some areas you can use to include extra data in your document.

207

Unlike a lot of other dialogs, this one doesn't have an **Apply or Save** button. This is because if you change a number in any of the boxes, the new data will be saved immediately. At the very bottom of the text box is a button that says "**Save as default**." This lets you save the information for this document so that it is used by default for all future documents. For instance, you might only want to save the Creator information so that it appears immediately in new documents. If this is the case, leave all the other fields empty and click the Browse button. After that, you can go back to filling out the rest of this document's details and close the dialog box. When you click the "**Use default**" button, the content will be replaced with the information you saved as the default.What's the point of all this metadata? For starters, anyone who reads your SVG file will be able to see all of the content that was saved in it. This will help them figure out who made it and how it can be used.

This information can also be seen and used by programs on the internet, which can search for the keywords you enter in the **Keywords** field. Thus, your file will show up in more search results for those terms. The **License** tab, which can be used to select a license for your file, is the last in the menu. The usual setting is "**Proprietary**," which means that you want to keep all rights to your artwork for yourself. If someone wants to use your picture, they have to get permission from you first. This dialog box has a lot of other options for less restrictive licenses, for people who want to give up some of their rights so that other people can use their graphics without asking them first. These other licenses are called **Creative Commons (CC)** licensing, and they let other people share your graphics as long as they follow certain rules. In this case, **CC Attribution-ShareAlike** lets anyone use and share your document as long as they give you credit for making it and share what they make with it too, under the same license. In the **URI** area at the bottom, when you pick a license from this tab, a web address that leads to the license text shows up.

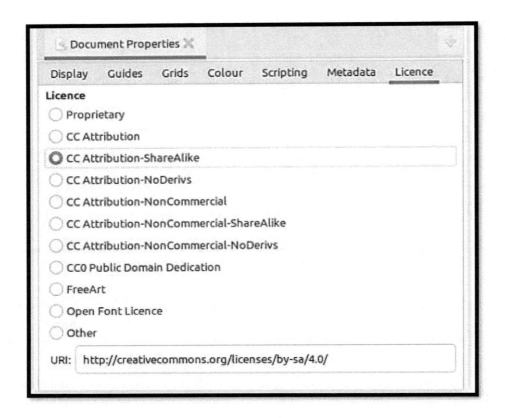

If you type that website into your favorite web browser, you can learn all about the license you choose. It is suggested that you carefully read all of them before picking one that works for you. Choose **CC0 Public Domain Dedication** if you want to share as much as you want with no restrictions. You can still put your name on the image as the author; the license just doesn't say that people have to give you credit or limit how it can be used. That's all there is to know about **Document Properties**. But what if your document needs more than one page? With Inkscape 1.1, we now have a brand-new tool for making documents with more than one page. Let's check out the **Pages** tool!

The Pages tool

This function has been asked for a long time and makes Inkscape much more useful. Before, you could only make one-page documents as separate PDFs that had to be put together in a program other than Inkscape. We can now add and remove pages with the Pages tool. When we save our document as a PDF, these changes will be saved as separate pages. When we click on the Pages tool, the Tool Control bar shows us options that let us add to or change the page that is currently chosen. You can click on and select pages on the board with this tool, and then you can move them around. The Pages tool and options in the Tool Control bar are shown in the image below.

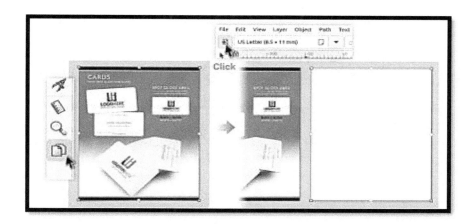

You'll see that the dropdown has a lot of different normal page sizes. If you choose a different one, it will change the size of the page that you have chosen. If you want to draw a new page by hand, start with the pages tool and click and drag on an empty area of the surface. Please keep in mind that this will not change the order of the pages in the final file. In this case, let's say we'd like our new blank page to come before the cards page. The **Move Page Backwards** button in the Tool Control bar lets us change the order of the pages after we've made a new one. The chosen (new) page will be put ahead of the cards page immediately, as shown below.

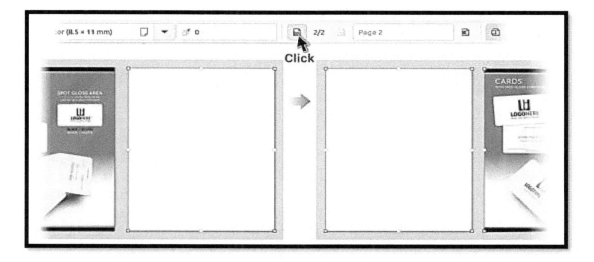

In the **Page Label** box, you can change the names of the pages; the labels do not change the order of the pages. If you don't want to move or delete the contents of the page along with the page itself, you can turn off the **Move Overlapping Objects** toggle, which is located at the bottom of the Tool Control bar. You can also delete the selected page by clicking the **Delete Selected Page** button (the one with the X). The borders box, where you can set borders for the currently chosen page, is a further useful feature of Inkscape 1.3 found in the Tool Control bar for the Pages tool. Just change the number **0** in the text box to something like **10**. The image below shows that this adds a **10 mm** space on each side of the page. To do this by hand, you can also pull the round handles on the page's edges.

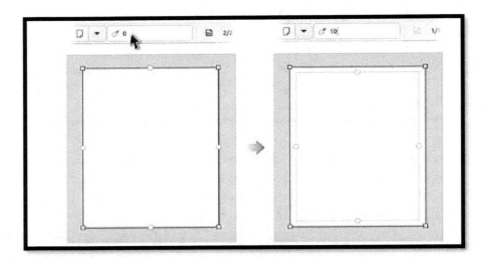

Keep in mind that the borders' units match the units you select in the Document Properties window. If the page measures are set to inches, 10 mm would be 0.39 inches. Now that we've added pages, we can set them up to save and export. The Export window has more options than those. Let's look at them all.

The Export dialog

When you want to use your Inkscape artwork for different things, the Export window is the best way to do it. It lets you save the page area, a selection, or even the whole piece of art (on and off paper) in some useful file types. Click on **File > Export** or press the **Ctrl + Shift + E** keys together to open this text box. Then we see the powerful Export dialog box, which has two tabs: one for exporting a single image, and the other, Batch Export, for sending many images at once. First, let's look at the **Single Image** tab, which is the tab that normally shows up when you **export. At the top, just below the tab, four buttons let you pick the area that will be copied. The options are the following:**

- **Document**: This exports the whole document, including the page area and everything else in it. This option saves everything you've drawn, even the page area.
- **Page**: Exports a section of the page area—anything outside the page area is cut off.
- **Selection**: The export area is the box around the currently chosen object or objects. Anything outside of that area is clipped off.

- **Custom**: This option lets you choose the exact page coordinates of the rectangular area that will be copied.

The image below shows the **Export** dialog box's **Document** option and the settings that go with it.

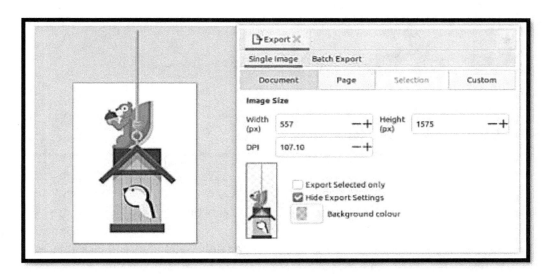

You can see that the line above the birdhouse goes past the **Page** area. We can still see the **Document** in the viewing area of the Export dialog box even though it is chosen. As well as changing the **Dots Per Inch (DPI)** of the image, you can also change its width and height in pixels. Don't know how big your image should be in pixels but know that your document units are inches or millimeters? DPI can help. For example, most printers need an image with **300 DPI** to print well.

In this case, you can use mm or inches as your measure and set **DPI** to **300**. Then, Inkscape will figure out the image's height and width in pixels on its own. It's useful, right? To save time, you should probably choose the "**Page**" option when exporting most of the time. This is because it lets you use the page area for cutting. On top of that, this is why the default document size in Inkscape is an **A4** page: this is the size of paper used by most desktop printers around the world. The Page area can be set to any size you want, and it helps you figure out how big your drawings should be as you're making them. The image below shows the same graphic as before, but this time the Page option is chosen rather than Document.

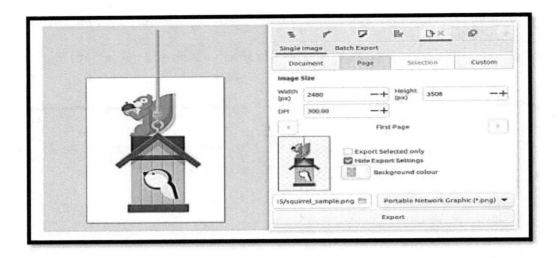

Not only are there more options, but there are also **Pages**, which has two arrows, and **First Page**, which has an arrow that lets you choose which page to export from. That's why this text box isn't grayed out if you've added more pages. The four export options may also have caught your eye because they all share a few options. The **Export Selected only** option lets you pick what is copied. You can use this to get rid of objects that are behind or in front of something and only keep the objects that are in the center. Select the objects you want to export, and then check the box that says "**Export Selected only**." The picture below shows what happens when you do this with the **Export Selected Only** option selected. This will crop the image to only include the objects that were selected.

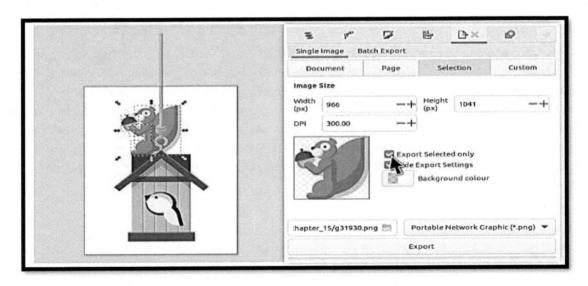

We will not usually use the **Custom** export option because the **Page and Selection** options give us a lot of control over what is copied. However, let's say you want to send the chosen squirrel but add some space to the edges of the image. When you select something on the canvas, the **Custom** options are filled with that selection instantly. To add the necessary padding, all you have to do is change the **Left, Right, Top, and Bottom** values. The results will be shown in the new video.

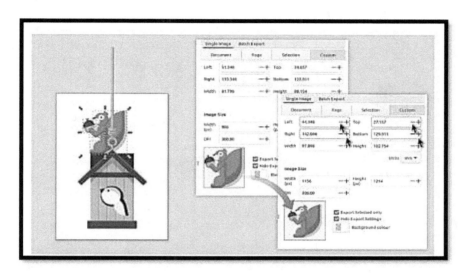

You'll need to fill in the title field at the bottom of the dialog box after you've chosen your choices. You can also pick your file type from this dropdown. PNG is chosen by default because it is a web file that can handle transparency. It is becoming more and more common for printers and print-on-demand services to only accept JPEG or PNG files. That's why the default of PNG works fine for us. After you pick the types you want, all you have to do is click the "**Export**" button, and Inkscape will send out an image file that fits the criteria you set.In the filename field, you can delete the title and file path. If you click on the file folder icon, your file browser will open, and your SVG will be saved where it already is. The PNG file will be named after the SVG file if you don't change the name of the file. You don't have to type a new title every time you save, and this method works well if you only want to save one file. What if you need to save more than one file? Now we're on the Batch Export tab!

When we go to the Export window box and click on the Batch Export tab, we see three export options:
- **Selection**: Export all selected items as individual files
- **Layers**: Export all layers, each as an individual file
- **Pages**: Export each page as an individual file

When exporting, the **Selection** option might be the most useful all-around because it makes a file for each of the objects that are chosen. If the **Export Selected Only** option is checked, Selection will show a sample of each object with a name that matches its name in the Layers and Objects dialog. This is yet another good reason to give your objects names! My chosen squirrel parts, which I must export to animate them, are shown in the image below.

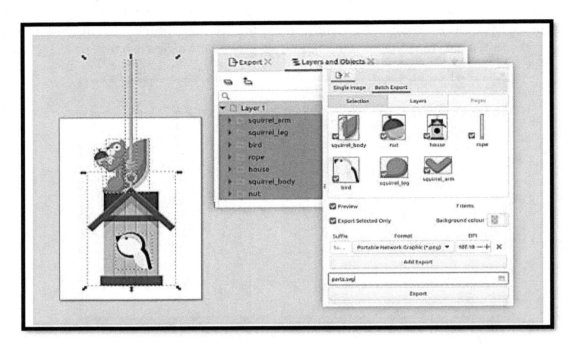

Inkscape will now join the filename with the object name and any text you put in the Suffix box. Export will then work the same way as before. In our case, this means that our **squirrel_arm** will be sent to **parts_squirrel_arm.png**. If you select multiple objects, Inkscape will name them all the same way. This will result in a folder full of images. When I need to import parts of an image for an animation, I use this tool a lot. I'm not going to go into detail about how I made this animation right now, but you can see that the moving parts are all different. Inkscape has a great feature that lets us save time by exporting and re-exporting images separately for many purposes, including animation.

You may have also seen the button that says "**Add Export**." You can now add more than one output with a different DPI. You can use this to your advantage if you need to make logos of different sizes for a client's website or to print. For graphics on websites that don't support SVG, a setting of 96 DPI usually works well. For printing, a setting of 300 to 600 DPI might work well. If you're sending more than one set of graphics, make sure you add a suffix that tells that set what DPI to use. That is, we might add 96 for the first one and 300 for the second if we wanted to add an output for 96 DPI and 300 DPI.

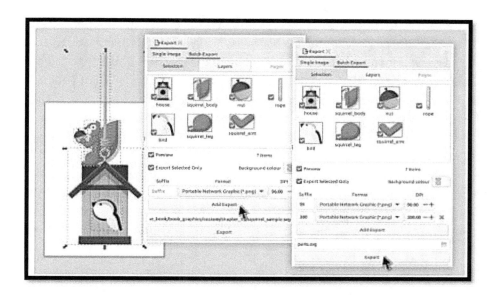

At the DPI size given, this setting will create files like parts_squirrel_arm_96.png and parts_squirrel_arm_300.png. What about SVG files, though? We do have a choice. Choose **.svg** from the dropdown to get a set of SVG graphics. More than likely, you'll also want to export SVG for the web, just in case the website system (like WordPress) supports them. If you can, always use SVGs because the edges stay sharp no matter how close you zoom in. It is possible to zoom in quite far on computers, phones, and screens with a high resolution, for example.

Save and export considerations

We will now talk about some choices that work best for different kinds of results. Since this is more of a recap than a tour, I'll keep it short by using a bulleted list.
It will be expanded upon in the parts that follow:
- Saving for printed magazine adverts
- Saving and exporting for email-friendly PDFs
- Exporting for the web
- Saving for CNC cutters and engravers
- Exporting for print-on-demand websites

Saving for printed magazine adverts

A lot of magazines want pixel graphics to have at least 300 DPI. Most of the time, I send exactly 300 DPI at whatever size the magazine page is. In most cases, they will want a PDF document, which you can select from the **Export** text box or by going to **File > Save As** if you need a multi-page document. If the printer wants you to convert the file to CMYK before sending it, you'll need to export it as a 300 DPI PNG and use software that specializes in print formats to export it as a

PDF. One of these free and open-source programs that I like is Scribus. When you convert, you can pick **FOGRA27** as the color scheme, and Scribus will make a PDF that is ready to print. Inkscape lets you save as a PDF file; all you have to do is change the.svg part of the title to.pdf. When you click the "**Save**" button, a window will appear with PDF saving options. All of your vector shapes can be added here as is, and the "**Convert text to paths**" option can be checked. This is because most printers don't want to deal with fonts they might or might not have. The text will become non-editable if you check this option, but the font will still look the same. Also, if you have any filter effects (like Blur), you might want to change the **Resolution for rasterization (dpi)** to **300 DPI** before printing. Also, pay attention to the **Bleed/margin (mm)** box. This will add the length you choose to the edge of your page. This setting is helpful if your graphics go all the way to the edge of the printed page because it gives the printers more room to cut off the parts that are written too much. You can add a 3mm gap area in this PDF text box, which is what most printers need. The following options are shown.

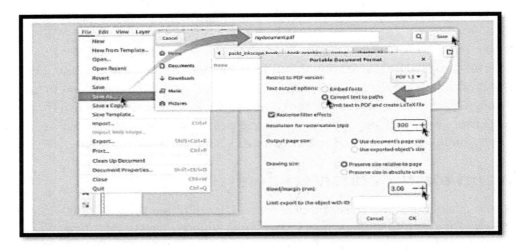

Saving and exporting for email-friendly PDFs

You will want to make your PDF as small as possible if you are saving it to send in an email. Aside from that, you probably won't want to change your text to paths. Leaving it as text will make it easier for screen reader software to read and for PDF users to copy by selection. If you want to save all of your pixel images as JPEGs, select "**.jpg**" from the Export menu instead of "**.png.**" You will then need to add these to your document and link them to the originals. They are still there, so you don't have to delete them. You can just put the original PNGs on a different layer and hide it. When you save as a PDF, Inkscape will automatically leave out any hidden layers, which will make the file much smaller.

Exporting for the web

People who work with computer graphics often change the document units to px. This is because I often have to build screens with different pixel sizes to make what are called "responsive websites." These are websites that load different graphics and layouts depending on the size of the screen being shown. If you're creating a website structure that lets you post and use SVGs, you don't have to worry about measurements at all. You can set the dimensions in the website code, and the SVG will automatically find the best resolution for the screen it's shown on. In this case, I send to SVG when I can and to PNG otherwise, since PNG can handle transparency. For big images with lots of gradients or features, this might make the file size too big. If you don't need transparency, you might also want to export as JPEG to make your websites load faster. Because of Inkscape 1.1, you can now send to the future. You can also use the webp format instead of JPEG or PNG. It has better quality and smaller file sizes, so you might want to think about that as an option.

Saving for CNC cutters and engravers

In general, you should send an SVG file so that the program that runs your CNC machine or engraver can read it. You can make something called **GCode** in Inkscape. This is a set of directions for how to move the etching or cutting head and it can be sent straight to the printer. Most of the time, though, the software that comes with your device will give you better results, and it may even keep you from sending directions that could damage your cutter. Still, you can change a lot of things by going to **Extensions > Export > Plot** and doing what you want there. If not, just save it as a plain SVG file (no fills or colors) and open it in your CNC program. Most CNC tools should be able to read this because SVG is a standard file.

Exporting for print-on-demand websites

When it comes to this, PNGs or JPEGs are the best formats. Large business printers realized about ten years ago that they could get more customers if they accepted popular formats like JPEG. This is because most consumer-grade cameras already have this format and don't need CMYK for printing. Also, if your printer needs a CMYK file, you can easily switch to a different printer that can handle sRGB-to-CMYK color conversion. A JPEG photo can be printed, after all. Most websites, like VistaPrint, let you print in high quality on a wide range of things, and PNG is one of the formats they accept. There are a few things you should think about before you print PNGs or JPEGs, though. Because most computer screens aren't color-corrected, it's hard to get the exact color you see on your screen in print. So, that pretty purple color you're seeing might be a dark blue color on the color-calibrated screens that printers use. What should we do?

Printing

You could get color correction tools, but before you spend a lot of money on one, there are some things you can try first that will get you close enough to the right colors for most people. You can email yourself the PNG file and open it on your phone to see if the colors you're seeing are correct. Most smartphones have color-calibrated screens. Most of the time, you'll be fine as long as the colors match. The color test chart I made (see image below) can be printed as another option.

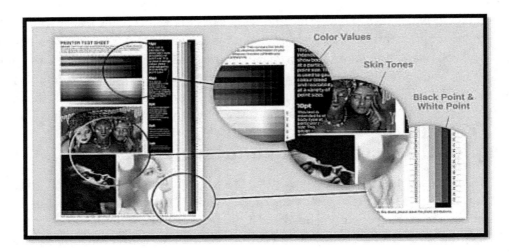

The trick is to make one copy of this PDF file that you made in Inkscape and then send it to the printer. You can check to see if there is any color shift between the print you got in the mail and the same file opened in Inkscape. After that, you can either change your monitor's color choices by hand to match, or you can just pick a color from the sheet that looks more like what you want. This sheet has a lot of useful tests on it, not just color tests. For example, it shows how accurate the skin tones are and what black-and-white points your printer can handle. In the same way, the black point shows how dark a color can be printed before it looks black. The white point shows how light a gray can be printed before it looks pure white. It's a good way to find out if, say, that light gray background will print the way you want it to. I also added a bleed test for white-on-black text. This should help you figure out what the smallest white-on-black font size is that you can use before the black ink starts to bleed and makes the text unusable. If you want to use different types of paper, you should print this sheet out on one of each type, with styles like gloss, silk, and matte. These different surfaces have very noticeable effects on the brightness of the color that you get, so you can change the colors based on what you see.

One last thing: If you can't get your Inkscape files to print on your desktop printer from Within Inkscape, try saving them as a PDF and then opening the PDF in a PDF reader... or even your web browser. PDF is a format for sending files to be printed, so it has all the size information you need to print. Indeed, this is why printers often require **.pdf** documents for magazines. As you print, make sure that the page is not automatically scaled. If it is, your numbers will be a little off. To fix this, go to your system's print settings and uncheck the "**Scale to fit page**" or a similar option.

Integrating with Other Design Tools

Integrating Inkscape with other design tools can enhance your workflow, allowing you to leverage the strengths of each tool for a more efficient and productive design process. **Here are some ways you can integrate Inkscape with other design tools:**

1. **Adobe Creative Suite**: While Inkscape is a powerful vector graphics editor, it may not have all the features you need for complex design projects. You can integrate Inkscape with Adobe Illustrator, Photoshop, or other Creative Suite applications by exporting and importing files between them. For example, you can create vector illustrations in Inkscape and then import them into Adobe Illustrator for further refinement or integration into a larger project.

2. **GIMP**: GIMP is a popular open-source raster graphics editor that complements Inkscape's vector capabilities. You can use Inkscape for creating vector graphics and GIMP for editing raster images, and then seamlessly combine them in your design projects. Exporting files from Inkscape in compatible formats (such as PNG or SVG) allows for smooth integration with GIMP.

3. **Blender**: Blender is a powerful 3D modeling and animation software. While it primarily deals with 3D objects, Blender can also handle 2D vector graphics. You can create vector illustrations in Inkscape and import them into Blender to incorporate them into 3D scenes or animations.

4. **Figma/Sketch**: Figma and Sketch are popular design tools known for their collaborative features and user interface (UI) design capabilities. While they are primarily used for UI/UX design, you can still use Inkscape for creating custom vector graphics or illustrations and then import them into Figma or Sketch for UI design prototyping or asset creation.

5. **LibreOffice/OpenOffice**: Inkscape's vector graphics can be integrated into presentations, documents, or spreadsheets created in LibreOffice or OpenOffice. You can export your Inkscape designs as scalable vector graphics (SVG) or other compatible formats and then import them into your Office suite documents.

6. **Web Design Tools**: If you're working on web design projects, you can integrate Inkscape with tools like Adobe Dreamweaver, Sublime Text, or Visual Studio Code. Exporting SVG files from Inkscape allows you to easily incorporate vector graphics into your web designs.

CHAPTER 18

TIPS AND TRICKS FOR EFFICIENT WORKFLOW

Using Inkscape as an XML editor

Even though we mostly work on design projects in Inkscape, the SVG format can be useful in some situations! If you want to learn more about SVG, you can look into it and, with some work, figure it out. You can edit SVG files even with a basic text editor because it uses the XML format to describe vector graphics. Don't worry—the goal isn't to use XML to make SVG graphics from scratch! No, that wouldn't help; that's still what Inkscape is for. Allow me to share a few tips on how to make the XML editing tools in Inkscape work better for you.

Searching for, selecting, and changing multiple elements at once

It's hard to work with a file that has hundreds of different shapes and objects, like small leaves on a tree drawing or many buttons and icons in a complicated user interface design. After that, you need to change the color of every file object. Not all of them, but enough that it would be difficult to select them by hand. This is when the simple **Find/Replace** tab comes in handy! This may seem like a small thing, but this is an important part of Inkscape that is often ignored. Let's try it out now. Say you need to change the blue color of the icons to orange just for fun. One way to change the color of the blue parts is to select them all by hand and then go into the groups they are in. **Since some of them are lines, they need to be colored differently. You can be smart and use the Find/Replace method instead:**

1. First, figure out which objects you want to change the color of. What do these objects all have in common? Like what color they are. You can get the code for a common color by clicking on one of the objects. In this case, copy the code for the original blue, which is **2ac1b5**, without the # symbol.

2. Press Ctrl + F to open the **Find/Replace** tab in the menu. For the image below, copy and paste the color code you want to find into the **Find** box.

3. Get the new color's code now. This time, we need orange with the code **ff9955** around it. This code needs to be copied and pasted into the **Replace** field.

4. This tab has a lot of settings and options, as you can also see from the image. You will only need a few most of the time.

5. Select the **Properties** option from the list of options under the Search in name. Inkscape will then know that you are not looking for this string of characters in the text but in the properties of the objects.

6. Click **Search in selection** under **Scope**. You can fine-tune your search terms to make sure you only find and select the elements you want and don't change or select parts of the

document by accident. You need to select all the icons you want to change colors for this to work. The rest will not be covered.

7. That's all there is to it! In the bottom menu, click "**Find**." This will select all the elements that have a property with the given value. You can now change their color, move them, or even get rid of them.

8. The old number will be replaced with the new one if you select **Replace all**. All of the parts will be chosen and given a new color value in this case. This is the better way to do the job at hand. Inkscape now only looks for the value anywhere in the chosen part of the XML. It doesn't matter if the color was set as a stroke or fill color.

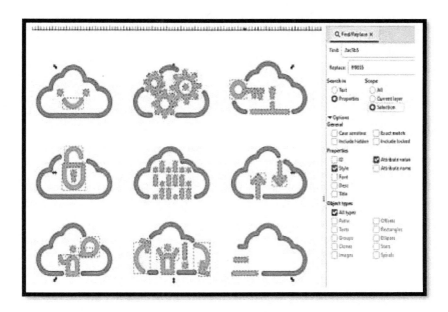

This easy trick can help you recolor many things at once and save a lot of time. With the Find/Replace tab, vector graphics in Inkscape can be used in a lot of different ways.

Naming and organizing your objects with unique IDs

As you already know, SVG files are made with XML, which means that both people and computers can read them. The layout of nodes, IDs, and characteristics makes it easy to understand. There is no complicated encoding. Your documents will be easier to find too if you use this open format. Inkscape lets you get any object, path, or group. Select **Object Properties** by right-clicking the object. Press Shift + Ctrl + O to select the object that way. You can change the ID for the chosen object in the Object Properties tab, which will be displayed. The document needs to have a unique ID for each object. By default, Inkscape gives each object an ID. Just give your object or group an

ID, like **icon001, btn002, character1_head**, etc. And finally, click **Set**. The object will now be correctly named.

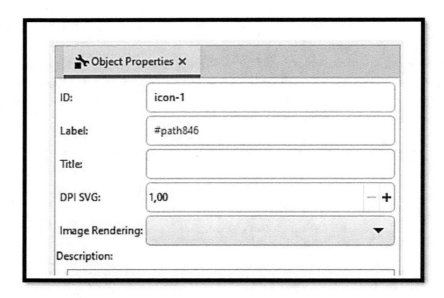

How does this help you then? Do you need to do this for every object? No, but changing the IDs that the computer sets for you makes it easier to find named objects. If you want to use the **Find/Replace** tab, you can also check the box next to the ID field. This will make Inkscape select all the icons or other things that match certain ID. Putting names on parts of your vector image is a good habit to get into if you are making game art, a complicated UI design, or sketches. Each group should have its unique ID. This will also help you when you need to select **Batch export multiple images**. In older versions of Inkscape, there is a box called "Batch export" in the Export dialogue that lets you export multiple chosen objects at once. This is not a new feature. Of the ways to do this, there is one that is very different between Inkscape 1.2 and the versions that came before it.

Let's check them out.

- **If you have an older version of Inkscape**: To begin, select several items on your page and check the box next to Batch export X chosen objects on the Export PNG images tab (press Shift + Ctrl + E to open this tab). This will save several PNG files in the place you choose.

- **If you are using Inkscape 1.2 or later**: There is a separate **Batch Export** tab under the Export tab since INKSCAPE 1.2. You can send more than one file in different types of forms from this page. It works with PNG, SVG, PDF, and JPG files. You can see exactly what will be exported and with what filename on this Batch Export tab, which shows samples of the chosen objects. This option is easier to use and helps you get things done.

- **Setting unique IDs**: Both versions agree on one thing: they both set unique IDs. If you didn't give the objects you want to export their unique IDs, the program will save them with filenames that are made from the IDs that were automatically given to them in the SVG. There will be files with names like **path4483.png, g5123.svg,** and more. Then you have to find them and change them by hand, which takes a lot of time when you have a lot of files.

These produced names can be a real pain when you are sending 50 icons at once, for example, because you have to check each one and name it based on what it is so you can use it later. However, Inkscape will save the PNG files with the filenames given as IDs if you did set the IDs in Inkscape for each object or group to be exported. Let's go back to the example of the icons. If you give each group of icons a unique ID in the **Object Properties** tab, then Inkscape will use those IDs as filenames. This will save you a ton of time in the future when you need to find and organize your images and files. Please think about using Inkscape as an available editor for your SVG file, even if you don't like thinking about the code behind your graphics. Inkscape makes it easy to find numbers in SVG scripts, which can save you a lot of time and work. Setting IDs is another simple and useful way to speed up the process of finding, organizing, and saving your graphics.

Working faster with custom templates

If you use Inkscape a lot, you will eventually find yourself doing the same things over and over again. You could make a business card every day or draw icons that are all the same size. This is why Inkscape lets you make a new document from a template when you start a new project. There are many basic templates, such as ones for normal paper sizes, the business card size that was already mentioned and even ones for making patterns that don't show up when you print them. In addition to these, you can also make custom templates for jobs that you do often. If you know you will be doing the same thing over and over again, you might want to make a template for it. This will save you time and effort, and it will quickly become an important part of your work.

Creating your custom template

It's very easy to make a template file. It's just an Inkscape SVG file saved in the **Inkscape Template folder**. You could make a general template file. For example, if you need to make horizontal ads that are the same size for all websites, you could make a new SVG with the right page size. You can also make a more detailed template for a job you do over and over for the same client.

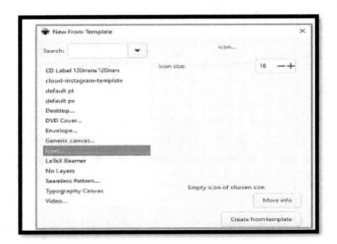

To practice, you will make a very specific template: an Instagram post template for our practice brand, **CloudUsers**. Brands and celebrities like to post text and quotes in the form of images to get people's attention, even though Instagram is mostly about pictures. All of these posts are the same size and have a background color, some sample text, and not much branding. If you've used Canva to make Instagram posts before, Inkscape could be a more creative and unique choice.

Here's how to make your vector files that are ready for Instagram:

1. Make a new document and draw a 1080 px x 1080 px square to begin. Right here is the usual size for an Instagram post. This is what our plan will be based on.

2. Press Shift + Ctrl + R after selecting the square to change the page's size to fit the text you chose. You can also use the Page tool and the scale icon on the Tool menu to change the size of the page.

3. Now we'll talk about the logo and colors. In your template, copy your color and the part of the background that has the gradient.

4. The background will be the same linear gradient color. Now use it on the square.

5. Now you see that templates can hold anything an SVG file can: colors, patterns, shapes, text, and even guides and text. To add the lines, make a new square that is 1000 pixels by 1000 pixels. Put it in the middle of your page, in the middle of the square background.

6. Select the second box and go to the top menu. From there, select **Object | Object to Guides**. This will make it into four lines, each 100 pixels from the edge of your background block. Every time you use this template after this, this will help.

7. Now, use the **bold Montserrat** font to add some title text to the background. As seen in the image below, add some smaller sample text below that.

CHAPTER 19

TROUBLESHOOTING COMMON ISSUES

What to do if Inkscape crashes

As an open-source tool, Inkscape comes in different versions that can run on different running systems. People work on computers that can do very different things but still use Inkscape on Windows, macOS, and GNU/Linux. Inkscape is always getting better. New features can make creation easier or more complicated, but they can also make bugs appear. And Inkscape will crash when it can't handle everything. You will learn what to do in these rare cases in the parts that follow.

Prevention

The best way to avoid accidents is to avoid them in the first place. When you use Inkscape, keep these tips in mind. Most of the tips can be used with other drawing tools as well.

Save your work and save it often

As soon as you finish drawing the first shape, you should save your work in the project directory as an Inkscape SVG file. After that, save your work every time you make a big change. To quickly save your work, make this a habit: press Ctrl + S. Even though it seems like a small thing, I've seen too much work get lost because someone forgot to save their design work.

You can set the auto-save timer.

Set up Autosave if you forget to save often. Pick **Autosave** from the **Input/Output** drop-down menu when you go to **Edit | Preferences**. You can choose how often your work should be saved here. When you lose your work and find that Inkscape saved it a few minutes ago, you will realize that this feature was working. That's so nice!

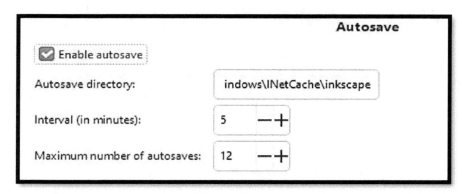

Don't overload Inkscape; organize your work

You can't overload Inkscape, but if you try to do too much at once, it will crash, which can also fill your computer's memory. There is a time to save, stop, and clean up your document when it starts to slow down because it has too many objects, effects, or imported bitmap images. Get rid of parts and objects that you don't need, link images instead of embedding them as much as possible, and save new copies of your documents after you're done fixing them up. This last tip also helps you keep your work organized since it's easier to work with several smaller files than one big one for each job. There's no reason not to copy and use parts of the idea in different parts. All of these things would be too big, slow, and hard to find your way around in one file, let alone work with it. For this reason, you should keep your information in different files.

Recover your work

Using the above safety tips will make it less likely that you will crash and lose your work. Also, Inkscape is getting more stable with each new version. You might still get a warning message and the software might just crash, though. In this case, you need to know how to get your graphics back in Inkscape.

Emergency backup files

When Inkscape crashes, it tries to make a backup file in the same project folder as the failed file or in the User folder on your machine. It will add a timestamp to the file's name so that it is easy to find and tell apart from the original. Find the file and make sure it has the right vector data in it. It works and has all the graphics you thought were lost. Change the name to get rid of the date, just so it's easier to find later and keep working.

Autosaved backup files

If you have the **Autosave** feature enabled, then Inkscape creates backup versions of your document automatically. To find these backups, head to **Preferences** again, and in the **Autosave** settings check the path to the Autosave directory. This is where your saved files are, so copy the directory location and go there. The files don't always end in .svg, but you can still open them in Inkscape and save them as normal Inkscape vector files.

How to open corrupted files

There are times when you save a file but can't open it. These things can happen with any tool; the files just get messed up. If an Inkscape SVG file won't open, try starting it with a different tool to see if the problem is with Inkscape. You can try Illustrator or another vector graphics program, but if you don't have any of those, most current computers can open and show SVG files. If you open your file in Chrome, check to see if it shows up as empty or broken. If the file shows up correctly, save it by hand with a different name, then open it in Inkscape again. It's possible to lose some settings that are unique to Inkscape in this way, like guides, but the important thing is that you might save most of your design. Use a different version of Inkscape the next time you want to open an Inkscape file that used to work. Most of the time, this problem can be fixed by getting the latest program. Should that not work, try a drop or look for an older version. You can still get most versions from the official website. Either way, if you can't read a damaged file, look for autosaves and try to get back to a previous version if you can. Remember to save often, turn on Autosave, and organize your files. The best way to keep your work safe is to avoid problems in the first place.

CHAPTER 20
INKSCAPE KEYBOARD SHORTCUTS CHEAT SHEET

File Management Shortcuts

- **Ctrl + N**: Initiates the creation of a new Inkscape document.
- **Ctrl + S**: Saves the currently open Inkscape document.
- **Ctrl + Shift + S**: Opens the "**Save As**..." dialog box.
- **Ctrl + Alt + Shift + S**: Creates a duplicate of the currently open file within the same directory
- **Ctrl + Shift + E**: Saves the currently open Inkscape document as a PNG image.
- **Ctrl + O**: Opens an existing Inkscape document from the user's file system.
- **Ctrl + I**: Imports an image as a graphics object into the currently open document.
- **Ctrl + Q**: Closes the currently open document.

File Properties Shortcuts

- **Ctrl + F**: Opens the Find and Replace prompt within the current document.
- **Ctrl + Shift + H**: Prints a history of all the undo actions performed in the current document.
- **Ctrl + Shift + D**: Prints all the available properties for the current document.
- **Ctrl + Shift + O**: Prints all the available properties for the currently selected object.
- **Ctrl + Shift + P**: Opens Inkscape's "**Preferences**" window.
- **Ctrl + Shift + L**: Opens a dialog box containing all the active layers in the document, providing an overview of the layer structure and allowing users to manage layer visibility and organization.
- **Ctrl + Shift + X**: Opens a dialog box displaying the underlying XML structure of the current document. This can be useful for advanced users who want to inspect or modify the document's structure directly.

Window Manipulation

- **F10**: Toggles Inkscape's Menu Bar, providing quick access to various commands and options.
- **F11**: Switches the current display to Full Screen mode.
- **Shift + F11**: Toggles the display of all the toolbars in the current session.
- **Ctrl + F11**: Toggles the display of all the toolbars and switches the display to fullscreen.
- **Ctrl + E**: Shows the guide rulers in the current document.
- **Ctrl + B**: Disables the scrollbars in the current document.
- **Alt + Shift + P**: Disables the Palette sub window in the current document.

- **Ctrl + Tab**: Navigates to the next document in the current session.
- **Ctrl + Shift + Tab**: Goes back to the previous document in the current session.

Layer Manipulation

- **Ctrl + Shift + N**: Creates a new drawing layer on the current document.
- **Shift + Page Up**: Moves the currently selected object one layer up.
- **Shift + Page Down**: Moves the currently selected object one layer down, altering its position in relation to other objects.
- **Ctrl + Shift + Page Up**: Moves the entire layer one level up.
- **Ctrl + Shift + Page Down**: Moves the entire layer one level down.
- **Ctrl + Shift + Home**: Moves the entire layer to the top of the document stack.
- **Ctrl + Shift + End**: Moves the entire layer to the bottom of the document stack.

Object Manipulation

- **Ctrl + Z**: Undoes the last change made on the currently selected object.
- **Ctrl + Y**: Redoes the last undo made on the currently selected object.
- **Ctrl + Insert**: Copies the currently selected object into the system clipboard.
- **Shift + Del**: Cuts the currently selected object into the system clipboard.
- **Shift + Insert**: Pastes the most recent object from the system clipboard onto the canvas.
- **Ctrl + Alt + V**: Pastes the object from the system clipboard on the original copy location.
- **Ctrl + Shift + V**: Pastes the style of the object in the clipboard onto the currently selected object.
- **Alt + D**: Creates a clone of the currently selected object.
- **Alt + Shift + D**: Removes the link between the cloned object and its original.
- **Shift + D**: Highlights the original object, providing visual distinction between the original and cloned objects.

Group and Alignment

- **Ctrl + G**: Creates a new object group using all the currently selected objects.
- **Ctrl + U**: Removes the group of the currently selected object.
- **Ctrl + Alt + H**: Vertically centers the currently selected group within the document.
- **Ctrl + Alt + T**: Horizontally centers the currently selected group within the document, maintaining symmetry in positioning.

Dialog Manipulation

- **Ctrl + Shift + T**: Opens the "**Text and Fonts**" dialog box on the current document, facilitating text editing and font selection.
- **Ctrl + Shift + W**: Opens the "**Swatches**" dialog box on the current document, allowing users to manage and apply color swatches.

- **Ctrl + Shift + F**: Opens the "**Fill and Stroke**" dialog box on the current document, providing controls for adjusting object fill and stroke properties.
- **Ctrl + Shift + A**: Opens the "**Align and Distribute**" dialog box on the current document, offering tools for precise alignment and distribution of objects.
- **Ctrl + Shift + M**: Opens the "**Transform**" dialog box for the currently selected object, enabling users to apply transformations such as scaling, rotation, and skewing.

Dialog Navigation

- **Ctrl + F**: Searches through the open dialog boxes in the current session.
- **Ctrl + W**: Closes the currently open dialog box.
- **Tab**: Moves to the next element in the current dialog box.
- **Shift + Tab**: Moves back to the previous element in the current dialog box.
- **Ctrl + Page Up**: Moves to the next dialog box in the current session.
- **Ctrl + Page Down**: Moves back to the previous dialog box in the current session, allowing users to revisit previously opened dialog boxes.

Editing Tools

- **S**: Switches to Inkscape's selection tool mode.
- **N**: Toggles the currently selected object's node points.
- **Z**: Zooms in on the currently active document, allowing users to magnify specific areas for detailed editing.
- **Shift + Z**: Zooms out of the currently active document, providing an overview of the entire canvas.
- **M**: Measures the distance between active objects in the current document, assisting in precise positioning and alignment.

Drawing Tools

- **R**: Draws a rectangle object on the current document, facilitating the creation of geometric shapes.
- **E**: Draws a circle object on the current document, enabling users to create perfect circles.
- **I**: Draws a spiral line on the current document, providing a versatile tool for creating spirals and helixes.
- **X**: Renders a 3D perspective box on the current document, allowing users to create three-dimensional shapes.
- **Asterisk (*)**: Draws a star object on the current document, offering options for customizing the number of points and other parameters.
- **P**: Toggles the freehand Pencil tool, allowing users to draw freehand lines and shapes.
- **B**: Toggles the point-to-point Pen tool, enabling users to create precise paths by clicking to define anchor points.

- **C**: Toggles the freehand Calligraphy tool, simulating the strokes of a calligraphy pen for artistic effects.
- **A**: Toggles the freehand Spraypaint tool, allowing users to apply spraypaint-like strokes to the canvas.
- **U**: Toggles the Paint Bucket tool, facilitating the filling of closed shapes with color or patterns.
- **G**: Toggles the Gradient tool, enabling users to apply gradients to objects for visual effects.
- **D**: Toggles the Eyedropper tool, allowing users to sample colors or properties from existing objects.
- **Shift + E**: Enables the Eraser tool on the current document, allowing users to erase parts of objects or paths.

Pencil Tool

- **Left Click**: Creates a non-freehand line between two points.
- **Ctrl + Left Click**: Creates a single dot.
- **Ctrl + Shift + Left Click**: Creates a dot twice the diameter of the single dot.
- **Ctrl + Alt + Left Click**: Creates a dot with a random diameter.

Pen Tool

- **Left Click**: Creates a new single node on the current document.
- **Shift + Left Click**: Creates a new node on the current document and adds it to a path.
- **Alt + Up Arrow**: Moves the currently selected node by one pixel up.
- **Alt + Down Arrow**: Moves the currently selected node by one pixel down.
- **Alt + Left Arrow**: Moves the currently selected node one pixel to the left.
- **Alt + Right Arrow**: Moves the currently selected node one pixel to the right.
- **Alt + Shift + Up Arrow**: Moves the currently selected node by ten pixels up.
- **Alt + Shift + Down Arrow**: Moves the currently selected node by ten pixels down.
- **Alt + Shift + Left Arrow**: Moves the currently selected node by ten pixels to the left.
- **Alt + Shift + Right Arrow**: Moves the currently selected node by ten pixels to the right.
- **Shift + U**: Converts the last pen segment into a curve.
- **Shift + L**: Converts the last pen segment into a line.
- **Enter**: Finalizes the current node path.
- **Esc**: Cancels the current node path.

Calligraphy Tool

- **Up Arrow**: Increases the angle of the brush, allowing for variations in stroke direction.
- **Down Arrow**: Decreases the angle of the brush, providing control over the orientation of strokes.

- **Left Arrow**: Resizes the brush's current width by one pixel less, adjusting the thickness of strokes.
- **Right Arrow**: Resizes the brush's current width by one pixel more, modifying the thickness of strokes.
- **Home**: Sets the current brush width to its minimum size, allowing for precise adjustments.
- **End**: Sets the current brush width to its maximum size, facilitating broader strokes.
- **Esc**: Cancels the current brush stroke, providing an option to start over if needed.

Spraypaint Tool

- **Shift + J**: Places the copied object anywhere inside the spray paint's spray radius, facilitating controlled distribution.
- **Shift + K**: Increases the number of object duplicates, allowing for denser spray patterns.
- **Up Arrow**: Increases the amount of object duplicates, controlling the density of the spray.
- **Down Arrow**: Fills the entire region with the bucket's contents and adds it to the current selection, streamlining the process.
- **Left Arrow**: Reduces the width of the spray radius by one unit, adjusting the spread of the spray.
- **Right Arrow**: Increases the width of the spray radius by one unit, expanding the coverage area.
- **Home**: Reduces the width of the spray radius to its minimum size, offering precise control over the spray pattern.
- **End**: Increases the width of the spray radius to its maximum size, maximizing coverage for larger areas.

Paint Bucket Tool

- **Left Click**: Fills the entire region with the contents of the bucket, applying a solid color to the selected area.
- **Shift + Left Click**: Fills the entire region with the contents of the bucket and adds it to the current selection, allowing for selective filling.
- **Ctrl + Left Click**: Changes the style of an object using the bucket's current properties, providing options for applying gradients or patterns.
- **Ctrl + Shift + Left Click**: Changes the style of either a line or a stroke using the bucket's current properties, offering flexibility in stroke customization.

Gradient Tool

- **Double Left Click**: Creates a basic gradient on the current object, enabling easy application of gradient fills.
- **Ctrl + Alt + Left Click**: Adds an abrupt step on the gradient of the current object, allowing for precise control over gradient transitions.

- **Delete**: Removes the currently selected abrupt step, facilitating gradient refinement.
- **Left Arrow, Right Arrow, Up Arrow, Down Arrow**: Moves the selected gradient nodes one step in the respective direction, enabling fine-tuning of gradient positions.
- **Ctrl + Left Arrow, Ctrl + Right Arrow, Ctrl + Up Arrow, Ctrl + Down Arrow**: Moves the selected gradient nodes one pixel in the respective direction, offering granular control over gradient adjustments.
- **Shift + R**: Reverses the gradient step on the current object.

Eyedropper Tool

- **Left Click**: Copies the color of an object and sets it as the document's foreground color.
- **Shift + Click**: Copies the color of an object and sets it as the document's stroke color.
- **Alt + Click**: Copies the color of an object, inverts it, and sets it as the document's foreground color.
- **Ctrl + C**: Copies the color of an object and places its RGB value in the clipboard.

Conclusion

Now that this guide is ending, I need you to know that Inkscape is a great tool for showing off your imagination. We learned how to make shapes, draw complicated patterns, and bring our thoughts to life with just a few clicks along the way. Anyone who loves to make things can use Inkscape, not just experts. You can use Inkscape whether you are a beginner just starting in design or an experienced artist looking for a tool that can do a lot of different things. The great thing about Inkscape is how easy it is to use. You don't have to be an expert to make beautiful art with its easy-to-use layout and simple tools. Inkscape gives you the freedom to do what you want, without any restrictions. So, as you start to be artistic with Inkscape, don't be afraid to try new things. Let your ideas run wild as you try out new styles and methods. You are one step closer to making your idea a reality with each mouse stroke and computer click. Inkscape isn't just a piece of software; it opens up a world of options. So jump right in and let your imagination run wild. You never know what great things you'll make next. You can do anything with Inkscape by your side.

INDEX

D

E

F

N

O

P

S

248

250